# SHORT WALKS
# IN LAKELAND

*Warnscale Head Hut, Hay Stacks (Walk 47)*

# SHORT WALKS IN LAKELAND

## Book 3:
# WEST LAKELAND

by

Aileen and Brian Evans

CICERONE PRESS LTD
MILNTHORPE, CUMBRIA
www.cicerone.co.uk

© Aileen Evans and Brian Evans 2000
First edition 2000
ISBN-10:  1 85284 308 X
ISBN-13:  978 1 85284 308 3
Reprinted 2010 (with updates)

Printed by KHL Printing, Singapore.

A catalogue record for this book is available from the British Library.

*For*
*Alison, Raif and Sean*

## ACKNOWLEDGEMENTS

Once again we are indebted to our chief check walkers Marjorie
and Maurice Tedd, who have followed most of our routes, in
fair and foul weather and have made invaluable suggestions.
Our thanks also go to Lake District National Park Authority
Archaeologist John Hodgson and to Malcolm Guyatt, LDNPA
Warden, for helpful up-to-date information.

*Front cover*: Ennerdale Water shore (Walk 32)

# CONTENTS

**WHEREVER YOU GO FOLLOW THE COUNTRY CODE**

Enjoy the countryside and respect its life and work
Guard against all risk of fire
Fasten all gates
Keep dogs under close control
Keep to public paths across farmland
Use gates and stiles to cross fences, hedges and walls
Leave livestock, crops and machinery alone
Take your litter home
Help keep all water clean
Protect wildlife, plants and trees
Take special care on country roads
Make no unnecessary noise

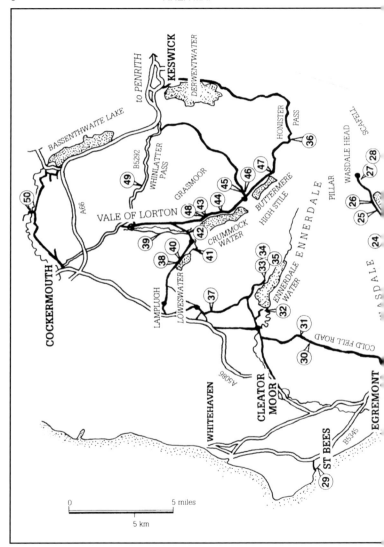

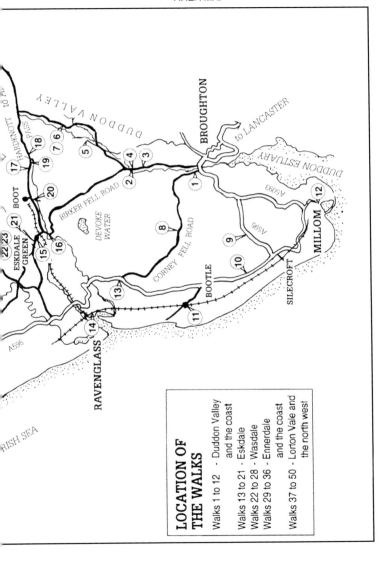

**LOCATION OF THE WALKS**

Walks 1 to 12 - Duddon Valley and the coast

Walks 13 to 21 - Eskdale

Walks 22 to 28 - Wasdale

Walks 29 to 36 - Ennerdale and the coast

Walks 37 to 50 - Lorton Vale and the north west

# PREFACE

Our final volume of the trilogy continues the pattern of the previous volumes. Our aim is to describe a wide variety of walks, averaging between 4 and 8 miles, ideal for a half-day or a leisurely full day, keeping mainly to the lower fells, valleys, woodlands and coast. Some classic walks are included, but we also point out quieter routes which will appeal to those who seek less popular but equally beautiful places. Many of these use old green paths, half-forgotten bridleways and retired peat roads.

Although this is not a primarily high-fell walking guide, the nature of the area demands a degree of effort and many of the walks visit a summit. Priority is given to the lower fells, which we have found to be as rewarding as their higher neighbours.

We have aimed to present a combination of comprehensive coverage, detailed route description and easy to follow maps in an interesting way. If you work your way through the walks you will, like us, come to form a very special relationship with this lesser known part of Lakeland.

*Aileen and Brian Evans*
*Preston 2000*

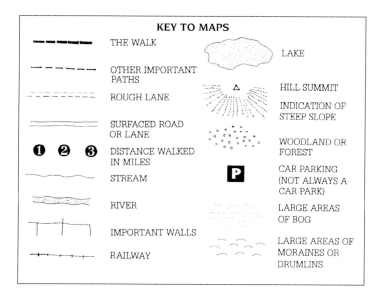

### KEY TO MAPS

| | | | |
|---|---|---|---|
| ▬ ▬ ▬ ▬ | THE WALK | (lake shape) | LAKE |
| ▬ – – ▬ – | OTHER IMPORTANT PATHS | △ | HILL SUMMIT |
| – – – – – | ROUGH LANE | | INDICATION OF STEEP SLOPE |
| ──────── | SURFACED ROAD OR LANE | | WOODLAND OR FOREST |
| ❶ ❷ ❸ | DISTANCE WALKED IN MILES | **P** | CAR PARKING (NOT ALWAYS A CAR PARK) |
| 〜〜〜 | STREAM | | LARGE AREAS OF BOG |
| ▬▬▬ | RIVER | | LARGE AREAS OF MORAINES OR DRUMLINS |
| ┬─┬─┬ | IMPORTANT WALLS | | |
| ─┼─┼─ | RAILWAY | | |

# INTRODUCTION

This book is split into five sections: Duddon Valleyand the coast, Eskdale, Wasdale, Ennerdale and the coast, Lorton Vale and the North West. The routes are carefully planned to incorporate interesting places with a minimum of walking on rough paths or surfaced lanes.

## Maps

To locate your chosen walk there is a complete map on pages 8 and 9 which pinpoints the start of the walks and shows the approach roads. The individual maps show each walk in detail and should be clear enough for you to follow the route. It is helpful to have the relevant Ordnance Survey map or the easy to read Harveys Superwalker 1:25,000 maps which show more of the surrounding area; these are specified in the route introductions with the following codes:

OL4 = OS Outdoor Leisure No.4
The English Lakes North Western Area 1:25,000

OL6 = OS Outdoor Leisure No.6
The English Lakes South Western Area 1:25,000

## Footwear and Clothing

Lightweight boots with a cleated rubber sole are the best footwear for almost all the walks, as there are usually some wet patches or rough ground to contend with. A wide range is available and, as almost all the walks are on tracks or paths, there is no need to choose the most expensive boots. Comfort is the chief priority. In a dry spell in summer, trainers *may* be adequate for some of the lower walks, although make sure the soles still retain good tread - care is needed on steep slopes, particularly when descending wet grass.

Clothing needs to be sensible - bear in mind that even on a warm summer day it can be cold and windy on the fells. In winter, snow and ice may render the high fells dangerous. The high fells can be wintry until May. Every year unprepared walkers die of exposure in unexpected bad weather. There are plenty of low-level woodland walks in this book which are ideal for a day when conditions on the higher fells are dangerous or unpleasant.

The Lake District is notoriously wet, and a wise walker never sets out without a waterproof/windproof, a jumper or pile jacket, and warm trousers - not shorts.

A small daysack completes the gear, with a torch for short winter days, a compass (you need to practise how to use one!) some spare food and drink.

A recommended book which tells you all you need to know about walking in the hills is *The Hillwalker's Manual* by Bill Birkett (Cicerone).

## Access

Almost all the walks are on rights of way or permissive paths, or over fell country with open access and a long history of use. On the higher fells the popular paths are stony and worn. These have had a considerable amount of repair work done on them in recent years, with great success. Please keep to paths instead of walking a parallel route which leads to ever-greater erosion. However, the majority of walks described in this book are on paths which are pleasant underfoot. Where the walk goes through farmland it is necessary to keep strictly to the paths and these are usually waymarked, often with tiny yellow arrows. Away from the rough fells and forests, some of the paths cross pasture with grazing animals. Normally they do not bother walkers, although cows may be alarmingly interested in your dog, particularly if it is black and white. Occasionally they may have a bull with them - if in doubt as to your safety skirt the field to avoid problems. Dogs should be under control at all times and on a lead, particularly during lambing time.

## Parking

The walks start where possible from recognised car parks or places where parked cars can be tucked well out of the way of other road users. Please park sensibly. Remember that the Lake District is no different from most other places in Britain and Western Europe with regard to thieving from parked cars. Take everything of value with you and leave doors locked and windows closed.

## Grades and Terrain Used in this Book

| | |
|---|---|
| Easy | - A walk on good paths with modest ascents. |
| Moderate | - Some short steep ascents, or longer well-graded ascents. Rough paths in parts. |
| Strenuous | - Longer steep ascents with rough paths. |
| Low fell | - Generally below 400m, |
| Medium Fell | - 400m-600m. |
| High Fell | - above 600m. |

## Points of Interest

These are indicated in bold type in the walk description and details are given at the end of the walk.

## Directional Instructions

L = left and R = right    ROW = right of way
w/m = waymark    CCW = Cumbria Coastal Way
C to C = Coast to Coast long distance footpath
C2C = Coast to Coast Cycleway

## Useful Addresses

Lake District National Park Office
  Murley Moss, Oxenholme Road, Kendal, Cumbria LA9 7RL
  Tel: 01539 724555    www.lake-district.gov.uk

Cumbria Tourist Board
  Ashleigh, Holly Road, Windermere, Cumbria LA23 2AQ
  Tel: 015394 44444    www.golakes.co.uk

## Scheduled Sites

Several of the historical sites visited on the walks are scheduled - that is
protected by law. It is an offence to interfere with them. Please look, enjoy
but do not disturb!

*Stile near
Peathouse
Beck,
Walk 1*

CHAPTER 1

# Duddon Valley and The Coast

Dunnerdale is one of Lakeland's most beautiful and colourful valleys with a richness of woodland, rocky hillsides and lively river scenery. It retains a quiet unspoilt charm, for the narrowness of its roads deter tourist traffic and development. For much of the year golden brown is the characteristic colour, for bracken is rampant, its expansion a threat to farming and in summer a hindrance to walkers.

The valley inspired Wordsworth to compose a series of sonnets which capture its character and changing moods so well.

The planting of Dunnerdale Forest in 1936 drew heavy criticism. Now much of the original dense growth has been harvested and replanting is in progress, with much greater sensitivity given to wildlife and aesthetic considerations.

Walkers must be prepared to deal with paths which are often very juicy, for the nature of the underlying rocks tend to favour water retention in the overlying vegetation.

Black Combe, with its great bulk and broad vistas adds another dimension to the walks in the area.

We also include two coastal walks in this chapter, one a short stroll packed with interesting reminders of the industrial past, the other a worthwhile and lonely section of the Cumbria Coastal Way. Other coastal walks are included in later chapters.

*The Isle of Man seen from Whitbeck, Walk 10*

# WALK 1: Duddon Furnace to Swinside Stone Circle

*Duddon Furnace*

**SUMMARY:** A little frequented, varied walk which links two important historical sites, the Duddon Iron Furnace and Swinside Stone Circle. A bonus is the ascent of Barrow, a modest hill with outstanding views. The beautiful woods which form the beginning and end of the walk are host to a wonderful display of bluebells in season.

**HOW TO GET THERE AND PARKING:**
Take the A595 to Duddon Bridge a mile west of Broughton in Furness. Turn on the minor road up the west side of the river for 200yds. Park on the left by the Furnace gate, or 100 yards further on.

| | |
|---|---|
| *Distance:* | 6 miles (9.5km) |
| *Grade:* | Moderate |
| *Terrain:* | Low fell and woodland |
| *Summit:* | Barrow - 886ft (270m) |
| *Height gain:* | 1280ft (390m) |
| *Map:* | OL6 |

**THE WALK:** *The Duddon Iron Furnace is one of the most impressive charcoal fired blast furnaces in Britain and was restored in 1992 by the National Park Authority and English Heritage. We recommend that you allow time to wander around the site* and stand in the heart of the furnace itself.

Walk up the bridleway as far as the highest building, the Later Charcoal Store, and turn L just beyond into a woodland path signed with blue arrow waymarks. Away now from the captivating furnace, the beautiful woodland, with celandine and sorrel peeping through discarded oak leaves, dispells any notion of industry you may have imagined. Cross the Dower House drive and keep straight on. At a signed fork go ahead (the path over the stream left is our return route) recrossing the divided stream. *There are spring bluebells as far as the eye can see bordering the path, now showing its origin as a hollow way over the fells to Waberthwaite on the coast.* Zigzag up through a larch plantation to cross and recross a rough forest track. Go through a gate (sign to Boadhole) in the fell wall. Clear of the trees, go ahead on a good path up a bracken slope and take in a retrospective view of the wind generators on Kirkby Moor, which extends as height is gained to include the Burlington quarries and the hills to the east of the river. Go over the brow and follow the blue arrows skirting the fields of Boadhole to a gate in the left-hand wall. (Ignore the more distant forest gate.) Turn L through the gate and along the path, the left wall is low enough for views down the estuary, but

*'Bracken-clearing machine' on the fell above Boadhole*

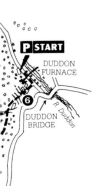

the right-hand one an intermittent remnant. Pass individual shapely rowan trees and a stone sheepfold, and reach a gate in a high wall.

Go through and turn L to the highest point of the bridleway by stones, boulders and an iron gate, where a sudden spread of Black Combe rises beyond the upper tributary valley of Black Beck.

Ignore the gate, carry on for 100 yards to just before a hog hole in the wall, then turn R up a little U-shaped valley. At a col, a level area with rushy pools, branch diagonally L on a rising path showing a fine tableau of the Coniston mountains to the north-east. When the path crosses exposed bedrock turn sharp back diagonally L to gain the summit of Barrow. *The problem is where to look first from this wonderful viewpoint: coastline and estuary, moorland and mountain, woodland and vale, or can your sharp eye spot the gas rigs out to sea or the stone circle in the second field left of Swinside Farm?*

Use the elevation to advantage by studying the lie of the land. Let your eye range north-west pinpointing the fell road to Waberthwaite. See our hollow way, having skirted between our peak and Thwaite Yeat Farm, rising over the moor to join the road at a Y-junction.

Set off in a north-west direction along the ridge-top turf to a cairn with a pole (to the left of the high point ahead). Just before reaching the poled cairn's rock promontory turn L, descend for 50 yards, then turn R into a wide gap. Go through and trend L, descending a tussocky hollow and cross its stream. Bend L again down the drier ground to the muddy tricklings in the valley bottom.

*View eastward from Barrow*

Look back left to discover that one of the stoneshod 'channels' is none other than the hollow bridleway and turn R along it. At a cross path when the way splits into two furrows turn L, heading for a small rock outcrop with a profile which would earn an exotic title if it was in the local park. The fell road lies completely hidden by a low grassy bank only a few yards to the right. Meet the surfaced road at a junction by the rock and cross over to continue along the non-cycling farm access road. Descend into a gill, where the buildings of Windy Slack can be seen to the left. Go up the steep concreted road out of the gill and over the brow where a sweeping view of Swinside Fell, White Combe and Black Combe makes the 1/3 mile to Fenwick fly.

Go through the gate, over the stream (three-way signpost), and follow the white arrow indicating the permissive path to a track junction at the isolated farm. Turn L for 25 yards then leave the track (public footpath sign) branching L to a stile in the wall. Go straight across to the next wall and through an old stile of character. A glance up right shows the prominent cairn on Raven Crag piercing the sky. Keep ahead to a wooden stile and steep descent to a footbridge over the cascades of Peathouse Beck. Carry straight on up the rise and the path disappears. Look back to Fenwick and maintaining the same line of direction, proceed ahead in expectation of a faint dent across the fellside and a green track leading to Swinside Farm. Our earlier summit looks impressive across the Black Beck valley, despite its modest height.

Go straight on behind the farm, turn L at the last barn and pass through the gates to the access track. Look for a stile in the left-hand wall with the renowned **Swinside Stone Circle** in the adjoining field - by the way, you might like to consult the sign on the next gate first!

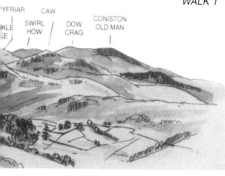

Go along the track with Knott Hill to the south and views over the sands of the Duddon Estuary. Gradually the surface improves and the track becomes a walled lane. Pass Crag Hall and a strip of woodland then look for a slit stile and turn L (public footpath sign just before a house). Go down the field to a gateway (making redundant the old slit stile) and a stone slab acting economically as bridge and wall support. Turn R along the bank of the Black Beck and cross it by stepping stones to the farm. Go through the left-hand gate and turn R in front of the house and on the access track to the road. Turn L to the main A595 road and turn L towards Broughton. The couple of hundred yards goes quickly as you ignore the first lane to Graystone House and turn L by a post box to Ash House. The lane is sheltered by mature trees, and the verges display a variety of flowers, wild and escaped, to immediately dispel thoughts of the traffic. Follow footpath signs, and as the drive loops back left go ahead on a narrow path by yew trees to the garden gate. Turn L over a stile then R along the wallside. The path heads through a gap and the knoll to the right

*Swinside Stone Circle*

has ancient standing stones but we failed to spot them. Go over a stile into an oak wood. The path rises gradually, then levels and descends every step through a glorious carpet of bluebells. At a wall turn R and stroll down the bluebell path to cross a little stream to join the outward route. Turn R to the furnace and start.

## Swinside Stone Circle (Sunkenkirk)

This second most important megalithic stone circle in Cumbria is little visited, in contrast to the well-known Castlerigg, near Keswick. Reputed to be about 3500 years old. It stands on private land.

## WALK 2:     Frith Hall and Beckfoot

*Ruins of Frith Hall*

**SUMMARY:** The gaunt ruins of Frith Hall, so well seen from around Ulpha Bridge, make a worthwhile destination for a short walk. The views over Dunnerdale from this old hunting lodge and inn are superb, while the surrounding ungrazed pasture is a botanist's dream. Take your flower guide with you. The access area with its rocky knolls makes a great picnic spot. The rest of the walk, along the old road with the return along the base of the woods is pleasant enough, especially in autumn, but lacks variety and has restricted views. Some lane walking is involved. A good walk for a wild day.

**HOW TO GET THERE AND PARKING:** Three miles up Dunnerdale from the A593, park near Ulpha Bridge over the River Duddon by the school.

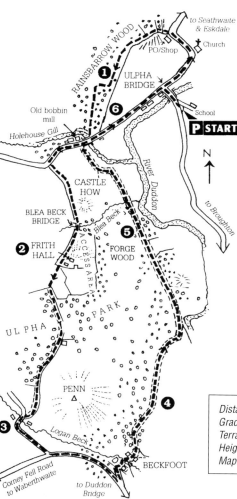

**THE WALK** *Before setting off just look across the River Duddon at the western horizon. It is possible to pick out the ruined walls of Frith Hall against the skyline. Also look at the attractive triple-arched bridge. Its underside shows where the older bridge was widened to allow an increase in traffic.*
Cross the bridge and turn R along the road. The Pike rises from the wooded slopes on the left as we walk past St John's Church (seventeenth century) and along to the Post Office, (sweets, groceries etc.). *The row of houses ahead on the right are the Almshouses.*
Immediately beyond the Post Office turn L (signed footpath) and climb 30 yards up the field to turn L at waymark and gate. Progress to a stile and a sudden view down

| | |
|---|---|
| *Distance:* | 6½ miles (10.5km) |
| *Grade:* | Easy |
| *Terrain:* | Woods and lanes |
| *Height gain:* | 425ft (129m) |
| *Map:* | OL6 |

HARTER FELL   CRINKLE CRAGS   WALLOWBARROW   GREY FRIAR

*Duddon Valley from Frith Hall*

the valley showing a variety of textures as the rushes, bracken and woodland swathe the valley floor and encroach on the enclosing fells.

The path clings to the wallside enclosing Rainsbarrow Wood, passes an old cross-wall and on descending becomes invaded by a stream. Find another way through the trees parallel to the wall, as this eventually becomes a better alternative. Where the wall swings away left the path becomes more distinct as it leads through a wood, mainly of beech and with some beautiful pollarded lime. *Go quietly, you may see a red squirrel or the shy dormouse.* The leaves give a bright mosaic carpet as the path makes a rising bend R, then swings left to widen, improve, and emerge near Holehouse Gill and a gate L accessing the road. Turn R and cross the bridge.

*The chimney ahead and its adjoining buildings have surely caught your eye. This was a* **bobbin mill** *using the water-power of Holehouse Gill.* Keep ahead up steep Mill Brow, the tarmac cutting a line through dense vegetation. There are views across the valley to Caw and, as height is gained, to Stickle Pike. Pass a large erratic boulder, and as the gradient flattens turn L onto a footpath signed Logan Beck via Ulpha Park. Walk along to a dramatic view of the valley with the little community of Ulpha centre stage. Pass the rock knob of Castle How and cross Blea Beck by the packhorse bridge to enter the Countryside Commission access area. Go along the path and up to the ruins of **Frith Hall. (Do not enter** as some stonework is in a dangerous condition.)

*The surrounding volcanic bedrock, smoothed by ice into flowing curves with deep grooves showing the direction of the glacier's passage, is more bizarre than the ruins*

themselves. The hall's window-less gables still stand as do the chimney breast with charred stone, where many tales will have been told round the crackling fire as the wind howled down the smoking chimney, for this was a staging post on the packhorse route to Millom. As you walk round the hall the views extend to the high mountain peaks of central Lakeland.

a) Either return to the path and continue through a gate and then to a kissing gate in the forest wall.

b) Or go through a gap in the wall to the right of the barn, which leads to ungrazed pasture and is awash with wild flowers: bluebells, foxgloves orchids, lousewort and a variety of grasses, sedges and rushes. Return to the main track.

The path becomes lined with myrtle before it enters the forest.

Descend to the Logan Valley and turn L on the lane at Logan Beck Bridge. At the T-junction turn L to Broughton. Cross a cattle grid and go down the road which descends beside the wooded Logan gorge. In ¼ mile turn L into a signed footpath to Mill Bridge (public footpath Broughton Mills, Ulpha). At Beckfoot continue ahead signed with a yellow waymark. Note the old mill machinery used as a garden feature. Cross the Logan gill on a picturesque old bridge. **Beckfoot Mill** *was once a woollen mill, now a sawmill and joiners' shop.* Keep ahead down an enclosed track bordered by woodland and ignore any side paths or stiles. *If you go quietly you may be rewarded by the sight of red deer as they graze the riverside meadows.* Go through a gate and straight on. The river is close by, but only glimpsed occasionally through the trees of Forge Wood. The next gate is at the woodland's edge, so keep ahead across a field with Castle How to the left. The way is now alongside Blea Beck and through a gate into a walled path which joins the road opposite the old bobbin mill. Turn R and along the road to Ulpha Bridge and the start.

## Frith Hall

The hall was built by the Huddlestone family, lords of Millom, as a hunting lodge in the early 17th century to replace the 16th-century nearby Old Hall.

It later became an inn used by travellers and pack-pony trains on the road to Millom, and had its share of rumours of smuggling, death and intrigue associated with lonely dwellings in wild places. For a time it rivalled Gretna Green as a runaway couple's wedding destination. It is now a ruin at the back of the farm.

**Bobbin Mill**

The bobbin mill was one of about fifty nineteenth century mills in the area and produced seven million bobbins per week. It was written into the apprentice workers' contract that they were not to be given salmon from the River Duddon more often than three days per week.

**Beckfoot Mill**

This was a fulling mill. Coarse, loosely woven cloth was immersed in water and fuller's earth and trampled in order to felt and shrink it into a warmer and more serviceable fabric.

*The old bobbin mill at Holehouse Gill*

# WALK 3: **Tarn Hill and Stickle Pike**

*On Tarn Hill*

**SUMMARY:** The attractive, isolated cone of Stickle Pike makes a fine objective for a walk; it has a lot of the characteristics of the higher fells but is attained with less effort. A dense mantle of bracken protects all but the highest tops, yet good paths provide adequate passage at all seasons. Tarn Hill is a wonderful area of rocky summits with a necklace of tarns; see how many you can spot.

**HOW TO GET THERE AND PARKING:** Park in Dunnerdale on the Common ½ mile south of Ulpha Bridge at a small quarry parking area (2½ miles from the A593).

| | |
|---|---|
| *Distance:* | 4¾ miles (7.5km) |
| *Grade:* | Moderate |
| *Terrain:* | Low fell |
| *Summits:* | Tarn Hill - North Top - 1017ft (310m) |
| | Stickle Pike - 1230ft (375m) |
| *Height gain:* | 1312ft (400m) |
| *Map:* | OL6 |

**THE WALK:** From the car park look down the east side of Dunnerdale and a good path can be seen rising up a narrow valley to crags. This path is our first objective.

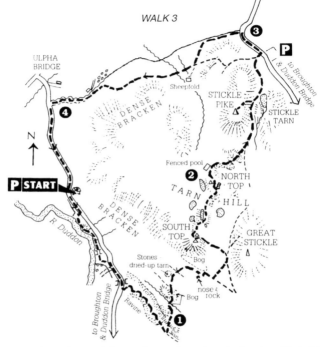

Turn L down the road. Do not be too hasty to gain the riverside but join it by a rock knoll, a popular family picnic spot with rocks, beach, cascades and sidestreams - in fact everything to delay children as the wet terrain gradually forces you to cross a bridge over a sidestream and head for the forest wall. Turn L to the road and turn R along it for 200 yards to the crest of the rise. After passing a fine ash tree turn L onto a public bridleway (the path we saw previously). The path climbs steadily beside a small stream and, across Dunnerdale, The Pike above Ulpha dominates the view (see Walk 4). *The path is well made and illustrates how walkers are now rediscovering centuries-old ways, once important connecting paths. It is known as Parson's Road, and was used in the 1770s by the parson to go from his home at Stonestar to his school over the fell in the Woodland valley. Individual trees of yew, hawthorn, sycamore and oak cheer the now dry ravine.* Go through the 'Khyber Pass', cross the stream, and in 100 yards bend sharp L on a small path up the slope to a gap in the rocky valley rim to see Great Stickle ahead (east) and Black Combe on the far western horizon.

*The Parson's Road, Duddon Valley with The Pike behind*

Go ahead to cross a shallow valley occupied by a chaos of rocks and climb out keeping on the dry path just in the bracken and to the left of two flat, boggy tracts. Pass a holly tree sheltered by a steep slope from the prevailing westerly winds and ignore a path on the left, keeping ahead towards Tarn Hill. *It is a scant name for the collection of fine little viewpoint summits and numerous picturesque tarns which it identifies.* Pass a tarn (or group of muddy stones according to the season), and from the gradually rising path take a retrospective view to the Duddon Estuary. The path bends round a 'nose' rock then over a slight rise to a wet grassy area beneath Tarn Hill. The path avoids the bog then forks (just before a perched boulder on the right). Fork L on the path, which slants dry underfoot through the bracken to meet a bigger path. Turn L between Great Stickle on the right and Tarn Hill on the left. The path steepens, and at a large boulder and small stone set in the pathway fork L on a narrow grassy trod with our target summit to the left. To reach it the trod tracks across the spongy ground to a cross path. Turn L, and as it peters out

*View from Tarn Hill*

attack the virgin slope to reach the south summit and a glittering seascape of the Duddon Estuary. *To the south-east the controversial wind generators on Kirkby Fell may not even catch your eye, but to spot the ruins of Frith Hall (see p.24) across Dunnerdale will certainly challenge it.* Go 30 yards north to stand on the north twin summit.

A jumble of rocky hummocks must be negotiated to visit our next summit of Tarn Hill, the cairned skyline point ahead with Stickle Pike just visible behind.

From the north twin summit scramble L down rocks (west) a few yards to a small green path which heads right, then winds about hither and thither and passes pools (right) and tarns (left). The tarns have their own individual, unexpected beauty. Keep to the R of the upper tarn. Just beyond the tarn a trod bears R, then forks immediately. Keep L, aiming for the summit of Stickle Pike and gaining height. Pass split, up-ended rocks, like stacked biscuits, and, on the rising trod close under the right-hand outcrop, don't miss the rocking-stone seat beside the trod. Keep to these right-hand rocks (the main path leads up the valley to a lake), then at the top of the rocks pop out onto a grassy shoulder and the cairn is diagonally left. *From the summit you can count the tarns of Tarn Hill, each one a reflective picture in its own right with the central Lakeland mountains forming the northern skyline of the 360-degree panorama.*

A few strides beyond the cairn join a double path and turn L along it. Round a knoll, pass a fenced tarn until a glance east reveals the upper Lickle valley which leads down to Broughton Mills; go a further 25 yards and leave the double path on a R fork. Cross a hollow and continue over the next knoll with a steep descent. Join a major path which leads easily up the right shoulder of Stickle Pike. At the first cairn on the shoulder a glance back will reveal the mirror-like tarn reflecting in the distance. Go to a second cairn then turn L, where the steep pink stony path to the summit promotes a real mountain atmosphere. Do not descend the stony path, but turn north at the summit cairn and make your way down the more amenable grassy slopes on the right returning to the second cairn. Turn L and down to pass Stickle Tarn bulging out of its hollow on the right. Keep ahead through the gap which frames Caw and amble down the wide path, gradually pulling round rightwards to the road at a parking area.

Turn L down the quiet road enjoying the views into Dunnerdale as far as the cattle-grid and intake wall. Do not cross it, but turn L along the wallside, passing boulders cleverly incorporated into the wall and a gate. The wall begins to descend, but our path keeps level below a rock slab to a fork beyond. Fork R on the lesser path which crosses a bracken slope. It is sound underfoot and makes a descending traverse which leads into a shallow valley. Cross the stream and carry on in the same direction up the bank and once more on the descending traverse, passing outcrops of rock dappled with white quartz. Pass above a spoil heap, and at a bridleway sign turn R and squelch downhill towards a plantation. Turn L by the wall to Big House and L along the access lane. At the main road near Ulpha school turn L along the Common for ¼ mile to the start (or R over the bridge for 400 yards to visit the shop).

# WALK 4:    Duddon Valley and The Pike

*Ulpha Bridge and The Pike*

**SUMMARY:** The Pike dominates the lower part of Dunnerdale, and the view from its summit is almost aerial over the patchwork valley below. Our circuit uses little-walked paths some of which, where bracken encroaches, will benefit from greater use. Perhaps it is wise to avoid the high summer when bracken growth is at its peak. Ever-changing views along the valley

| | |
|---|---|
| *Distance:* | 7¼ miles (11.6km) by the stepping stones A & B. |
| | 8¾ miles (14.7km) by Hall Bridge A, D & E. |
| | Short return reduces the route by 4½ miles. |
| *Grade:* | Moderate |
| *Terrain:* | Valley, woodland and low fell |
| *Summits:* | The Pike - 1214ft (370m) |
| *Height gain:* | 1375ft (420m) |
| *Map:* | OL6 |

are a delight and the variety of walking is always interesting: riverside, balcony, old quarry tracks, moorland and woods.

In low water the stepping stones (see route B) offer an interesting shorter route, but they quickly become impassable when the river level rises. The stepping stones are dangerously slippery if damp. The longer route includes one of the most pleasing green paths in Dunnerdale, once used as a bridleway, now a little used gem.

**HOW TO GET THERE AND PARKING:** Park at Ulpha Bridge on the common. A Post Office/shop is 500 yards up the road towards Seathwaite.

**THE WALK:** Check the water level at the bridge. If the concrete foundations are clear of the water the stepping stones upstream should be passable.
**Caution:** If the stepping stones are wet they are very slippery.

**A - ALONG THE VALLEY:** From the cattle grid the bridge leads the eye to locate the shapely peak of The Pike - our ultimate objective. Set off over the stile, signed 'Public footpath', along the delightful riverside meadow and through an oak glade. At the woodland ignore the continuing riverside path and enter a gate, yellow waymark arrow. Take the path diagonally R for a brief stretch uphill, just enough to get the circulation going before reaching a bridle-path. Turn L to leave the wood at a gate. Fork R up the wallside stony track, which soon turns into a scenic green path, previously an old road between farms. Across Dunnerdale, heavily wooded slopes hide the Ulpha road over to Eskdale, and to the north the

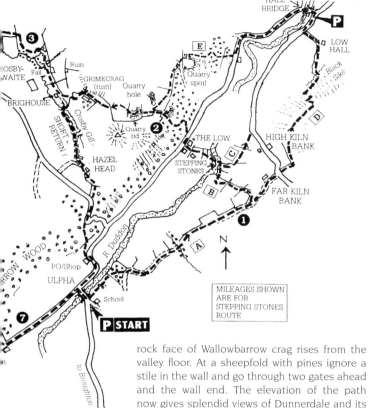

rock face of Wallowbarrow crag rises from the valley floor. At a sheepfold with pines ignore a stile in the wall and go through two gates ahead and the wall end. The elevation of the path now gives splendid views of Dunnerdale and its surrounding peaks. Carry on through another gate, and in 100 yards find a waymarked stile on the L.

To continue choose either **B** (Stepping Stones over the River Duddon) or **D** (Pony path to Hall Bridge).

## B - TO THE STEPPING STONES AND THE QUARRY

Leave the old road here and either go over the stile and down through deep, steep midgy vegetation or cross the stream and turn L down the lubricated animal path, to follow the stream descending through two walls to the river. (If you reach Far Kiln Bank Farm you have missed the waymark.)

Turn R over a stile by a huge boulder in the right-hand wall. Go upstream and take an energetic stride over a ditch and climb over a stile, then walk on to the next wall, also with a stream and high stile. Climb over this, ignore the fence stile to the right, and a few yards ahead discover the stepping stones. *They are but a few years old; renewed by the National Park authorities, they are large, flat and comfortably spaced - or they were - the last three moved when nudged by a freak flood soon after their installation.* (**Take care** - *the stones are very slippery when wet.*)

*If you arrive at the stepping stones and find the water level too high, or the stones too daunting, take **alternative** C. You are sure to conquer this lesser challenge*

**To continue** step over the River Duddon on the stones, and turn R along the bank for a few yards to find a low gap in the wall. Go ahead through the flower-strewn pasture to a gate in the right-hand wall, and turn R along the track from the barn. Carry on through the 'Danger of Death' gate and up to the road at Low Wood. Turn R.

A signed footpath leads into the woodland, and if the wild garlic is in flower progress uphill will surely be speedy. *The path underfoot has sections of set stones remaining, hinting at an important reason for its construction: it serviced quarries and mines which now lie forgotten and tranquil.*

Soon the first ruined quarry building and dressing floor are reached. A *brilliant expanse of wild flowers - speedwell, birdsfoot trefoil and foxglove - are shaded by the dainty silver birch.* Go on through a gate then a gate with stile. The path now runs between a wall and quarry rid to pass the awesome blue face of the Old Quarry (50 yards off to the right). The songs of the many birds neutralise the sombre atmosphere and liven the air with their chatter. Keep on the path. **Route E from Hall Bridge joins here.**

## C: ALTERNATIVE FROM THE STEPPING STONES TO THE ROAD AT HALL BRIDGE:

From the stones return to the stile in the fence, go over and look left. You will see two fields with stiles in their walls. Because of the rising hillside sight of the stiles will be lost as you cross the fields. Simply keep in the direction set by the fence and you will meet, and climb over, two of the highest stiles imaginable. At the road turn L, meet the pony path people, and follow the road to Hall Bridge. **Continue at E.**

## D: To HALL BRIDGE VIA THE PONY PATH (avoiding the stepping stones):
Keep ahead on the old lane above the buildings of Far Kiln Bank Farm and through the gate giving access onto the fell road to Broughton Mills. Go straight over the road and along the public bridleway above the

The Wallowbarrow Gorge is a challenge for canoeists when water conditions are suitable (Walk 5)

The path to Seathwaite Tarn gives fine views over the Duddon valley to Scafell (Walk 6)

Approaching the Horse Back Ridge of Black Combe (Walk 9)

The western flank of Black Combe seen from the top of Gutterby Banks (Walks 10/11)

*Stepping
stones across
the River
Duddon*

wall. Do not be put off by the mud or the cows which shelter under the high wall. Bend L over a stream, go through a gate and the green path is underfoot. This beautiful scenic old way runs over a knoll passing through two gates, then makes a gentle zigzag descent of the steep slope, giving a wealth of views along Dunnerdale. At the valley floor go L through a gate in the wall, and choose from three bridges over the Black Sike and along the left-hand wall to Low Hall Farm. Go between the house and the barn to the access lane and along to the road. Turn R, and in 100 yards, and well satisfied with your choice of the pony path, meet the wet or the wise coming from the stepping stones, then carry on to Hall Bridge. **Continue at E.**

## E: HALL BRIDGE TO THE QUARRY

Cross Hall Bridge and turn L along the road for 500 yards. Pass Crowberry House and in 50 yards discover a public footpath sign and stile on the right. Climb over. Branch diagonally L up the pasture to a gate in the woodland wall, avoiding a spring. Go through and keep ahead up the path-cum-waterway, which quickly improves. Pass a waymark still going ahead, then go slightly L, guided by another waymark to the quarry rid. Turn R along the base of the rid and straight on at the second tier. Turn L across the front of a roofless hut to cross a stile in a fence. Go ahead through a wooden gate leading onto the fell, and make a pleasant stroll along the top edge of the wood to a gateway lined by fine pole gateslabs. Ahead is a second quarry. Keep ahead on the main track, and when it forks turn R to the upper dressing floor, where a pause is rewarded by a fine view.

**Walkers of alternatives B, D & E meet here.**

## QUARRIES TO BRIGHOUSE FARM:

Ignoring the approaching gate, turn R over a waymarked stile in the fence and along the foot of the rid to follow the waymark pole L back along the top of the stones to an upper dressing floor. Go across, pausing to see The Pike ahead. Find a narrow path rising diagonally L through the bracken to a stile in the fence above. Keep ahead over the shoulder of Gim Crag to a sudden view across the Ulpha road to The Pike, with Hesk Fell on its right and Whit Fell peeping through the gap beyond.

Go through a gate in the wall ahead, then R on an indistinct path along the edge of a flurry of cotton grass towards a clump of walled trees. Ignore the stile in the wall left and follow the wallside path past an unsafe building to swing left through its back yard. Go along the pasture to the second gate in the right-hand wall. Go ahead to join the track near Brighouse Farm.

## SHORT RETURN

At Brighouse Farm turn L along the farm access track. Cross the bridge over Crosby Gill and continue along to Hazel Head Farm. Turn L through the yard, pass the front of the farmhouse, and turn R beyond into a track leading down past a barn and ahead through a gate into the field ahead. (**Note:** the ROW path should turn right through the slurry, but at present is not passable) Keep by the right-hand wall, turn R at its corner then diagonally left as the path angles down the pasture to cross a stile at the Ulpha road. Turn L down the steep tarmac and find a stile leading R just above a plunging hairpin. A dampish path leads through the wood to an interesting stile over the left-hand wall. Go over and down the field to a corner gate near the Post Office (shop). Turn R and follow the road to Ulpha Bridge and the start.

**CONTINUATION FROM BRIGHOUSE FARM:** Turn R into the farmyard (w/m) and pass to the right of the barn. Just beyond, go along the gated, walled green lane. Keep on, now in the valley of the Crosby Gill, which tumbles over a fall and splashes down its bouldery bed. A belt of pines line the far bank, sheltering a stone barn by the pathside. The footstones of the barn make an opportune seat before going on through a gate. Keep by the fence of the new deciduous plantation and cross a stone-spanned ditch to the fell gate.

Turn L and in 50 yards cross a boggy ditch. Then, keeping the wall off to the left, follow it round to a gate and turn L through it. From here our objective, The Pike, is an alluring peak rising above the pines, with its watershed wall leading the way to the summit. There is no onward path, but keep parallel to the left-hand wall. When the wall turns away at a corner, hold your direction over the rough ground (note: the gate seen by the road bridge is not on the ROW path) until you reach the signposted stile and gate at the Ulpha road.

Turn L down the road, cross the bridge, pass by the Crosbythwaite Farm lane, and in 200 yards turn R on a public bridleway. The track soon disappears, but keep on shadowing the fenceline to a gate in the upper cross-wall with ROW sign. Keep ahead, parallel to the groove of the old path, now invaded by water seepage, as you aim for the col between The Pike and Hesk Fell. Stones to the left of the way lie on the site of ancient settlements and continue beyond the next cross-wall gate (wet but with step-stones among the water, peat and chickweed), and the views are extensive. At the watershed wall gate* choose to ascend The Pike and return to this spot (highly recommended) or carry on.

## TO THE PIKE

Turn L (south) and follow the watershed wall to a cross-fence. Go over the stile then follow the wall to the summit. It is completely unadorned, a mere high point in the wall, yet with a superb outlook all the more spectacular because of its sudden appearance. (To identify the panorama see p. 18/19). Return to the fence stile and continue on the ridge path to the lowest part of the wall and the gate*.

**TO CONTINUE** Turn L through the watershed wall gate to another brilliant seascape view as you turn diagonally L (south-west) towards farmsteads in the valley of Hole House Gill. Join a bridleway from old copper mines higher up the valley and turn L on the waymarked path. Pass through a gateway in a broken wall and beyond turn R, descending towards Hole House Gill through meadows to a gate (ignore the stile and gate on right), join the farm track. Turn L up the track to Pike Side. The way is clearly marked through the yard, between the barns, and into the field beyond.

Using your ingenuity go ahead for several yards then, without losing height, bear slightly left on the old green ROW path. The way is disguised by rushes, so track round the hillside to a gate staying at the same level, towards trees to a stile located 30 feet down from the wall corner. From the top of the stile the way ahead may appear like virgin territory, but it is a ROW.

Do your bit for posterity by descending left of a small oak into bracken on the line of the path, which descends gently, staying about 30 feet below the horizontal wall, into the wood, where the path is clearer and some steps have survived the encroachment of the oak leaf- mould. At a broken wall turn R and, using paths on either side and passing giant ant hills, come to a cross-wall at the end of the wood. Go over a ladder stile into a rough pasture. Keep ahead for 100 yards then bend R towards a wood corner. Pass a pile of stones in the centre of the pasture and gradually move closer to the right-hand wall to a ladder stile and gate. Go over and keep the wall to the left and the new barn at Old Hall Farm in the valley as a guide. The ruins of Frith Hall and the woods of Ulpha Park are seen ahead. Find your way down the slope until it is possible to cross L, avoiding the orchids which spring from the damp slope in June, to a gate in the left-hand wall. Go ahead between the converging woodland to a wall gap and stile in a double fence. A path now leads through the larch plantation, but take care not to stray into a drainage channel or side trods. Join a nature trail marked with green-topped posts and keep going downhill to meet a wider track. Turn R to a gate at the Millbrow Bobbin Mill. At the road turn L and continue for ¼ mile then turn R at the main road near Ulpha Bridge and the start.

*Old gatepost with The Pike behind*

# WALK 5:  **Wallowbarrow Gorge, Birks Bridge and Dunnerdale Forest**

*Wallowbarrow Farm*

**SUMMARY:** A fine valley walk which follows the River Duddon through its wooded gorge to the renowned beauty spot of Birks Bridge, then returns through the forest above. At its best after rain, in spring or autumn, when the colours are resplendent and the lively river can be seen through its cloaking trees. The riverside path is rocky and rough, whilst a long, boggy stretch has welcome duckboards. **Note** that in spate the path is impassable. Forestry clearance in 1997 has revealed the craggy lower flank of Harter Fell. Despite a return through the forest there is remarkably little forest

| | |
|---|---|
| Distance: | 4½ miles (7.25km); short return A 2½ miles (4km) |
| Grade: | Moderate. Rough walking through the gorge with wet patches |
| Terrain: | Valley and forest. Some rough paths. Dog flaps by stiles. |
| High point: | Dunnerdale Forest - 918ft (280m) |
| Height gain: | 721ft (220m) |
| Map: | OL6 |

road, as almost all the way back is along footpaths or the old bridleways which linked farmsteads.

   If a shorter walk is desired then the crossing of Fickle Steps provides amusement (if the water level is not too high) to gain Tarn Beck, the Duddon's sister stream, and finish through Seathwaite.

   Refreshments at the Post Office/shop, Ulpha and the pub at Seathwaite.

## HOW TO GET THERE AND PARKING:

From the hamlet of Ulpha in Dunnerdale continue north up the valley.

**Parking 1:** Where the main road bends to cross the River Duddon go straight on along a narrow unsigned lane to its end at Wallowbarrow Farm. Park on the wide verge left. On the wall is a voluntary heart charity box for a small parking fee.

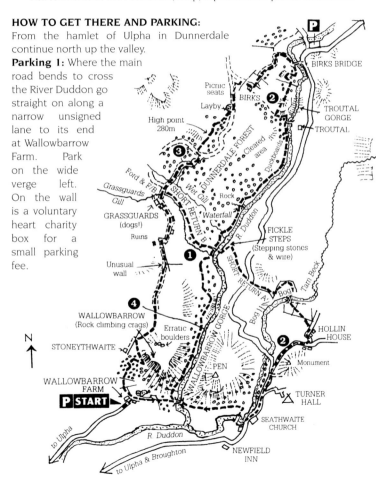

**Parking 2:** Drive past Seathwaite village and in a further 2 miles, just past Birks Bridge, **Hinning House car park** (picnic tables) is on the left.
To join the walk turn R down the road 500 yards to cross Birks Bridge **.

**THE WALK:** Start at Wallowbarrow Farm by going through the farmyard gate and past the house. Fork R signed to Seathwaite. The green path through the meadow allows a good view of Wallowbarrow Crag (ahead left), a favourite crag for rock climbers because of its sheltered position. To the east over the valley stands Caw, with the fell road over to Broughton Mills. Go through the gate into the birch wood to the packhorse bridge over the River Duddon. Do not cross over it to Seathwaite but carry on along the western riverbank, although, who will not peer over the parapet perhaps to see canoeists shooting the rapids in high water?

At a wallend thread your way through large boulders, and as the path resumes notice a pinnacle up left as the ridge of Low Crag forces the river into a narrow gorge. The rising path gives occasional glimpses through the trees of the waterfalls below and birds soaring above. The valley widens and crags rise above screes on both sides from old oak woodland.

Go over a stile and a stream which marks the edge of the National Trust property. The path now climbs, and the reward is a view east of the Dow Crag, Buck Pike, Brown Pike Ridge and the Walna Scar packhorse route over to Coniston. Skirt the boggy bits as the path follows the fence and tops a crag where Harter Fell appears to the north-west.

Descend to the river, heeding the white waymarks, to duckboards through a myrtle bog. The bushes grow just at the irresistible height to bruise a leaf between your fingers and enjoy its aromatic fragrance. Cross a footbridge over a tributary and stiles, then, if other walkers are about, shrieks of laughter may announce your arrival at

*Fickle Steps*

Fickle Steps. A *stout hand-cable aids the crossing of the stepping -stones, but they always produce a good giggle and, if the water is high, wet feet.*

The main route continues at 'To Birks Bridge'.

**SHORT RETURN A:** (only possible if the water level allows a crossing of the stepping-stones): Cross the Fickle Steps and mount the zigzag fellside path from which there is a wonderful view of Harter Fell rising from its forest. Cross the previously hidden road and move right to the wall corner (public footpath sign). (Do not be tempted to go straight across the road and down the green path which leads to a boggy area.)

Go down the wallside towards the valley of Tarn Beck. The quarries of White Pike show spoil on the facing hillside. Pass through a slit stile, turn L and totter on the tussocks past a shelter boulder. Circle the bog clockwise (ignore path left), aided by duckboards, to a footbridge over Tarn Beck.

Make your way across two fields (yellow waymarks) and, relieved of concentrating on every footfall, glance west where the rocky ridge of Pen separates Tarn Beck and the Duddon and at the valley head Crinkle Crags spread across the horizon. The second gate is slightly R. Next head for a gate diagonally L skirting a rushy spring to reach it. Go into the lane (notice the fine old stone gate slabs with pole holes, square on one side, round on the other).

Turn R along the lane and pass Low Hollin Cottage and Hollin House. At the junction with the Walna Scar road turn R. (In the field to the left is a prominent cairn.)

Ignore a stile on the right and at the junction turn L to Broughton. Pass the lane to Turner Hall Farm (campsite) and continue, not unpleasantly, down the road beside the Tarn Beck, where signs 'No Camping. No Fires' can be translated into 'beautiful picnic spots with waterfalls'.

At Seathwaite pass the parish church. By *the porch is a sundial mounted on an old stone which was used as a clipping stool at a local farm by the Rev Walker. An old newspaper article in the church recounts its history.*

Turn R opposite the church, go through a narrow slit stile, along the stream side, over a footbridge and a slab bridge, cross a leat and follow the path across the valley. The path skirts the woodland edge then leads along a wall constructed of water-worn stones to the packhorse bridge over the River Duddon. Turn diagonally L and retrace the outward route to Wallowbarrow Farm and the start.

**SHORT RETURN B\*:** If the water level is too high to cross the Fickle Steps, take a path which climbs through the woods close to the tributary stream to join the return route at Grassguards.

*Birks Bridge*

## TO BIRKS BRIDGE (main route continued):

Leave the Fickle Steps, still on the western riverside path through the beech wood to the next bit of fun, the crossing of a lively stream. Go to the foot of its waterfall pool and balance over. Fifteen yards downstream turn left across the bank. The path may be obscured by fallen leaves, but over the rise its line can be seen descending ahead. When below an old wall the path rises again, traversing below a perched block and the forest edge, and allowing views over the river to the cascades of Tarn Beck pouring from Seathwaite Tarn, lying unseen in its corrie on the opposite fellside.

Enter the forest again and, if you have chosen a wet day for the walk, proceed with the caution of a novice skater along a series of duckboards through the plantation. The proximity of the road across the diminishing stream is hardly noticed, and soon Troutal Farm is visible and the ROW path with river footbridge is reached. Do not cross but turn L up the bank and take the rising path through the plantation. At a three-way path junction turn R on the permissive path to Birks Bridge. (** The yellow waymarked path left is a short-cut to Birks if you are returning to **Hinning House (Birks Bridge) car park.)** Mount to a rock knoll which avoids Troutal Gorge, hidden below, with the bonus of a fine view of Harter Fell and the mountains surrounding Seathwaite Tarn. Descend to a stile in a fence/wall then through lighter oak woodland to face a rock outcrop. Turn R at w/m and a minute will bring you to Birks Bridge.

*Who can resist leaning over the parapet of this much photographed packhorse bridge and gazing into*

> *"..this hidden pool, whose depths surpass*
> *In crystal clearness Dian's looking glass"*

*Wordsworth certainly couldn't.*

For the return to **Hinning House (Birks Bridge) car park** cross over the river and turn L |500 yards upstream|.

Do not cross the river but keep L on the broad path curving through rough grassland. (Paths branching right lead to the car park via the new bridge.) As height is gained upper Dunnerdale stretches into the heart of the Lakeland mountains. Go through a gate into a walled path and across the ensuing pasture to Birks, now a field study centre. *In 1999 the face of Harter Fell stands bare, its many rock outcrops revealed by the harvesting of the timber, the first to be planted in the* **Duddon Forest** *in 1943.*

Go through the gate (** the path from the three-way junction joins here), turn R and over the cattle grid and through the 'Welcome' access gate. Turn L up the zigzags to the forest road or take a break at one of the picnic tables and enjoy their situation. Turn L along the forest road for a short way looking for a vehicle turning space cut into the right-hand verge. Immediately beyond a yellow waymark indicates our old ROW path. Fork R on the old path from Birks to Grassguards, with maturing trees to its left and young trees peeping above the heather on the right.

On meeting the forest road again cross diagonally L and go down the path, now wider, into dense forest. Keep on the main path ignoring other ways off into the trees. Paddle a shallow stream crossing and meet the road once more at a bend. Keep ahead, through a gate with waymarks left indicating a coast-to-coast cycle route. *Short return B joins here. At Grassguards go straight on over the ford (or make a detour over the footbridge), then to the left of the barn and out of the yard on a green fenced bridleway. The forest is left behind and the open aspect allows a view down the dale with the Walna Scar road over to Coniston just visible and to the south, the lesser peaks of White Maiden and Caw terminating the ridge.

Pass ruined barns and go up to a gate. Turn L between high walls to a gate and ladder stile. Through the next gate the walls are unusually massive but quickly give out onto the open fell. Pass an outcrop of ice-smoothed rock cut by a ribbon of white quartz. *The knob ahead with a crowning cluster of perched boulders is Wallowbarrow seen from its more gentle side. To the north-east across the dale the waterfalls of Tarn Beck pinpoint the hidden Seathwaite Tarn surrounded by, left to right, Grey Friar, Swirl How and Dow Crag.* Go through a gate or ladder stile and descend towards Stoneythwaite, a refurbished farmstead with crafts and refreshments. Turn L and go down the steepening path overlooked by the crags popular with rock climbers. Cross the stream on red foot-worn stones and carry on down to the intake wall gate and on through the garden gate to Wallowbarrow Farm barn. Notice the old datestone used as a doorstep just as you go through the adjacent gate. Turn R and through the yard to the start.

## Duddon Forest

In 1935 the Forestry Commission acquired 7,000 acres of land in Eskdale and Dunnerdale which they proposed to plant as the huge Hardknott Forest Park. Due to objections, the Commission consulted with various local bodies which resulted in the preservation of the ancient farmsteads and the attractive woodlands we enjoy today.

## Wallowbarrow Farm

This is a typical Lakeland hill farm, owned by the National Trust. During the 1990's it was a rare breeds farm which did a good job in rearing 300 New Zealand spotted pigs, whose numbers had been as low as 200.

## 'Wonderful Walker'

Reverend Robert Walker became minister and schoolmaster at Seathwaite, where he was a fine example of thrift and industry to his parishoners. He combined his duties with that of farming and shepherding. He spun wool and made his own clothes, even his boots. He was a butterfly collector and father of twelve children. He died at the age of 93 in 1802.

*Dipper*

# WALK 6:

# Seathwaite Tarn and Shudderstone How

*Seathwaite Tarn. Shudderstone How is the rock knoll on the right*

**SUMMARY:** Seathwaite Tarn in its deep glaciated combe makes a pleasant objective if you choose a period of dry weather. A wet spell, however, can turn sections into a morass, and if the stream at the tarn head cannot be crossed the traverse of Shudderstone How is curtailed. Rock scenery is splendid throughout, whilst the prospect over Harter Fell from Shudderstone How is something to savour.

**HOW TO GET THERE AND PARKING:** Park at Birks Bridge (Hinning House) car park, Duddon Valley.

| | |
|---|---|
| *Distance:* | 5½ miles (8.8km) |
| *Grade:* | Moderate |
| *Terrain:* | Low fell and valley, very boggy in places |
| *Summits:* | Shudderstone How - 1444ft (440m) |
| *Height gain:* | 1181(360m) |
| *Map:* | OL 6 |

**THE WALK:** Gain the road and turn L. In 100 yards ignore a footpath to the right (our return path), and 75 yards beyond branch R on a green forest track which rises gently and curves. Turn R at a small waymarked pole on a footpath rising through larches, a wonderful place for autumn fungi.

The path joins and runs by an old wall, moves over a crest and descends steeply to a stream. A R-pointing waymark directs a turn downstream to meet a wall. Cross L over the stream, go over a fence stile and through a gap in the wall which marks the edge of the forest and is a nesting place of wrens. The view, looking down the valley, gradually takes shape as you turn L up the side of the wall. Note a gap in the wall, used by the defunct ROW path, by a red streaked rock with a wall standing on top. Above is a rock barrier. Zigzag up a further 15 feet then turn R along a grassy shelf with the full expanse of Harter Fell standing proud above its shorn forest to the west.

Go ahead for 25 yards then slant L under a crag-grown holly on a narrow path rising through the bracken and crossing a stream. Above the intake wall are the crags of Blake Rigg, a playground for climbers and scramblers. The path converges with the wall as it climbs. On reaching a knoll turn L through a gate signed 'Public footpath to Seathwaite Tarn'. The path now climbs rightwards to an assortment of rocks, a perch for picking out the mountains on the northern horizon.

Pass through a gap by a holly and curve L round the foot of the rocks

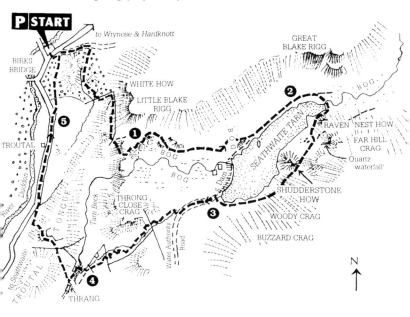

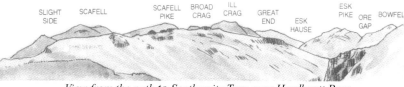

SLIGHT SIDE · SCAFELL · SCAFELL PIKE · BROAD CRAG · ILL CRAG · GREAT END · ESK HAUSE · ESK PIKE · ORE GAP · BOWFELL

*View from the path to Seathwaite Tarn over Hardknott Pass*

to climb more steeply, either by the old zigzag path (which may be obscured by bracken) or a modern frontal attack, until you can see in the middle distance ahead two sentinel perched blocks which face out over the Seathwaite valley. Turn L (waymark) on an indistinct path with quartz-streaked boulders on one side and a bog to the other. Skirt R (w/m) using the drier ground above a rock guarding a second bog. From here a glance south shows the glaciated form of the lower Duddon Valley. Leave the bog behind and, ignoring farm vehicle tracks, trek up the valley within sound of the chuckling water of Tarn Beck, until mounting a squelchy slope well to the left of the dam. At the side of an elegant perched boulder is an ice-scratched hump of rock, a panoramic seat on the lip of Seathwaite where the glacier paused before plunging steeply into the valley. The fellsides disclose vast stone-shod slopes, draped in drab grass and heather, and a deep ice-gouged combe duplicated in the dark surface of the reservoir. *It is hard to believe that as recently as 1090 BC the scene was one of birch forest, with areas cleared for cultivation by Bronze Age man. Rich soil supported more exotic plants such as Jacob's Ladder and rock rose, yet today's scene forms its own beauty. At the head of the valley is the pass of Goat's Hause, where a continual stream of minute ant-like figures move almost imperceptibly on their way to the summit of Coniston Old Man but few descend into lonely Seathwaite.*

BLACK COMBE

STICKLE PIKE

As you set off again take care, you are on top of a small quarry which is disguised, as the grass at its edge blends into the further grassy background. Descend to the shore path and progress up the valley. No further description is needed until you reach the end of the tarn. Above left towers the crag of Great Blake Rigg (climbs and scrambles). Turn down R to the colourful deep water sign, not missing a memorable display down the tarn-varied tones, now lighter and brighter, dance as the water reflects the skyscape. Cross the inlet stream on stones dry-shod - if you have chosen your weather well. (If crossing is impossible it will be unpleasantly boggy higher up the stream, so return to the dam and rejoin the route at *. Backtrack the route to climb Shudderstone How.)

Circle R to find a tarn-side path - a narrow trod below Raven Nest How. Mount to the bottom of the crag, where a cairn stands on a boulder. Continue the direction on this higher trod to approach a boulder-filled depression. Cross the gurgling lower boulders, then work diagonally up the hill on a wide grassy break to join a path coming from the gap behind Raven Nest How. Notice the fine quartz-filled cracks - easily mistaken for icefalls spilling down Far Hill Crag. The path you are making for is cunningly hidden but unmistakable when you reach it. Ignore a tiny cairn on a boulder

WHIT FELL    HESK PIKE    *The valley of Tarn Beck*

E PIKE

which is 30 feet below the path. Turn R along the traversing path to the gap behind Shudderstone How. Turn aside R to climb a few extra feet and park on the summit rocks for a panorama of infinite variety.

Return to the path and make a descending traverse across the boulder-strewn slopes of Woody and Buzzard Crags with a view of Greyfriar across the tarn. Too soon the scenic path reaches the shoreline and the braced wall of the dam*. A series of rain gauges, current and abandoned, are sited hereabouts.

Join the road from the dam and turn L, marching along until a slight bend and a waymark on the right. (If you reach two leaning stones you have overshot the path.) Turn R on an old green path which leads across a slight stream gathering in an emerging valley and turns down its throat to a gate by a sheepfold. Go through, still on the old path, and gradually the shining ribbons of the Tarn Beck valley glisten below with the line of our path making a brave attempt to stay on solid ground as it crosses the valley (see drawing).

As the descent steepens do not lose the path but cross the stream and go down its old hollow way, parallel to the wall and still retaining some of its set stones. The path gradually bends away from the wall, with the rocks of Throng Close Crag now rising in an impressive wall above. Look ahead and let your eye track back from below to locate the path as it negotiates rocky humps and eventually reach a ladder stile by a gate.

Go over and ahead through a pasture to a gate. Through this, bend R to a ladder stile in the right-hand wall. Cross the footbridge over the gorge of Tarn Beck and amble over to the gate in the left-hand wall. The path now leads along a wooded slope towards Thrang Cottage.

**TO TROUTAL TONGUE:** Before reaching the cottage turn sharp R up a path climbing through the woods (a brief ascent) and over the remains of a low wall to emerge on an attractive moorland dotted with myrtle and silver birch. The path is now more obvious and level. Go over a stile in a crosswall - a balcony with splendid views of Tarn Beck cascading into the valley - then cross a bog by means of a wooden walkway. A brief rise breasts Troutal Tongue and wooded Dunnerdale; the river in its crag-lined gorge is ahead. To the right is a fence corner. Advance 25 yards and turn R onto rock (avoiding the mistake of going ahead into a bog) and walk along the top of smoothed stone (mud free) for 100 yards to bend L with the old path and descend to the road.

Turn R, taking care on the road, which becomes narrow and walled. Pass Troutal Farm and a gate to Browside. The road becomes unfenced, so walk along to a gate in a fence on the right (public footpath sign). Go through and keep ahead, heading for an electricity post, to find a stile about 25 yards to its left and an ensuing fence stile. Go ahead through the forest on a firebreak path. At the road turn L and the car park is 100 yards on the right.

# WALK 7:  Circuit of Harter Fell

*Harter Fell from Eskdale, Walk 17*

**SUMMARY:** A satisfying circumnavigation of Harter Fell, which begins along a gentle riverside before a rough, wet ascent, in fleeting company with the Roman road, gains Hardknott Pass. Easier walking through the Roman fort descends into Eskdale. The return is a steady climb enlivened by the outlook both down the dale and up to the cirque of high fells at Eskdale's head. A final stretch through the Dunnerdale Forest completes this varied walk.

| | |
|---|---|
| *Distance:* | 6½ miles (10.5km) |
| *Grade:* | Strenuous |
| *Terrain:* | Low fell. Rough with wet patches |
| *High point:* | First pass - 1287ft (390m), Second pass - 1170ft (355m) |
| *Height gain:* | 1525ft (465m) |
| *Map:* | OL 4 |

**HOW TO GET THERE AND PARKING:** Park at Birks Bridge car park, Dunnerdale.

**THE WALK:** Cross the modern bridge over the River Duddon pausing in the middle to let the gentle

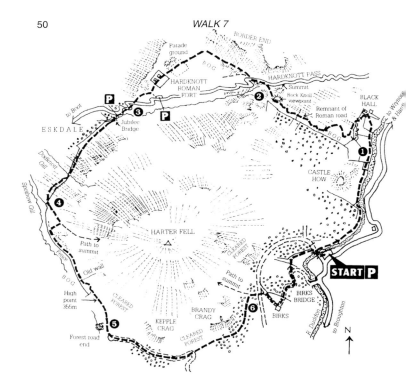

beauty of the valley set the mood for the walk. Turn R on a path between a treacherous-looking ditch and the river, which leads to a delightful green path up the riverside with comforting bridges over any oozy bits. Beyond a grove of silver birches the forest meets the river and Hinning House, an outdoor centre, can be seen across the valley. Go over a stile and along the fenceside. Castle How is the appropriately named crag on the left (west) and up the valley is Little Stand, the end of the Crinkle Crag range of peaks. Cross stepping-stones over a beck then go through two fields and gates into National Trust land. On approaching Black Hall Farm ignore the gate ahead into the yard but keep L to the stile with waymark. *Black Hall Farm is on the* **Roman road** *from Hardknott Fort to Galava at Ambleside.* Turn L on a rising path to a sign. *You are now on the Roman road. Later it was also an important snuff and wool packhorse route. This route ran from the port of Whitehaven, south to Gosforth, over Hard Knott and Wrynose passes to Kendal, the centre of the snuff industry in the 18th century.*

**a)** If you are content to enjoy the sight of the pristine, level, green Roman Road from the sign, go through a gate in the wall, signed 'to Hardknott Fort', and take the leftward climbing path towards the forest.

**b)** If you feel you must tread the road, go left, signed 'Roman Road', to the next gate in the wall. Go through and diagonally left up the field to a very high stone stile and gate. Go ahead to join the a) path.

From here on, it is a continuing puzzle to speculate on the small remaining sections of the road, but a retrospective view leaves no doubt of its onward line, now the farm drive, heading straight up the valley to Wrynose Pass. At the remains of old walls do not be fooled by farm vehicle tracks up the slope ahead, but circle right round the wet slope then back to the path close to the forest wall. Forge uphill, with butterwort, the fly-eating plant with a single purple flower in summer, and stunted violets with many purple flowers in spring adding a little colour to the barren fellside. Go over a ladder stile in a cross wall and from here Harter Fell is impressive to the left between the forestry sections. Continue by the wall and, on leaving the forest behind, arrive at a gap with Rock Knoll to the right. Turn aside R and climb the 20 feet or so to the rock top, the highest point of our circuit, with a rewarding view. Across Dunnerdale the horizon shows the characteristic whaleback of Coniston Old Man supported by Dow Crag (right) and Greyfriar (left). Return to the path, go through a gap in a broken wall and down to the road near the top of Hardknott Pass.

Turn L down the road (or briefly use an old path on the left). The Roman

*Castle How*

fort can be seen below on the right and beyond it the green meadows of Eskdale.

At the start of the hairpins turn R (public footpath signpost) and in 15 yards bend very slightly R (ignore the broad, obvious path descending left which runs into boggy places and eventually returns to the road). Keep ahead to the right of a little knoll, using the line of a shelf which carried the Roman road. Cross an old wall and keep level on the shelf to another gap by the next knoll. The path now descends leftwards to a wide flat area, the parade ground, and crosses it. The mound on the right, constructed of small stones, is the vantage point from which the Commandant reviewed his troops. Carry on to the fort, entering by the north-east gate. *Much preservation work has been done, and excellent information plaques ensure that the time spent looking round is amply rewarded.* Leave by the south-west gate.

Set off ahead, keeping left of the knoll, then turn L down the side of, and under, a rock band (ignore paths descending left to the road and parking areas). Descend ahead more steeply to a wall, and (ignore a slit stile) follow it down to the road. Turn R, cross the road and, with a view of our onward path climbing above the trees on the southern slopes of the valley, use the tarmac or the short-cuts on the grass to go down to the car park and the ford, with Jubilee Bridge over Hard Knott Gill.

Here take your pick: cross the gill by the attractive arched bridge, the stepping-stones or paddle the ford. All may be occupied by giggling youngsters on a fine summer's day, as you make your way over and up the stony path beyond to kissing gates then along the well-made old path stretching ahead up the fell. Hawthorns and rowans, overburdened with blossom, give a rich scent, and views of verdant meadows add to the

*Upper Eskdale from the Harter Fell path*

SCAFELL    SLIGHT SIDE    SCAFELL PIKE    ILL CRAG        ESK PIKE        BOWFELL        CRINKLE CRAGS

pleasure, minimising the grind of the steady climb. Pass scree held by the wall which envelops the path briefly. Brotherilkeld and the mountains of upper Eskdale now come into view (see drawing). The climb seems relentless, but does level to cross Doddknott Gill. Go through a gate then climb again until the path eases into an upper balcony overlooking the woodland groves, heaths and pastures of middle Eskdale (see Walk 17). Go through a gate in a cross-wall and carry straight on, ignoring a stile on the right. The tree-lined ravine of Spothow Gill cuts down the fell over the fence to the right, draining the moor we eventually cross. A little tributary flows between the fence and the path. Dog-leg round two cairns on the left and along under a line of low rocks, with the stately west face of Harter Fell behind. At a flat area stop at a prominent cairn. (Ignore the cairned path onward which leads to the summit of the mountain.) Turn R and cross the level area, avoiding deviating paths to the right, to reach a fence and stile. Do not go over, but turn L up the fence-side on a clear path. Ignore a gate right and keep straight on, gradually rising to a broad col but keep an eye out for the path suddenly winding, usually left, round a boghole, for there are some deep evil-looking mires. Across the moor are (L to R) Green Crag, the summits of Crook Crag and the Pike being the highest, and another Dow Crag. Go through a gap in a cross wall and skirt left round a quaking bog.

At the highest point of the col reach the forest 'welcome' gate and go through into a replanted area with an open aspect over the moor and ever-present Harter Fell. Progress is somewhat slower, but the downhill path soon improves. At a signpost with blue waymarks go L onto the terminal circle of the forest road (the path right descends to Grassguards in Dunnerdale).

The forest road is pleasant underfoot after the cleared area and aesthetically pleasing, with silver birch and rowan lining the road, groups of rowan/ash saplings in their protective tubes, and rising above on the left, the long unnoticed Kettle Crag and Brandy Crag. Go over a slight rise and at the next bend turn L at a faded blue waymark pole onto a narrow path. Looking across the Duddon valley once more, the dam holding Seathwaite Tarn and the milky cascades of Tarn Beck can be seen. *Our narrow path is occupied by immaculate clumps of deer grass, an interesting plant with triangular-sectioned stalks each topped by a minute pale yellow glume*. Enter the cleared forest and continue until the bridge at the start comes into sight. However, we are not there yet. Descend more steeply, then go straight across a rough work road and on to a path junction with waymark signs to Harter Fell and Eskdale. Heed neither, but turn R down by an old wall and overgrown enclosures to the forest road above Birks (picnic table up the road right).

Go straight on across the forest road, down the bank and along the drive to the Forest Enterprise gate at Birks. Go over the grid and to the left of the house, now an outdoor centre. Turn L through a gate and across the pasture to the woodland wall and along a short enclosed track. Go through the next gate and follow the main track through the oakwood, passing a split boulder on a bend. At the next bend leave the track (winding right to Birks Bridge, the old packhorse bridge over a gorge, see p.41 - well worth a visit) and turn L through a gap in a wall, over a plank bridge and turn R (ignore the stile) along the fence to the forest road, bridge and the car park.

**The Roman Road** Built in the late first century the Roman road linked the forts of Glannaventa (Ravenglass) to Galava (Ambleside). It was a well-engineered track, normally 20 feet wide, and crosses of two inhospitable fell passes. Defended by Hardknott Fort it was an important route taking men and supplies from the port of Ravenglass.

# WALK 8:     Buckbarrow and Whitfell

*Looking up Buckbarrow Beck to Hare Raise*

**SUMMARY:** If you like widespread views over sea and mountain, and enjoy the challenge of some rough untracked upland walking in lonely places, then this walk will prove a peaceful antidote to the more crowded fells of Lakeland. The high starting point on the Corney Fell road minimises the effort required to gain Burn Moor and the cone of Whitfell, a fine viewpoint. The return traverse over the rocky tops of Buckbarrow gives a complete, but short-lived, change of character.

**Beware** of low cloud, which can rapidly clothe these hills as warm, moist air from the sea is forced upwards. In mist the route can be confusing. A map and compass are essential.

| Distance: | 6 miles (9.6km) |
|---|---|
| Grade: | Moderate |
| Terrain: | Low fell and grassy moorland |
| Summits: | Hare Raise - 1673ft (510m) |
| | Whitfell - 1880ft (573m) |
| | Buckbarrow - 1801ft (549m) |
| Height gain: | 1263ft (385m) |
| Map: | OL6 |

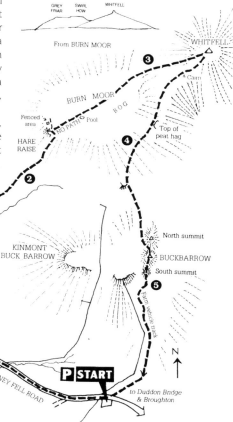

## HOW TO GET THERE AND PARKING:

**1.** From the A596 near Duddon Bridge turn up the west side of the valley to Corney Fell. (In 100 yards is the restored Duddon Iron Furnace, which is well worth a visit |see p.15|.) Continue for 1 mile then turn L on the fell road to Whitehaven (narrow road with passing places). Park on the hillcrest.

**2.** From the A595 west coast road take the Corney Fell road just south of Waberthwaite. Park on the hillcrest.

**THE WALK:** Face the sea (west) and freewheel for 1 mile down the Corney Fell road as far as the sharp hairpin over Buckbarrow Bridge. Turn R and walk upstream on the left (west) bank, gaining the moor and following edge of the trough to avoid an eroded area along the beckside. *On closer inspection the vast expanse of treeless moorland rising east of the beck to Kinmont Buck Barrow is not without interest. Buzzards wheel overhead and skylarks sing. The blue mountain grass is starred with yellow quatrefoil, and clumps of white cotton grass (not a grass but a reed) wave in the winds that race across the Irish Sea.* Pass some old cairns, the remains of a Bronze Age settlement, now a Scheduled Ancient Monument. Cross a farm vehicle path which leads to a sheepfold by the beck. Keep on upstream until the path branches slightly leftwards to join a ROW path running below Whit Crags. A fine retrospective view has opened south to Black Combe, the last peak of the mountain ridge which rises from a patchwork coastal plain. Turn R and, as you mount the zig zags, you may have noticed a wooden sign down by the stream: it is blank, but possibly contained a warning relating to the old mine workings. Carry on up the green path and to the west you see the Eskmeals viaduct carrying the railway line over the River Esk; on its left is the Eskmeals military establishment, and far right are the cooling towers of Sellafield Nuclear Power Station. The path bends to face Littlecell Bottom, the gathering grounds of Buckbarrow Beck, then swings north again towards Hare Raise. To the north the dark wooded ridge hiding Eskdale is Muncaster Fell (see Walk 15). As you progress, notice the line of the old hollow way to the left, which our path soon drops into. At a crest look right where the rock summit ridge of our final objective, Buckbarrow, appears from behind Kinmont Buck Barrow, which has so far dominated the eastern skyline.

An old fixed oil drum and cairn pinpoints the arrival at Hare Raise, but it is the next rise, gained by the gradually steepening path, which gives a wider view over Eskdale to the fells beyond.

The path now strikes out over Burn Moor, so, with your back to the sea (a north-easterly direction), head for Whitfell, the dome like a bun with a cherry cairn on top almost a mile away on the skyline. As the path

*The rocky top of Buckbarrow*

disappears watch for bog holes as you admire the expanding panorama of central Lakeland peaks. Hold the line of the route as the 'cherry' is obscured by a nearer horizon, with a guiding eye on Buckbarrow off to the right (south). As you climb up Whitfell the 'cherry' proves to be a handsome circular cairn with a wind shelter, triangulation point and small cairn on the summit. There is an exceptional mountainscape to enjoy from this modest peak.

Set off (south-south-west) from the small cairn towards the col, on a narrow path, taking care not to drop down right towards a vehicle track, but keep to the highest ground passing various stones. At the last upright one which is set in a cairn, make a leftward traverse of the fellside to the saddle below Buckbarrow without losing any height. There is a narrow sheep trod which is helpful. It runs above a peaty hole, then about 50 yards above a patch of rushes and along through scattered stones to a sheep-sheltering area, finally arriving at the saddle by a mound used as a lookout by sheep.

A path can now be seen heading up Buckbarrow. Go straight along and aim to arrive at the summit rock-fin left of centre. Clamber up choosing rock or grass to suit, to a golden view over Dunnerdale down the sands of the estuary.

Turn down L (east), cross the bouldery gap and climb up to the south dual summit. (If you have conquered sufficient heights for the day turn R in the gap, negotiate the stones and at their edge circle left below the scree to meet the route from the summits.) The first top is defended by a smooth slab which proves amusing to climb for the ego and equally so for a slide back down the same way. Turn the rock on its left and go up the second top. From here survey the onward route.

Looking south (towards Black Combe) there stretches a wide moorland ridge with a wall and a vehicle track running parallel. Pick your way down around the rocks to meet the way from the gap, but do not deviate from the general direction south towards the wall. Merge with the track and the wall, aiming for a fine upstanding cairn which proves to be merely part of the wall on a crag. The distance between the track and the wall varies but it leads easily down to the Corney Fell road (parking).

## WALK 9:          **Black Combe East**
### (from Beckside via the Horse Back Ridge)

*Whicham Mill*

**SUMMARY:** Travellers to the Lake District from the south will be familiar with the sight of Black Combe, the first rise of the fells from the sea. Despite its gentle profile, steep slopes abound, especially around the deep valley which cuts into its heart. Our walk explores this valley, Whitecombe Beck, then climbs out steeply by the Horse Back ridge, which makes a fine way to the moorland plateau. Views into the aptly named Black Combe are impressive. The ever expanding vista over the Duddon Estuary and central Lakeland fells makes a good excuse for a rest. Once the rim is gained it is an easy stroll to the summit, where the west Cumbria coast and the Isle of Man add to the scene. It was here, in 1813, that Wordsworth was inspired to write his 'View from the top of Black Combe'.

The return is very easy walking, back along the moor to the head of the valley where an old, well-graded, smooth green path zigzags down to our starting point. Black Combe, being so close to the sea, gets more than its fair share of cloud and

| | |
|---|---|
| *Distance:* | 5¼ miles (7.5km) |
| *Grade:* | Strenuous |
| *Terrain:* | Medium fell, mainly dry underfoot. Easy walking, except the Horse Back Ridge (steep with path, brief alternative avoids steep section). |
| *Summits:* | Black Combe - 1968ft (600m) |
| *Height gain:* | 1804ft (550m) |
| *Map:* | OL6 |

is often enveloped when hills further up Dunnerdale are cloud free.

**HOW TO GET THERE AND PARKING:** Park at Beckside Bridge on the A595 around 4 miles south-west of Duddon Bridge, 2 miles north-east of Silecroft. Park on the widened roadside by the farm.

**THE WALK:** Cross the road (post box and footpath sign), and set off along the lane which once served both farm, mill, mine and traveller alongside Whitecombe Beck. Go straight through Rallis Farm and on past Whicham Mill, now cottages.

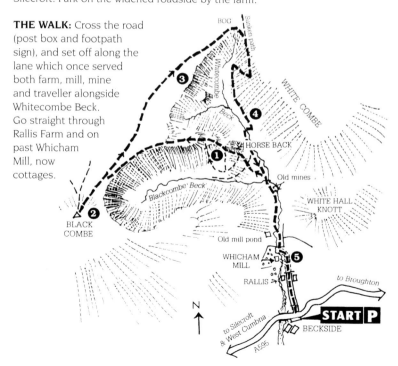

*Looking up Whitecombe Head from the Horse Back Ridge*

The valley bottom with its plantation is a gentle contrast to the steep bare flanks of Sty Knotts rising on the left and those of White Hall Knott to the right. Go through a gate, then in 50 yards fork L on the lower way to reach the gate in the intake wall.

Cross the sleeper bridge and notice to the left a reedy pond, once used by the mill. The valley has now taken on a wilder aspect. The domed slope of White Combe gradually appears behind White Hall Knott and a retrospective view shows the low wooded ridge of Millom Park. *Beside the track a boulder of Skiddaw slate confirms the mineral-bearing country rock, as do the remains of iron mines between track and beck. Black Combe is an isolated mass of the Skiddaw slates, which, as in northern Lakeland, results in generally smooth, but steep, valley sides and gently rounded summits.*

Ahead left is the rocky ridge of Horse Back. Cross the sidestream of Blackcombe Beck, and as the track begins to climb it offers a view of waterfalls in the valley and our return path cutting a line across the slope of White Combe.

At the top of a rise fork L on a narrow path traversing to the rocks of Horse Back. Meet and cross a major path (the farmer's way into the combe). The path now dwindles as the ground becomes steeper and passes through an area of grass clumps to approach the rocks. Turn L up the grass, keeping under the rock ridge. It is steep and requires effort but the views continually expand to look out over the Duddon Estuary. (To take the steepness out there is a narrow trod slanting away left across the slope - this may be obscured by the short bracken - and returning to the ridge via a smooth spur which rises to the flat reedy shelf with the sheepfold.) Bend R round the top of the rocks then keep R to reach a saddle on the ridge. Go up the ridge by up-ended plates of rocks then turn L to reach a flat reedy shelf with a fenced sheepfeed area where many animal paths converge.

Pass the fence and choose one of the paths leading onwards and upwards, avoiding the ones shedding off left. Keep up the broad ridge on a more distinct path now, pass between quartz-flecked rocks and gain the top of the Horse Back which offers a seascape scene east to Walney Island and the coast to Peel Island and Morecambe Bay.

Our onward path can be seen ahead shadowing the edge of Blackcombe Screes. We now have a dramatic view into the heart of Blackcombe and beyond to the slope of Swine Crag which is seamed with the horizontal lines of solifluxion (soilcreep). Look right (north) to note* where our return path quits the main moorland ridge, just north of Whitecombe Beck Head, to begin its descent into the valley.

Follow the path round the edge of the combe (take care if mist descends) to reach the wide moorland summit ridge, where the sudden view of the west coast and central mountains of Lakeland demands a halt.

When the edge of the combe turns away left a host of paths and trods merge into two prominent paths. **Remember them. Take the left-hand one and arrive at the windbreak wall and trig point to a unique view from the summit. T*his dark peak at the extremity of the Lake District is a familiar sight from the Isle of Man to the Pennines. A bastion in the teeth of every gale it acts as a measure of visibility for seamen and layman alike, as a marker of cloud level for walkers from their distant homes, and, however many times you visit Black Combe, the vast outlook is never quite the same.*

Retrace your steps, taking care in the first 100 yards to get on the same path, now the right-hand of the two paths (north). (The left-hand path will soon veer away to descend west towards Bootle.) ** Make sure you are on the path leading along the highest part of the moorland ridge and parallel, but well away from, the edge of Blackcombe Screes. Once located the path runs clear ahead down the moor and across the top of Whitecombe Beck Head. Pass patches of rushes, then plough through a rushy swathe, using their rootballs as support in a nasty peaty bog. Bend R to join an old green grooved path and turn R along it. This is the path seen previously*.

Follow the zigzags gently down to the valley and jump across the infant beck just above where it plunges down a gorge at the foot of Horse Back ridge. Turn L down the valley to the start.

# WALK 10:

# Black Combe West
## (from Whitebeck)

*Tarn Dimples*

**SUMMARY:** The neglected side of Black Combe deserves a visit. Its flanks are incised by steep gills which cut into ice-shorn slopes. Above is an unbroken moor which has a windswept wilderness atmosphere. Old bridleways encircle the fell and pass close to the summit. We use parts of the bridleway, but choose a less circuitous route which ascends by a more interesting way and short-cuts back to avoid a tedious stretch of busy road.

The sea is your companion, with extensive views along the west Cumbrian coast, including the landmarks of Sellafield and the Isle of Man.

Walking on the bridleway is easy with grassy sections. Paths dwindle on the moor but still provide easy going as narrow trods. On the lower

| | |
|---|---|
| *Distance:* | 6 miles (9.7km) |
| *Grade:* | Moderate |
| *Terrain:* | Easy underfoot, moorland, medium fell |
| *Summit:* | Black Combe - 1968ft (600m) |
| *Height gain:* | 1870ft (570m) |
| *Map:* | OL6 |

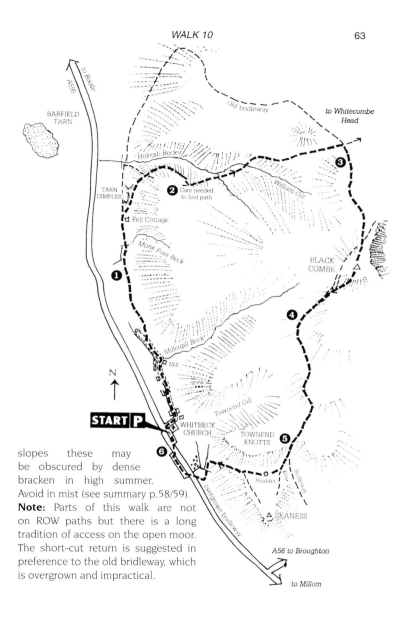

slopes these may be obscured by dense bracken in high summer. Avoid in mist (see summary p.58/59).
**Note:** Parts of this walk are not on ROW paths but there is a long tradition of access on the open moor. The short-cut return is suggested in preference to the old bridleway, which is overgrown and impractical.

**HOW TO GET THERE AND PARKING:** Park at Whitbeck church on the A595 between Silecroft and Bootle.

**THE WALK:** Turn alongside the church on a surfaced lane which passes a farm, bends left, loses its surface and gains enough height to produce a view. *To the west is the coastal plain, which was smoothed some 12,000 to 20,000 years ago by a southward moving ice sheet, and to the east is the steep ice-shorn slope of Black Combe. The walls are mainly of Skiddaw slate, the country rock, but boulders of ice-transported, large-crystalled granite are easily detected by the untrained eye.* Pass Midtown Farm and Combe Cottage then arrive at **Whitbeck Mill**. Branch L down to cross Millergill Beck. *Take a few strides up the grass bank and you can see the waterfalls in Millergill, the old overshot wheel and the remains of the stone leat which carried the water from a header dam above.*

Carry on along the old lane. Pass Gate House farm and 100 yards beyond branch R on a path above a quarry and leading to a brow. *From here is a fine view of the coast which will become familiar as the walk proceeds: Sellafield and St Bees Head to the north, and out west the Isle of Man on its misty couch.*

*Whitbeck Mill*

Walking the pebble beach north from Silecroft on the Cumbria Coastal Way (Walk 11)

Looking across Devoke Water to Harter Fell, on the descent from White Pike (Walk 13)

The Eskdale Needle with the cascades of Esk Gorge in the valley below (Walk 18)

The modest summit of Whin Crag makes an attractive objective (Walk 20)

The way is now a comfy green path which undulates with a narrow short-cut R. Cross a sleeper bridge over Monkfoss Beck and glance up at the cascades as you pass.

Just beyond Fell Cottage fork R and go through a little hidden valley formed by quartz-speckled rock outcrops, attractively named Tarn Dimples (there is a dwarf-size shelter under a flat stone). Bear R to climb up the rise to view the deep valley of Holegill ahead. Its water, emerging from the fell, flows hidden in a yellow stream of spring gorse as it winds through the meadows to Barfield Tarn. Keep ahead across a spur then turn R up the slope of the fell towards Holegill Beck. (Do not be sidetracked onto a path right up a spur appearing to make straight for the summit.) At cross-paths keep ahead on a narrow path; this makes towards the gill, then climbs steeply well above it, through bracken which gradually gives way to bilberry and heather. Look ahead up the valley, where streams converge and the young Holegill Beck runs under its maiden name of William Gill. We intend to cross just above the junction and mount the moor left of William Gill.

The angle eases and the path becomes a mere thread in deeper heather ahead. Now is the time to move to a better parallel path about 40 feet higher up the right-hand slope. To attain this turn R on a trod for 10 yards then fork L up through the bilberry, ignoring trods for about 100 yards, to meet the better path. Turn L (low- lying quartz stones) towards a side gill and drop down to cross the tributary. Keep ahead, circling round bog holes and not missing the pretty cascading chute in Holegill Beck which is met just above the name-changing stream junction.

The stride over William Gill in the heart of the desolate vale has the finality of having burnt your boats. The path has disappeared in the soggy ground between the streams and the summit of Black Combe is nowhere to be seen on the southern horizon. This is all character building, as you find the improving path beyond the bog and make height parallel and well above William Gill. Pause now and again to enjoy the superb seascape to the west then continue the straight, steady climb to meet and cross a pink-stone trickle (which is usually dry). Keep up the left bank of the pink trickle (Will Gill is well away right by now) until the gradient eases. Ignore a cross-path and carry on until the pink trickle gill is no more and the main ridge path is met. Turn R and proceed up the broad ridge. Looking north the moor is cut by the Corney Fell road, the only sign of civilization. As you proceed to the summit a word of caution. Be aware of your surroundings, as Black Combe and its neighbour Buckbarrow are often covered by cloud when other mountains are clear. Remember the crags of the Combe are well to the left (east) (see p.59) and take careful note of your angle of approach before you leave the old main path, which circles the west side of the summit, to dash ahead into the wind shelter at the summit triangulation point. It is an experience to gaze skywards and see the cloud forming over your head.

Go straight over the summit (south), and just over the summit dome rejoin the old path to stride off down the broad cairned descent route running on the right flank of the ridge. The deep gill on the right is Millergill Beck.

The view south is of the Silecroft wind farm, Haverigg prison and village, and the Hodbarrow embankment (near Millom) and over the Duddon Estuary to Barrow and Walney Island.

Cross the top of Townend Gill with its old mine/quarry down right, and carry on past Townend Knotts (to the right). Look ahead to the flat area on the right. We aim to cross the flat shelf between the Knotts and Seaness.

Leave the path where it divides and fork R before the ROW drops into a steep valley. Go about 100 yards then turn R and cut across the moor to a huge erratic boulder. Pass it and, staying on the same level, keep above the bracken to join a path coming from the cairn on Seaness. Turn R (this is not a ROW) and walk on down to a fence and gate. Do not go through but turn L and go down the fence-side to a gate level with an oak plantation off to the right. Go through the gate and straight down to the road. Turn R along the road for 500 yards to the start.

**Whitbeck Mill** A corn mill which was closed, then re-opened for a few years during the Second World War.

*Erratic boulder, Black Combe*

# WALK 11:

### A sample of the
## Cumbria Coastal Way
### (Silecroft/Bootle via train)

*On the Cumbria Coastal Way below Gutterby Banks*

**SUMMARY:** Completely different from other walks in this book, it traverses a quiet part of the Cumbria Coastal Way. At first it crunches along a shingle beach below cliffs of red clay, then winds along the grassy cliff top, where storm erosion has bitten deep into the path. (The problems caused by erosion are being dealt with, and an inland alternative is included.) Continue along the pleasant grassy flat of Hyton Marsh, and the River Annas backed by a vivid gorse bank.

There are views from the cliff top to the bulk of Black Combe and into the heart of Wasdale's mountains. Looking north along the coast, the vertical profile of St Bees Head and the constant, but subtle, presence of the Isle of Man add to the seascape. Some may find the initial stretch along the beach boring. Others will be soothed by the rhythm of

| | |
|---|---|
| *Distance:* | 7½ miles (12km) |
| *Grade:* | Easy, but rough underfoot |
| *Terrain:* | Rough pebble and sand beach, cliff-top, fields and lanes |
| *High point:* | Annaside Bank - 164ft (50m) |
| *Height gain:* | Negligible |
| *Map:* | OL6 |

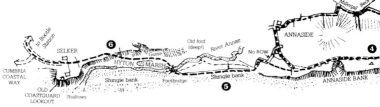

the waves, and the accompanying oystercatchers which gradually move ahead at your approach. The walk starts at Bootle railway station, with a short train ride to Silecroft. Make sure to tell the driver or conductor to stop at Silecroft. Dogs ride free.

**Note:** no trains on Sundays.

**HOW TO GET THERE AND PARKING:** Park at Bootle station, which is located 1 mile north-west of the village. Board the train in the direction of Barrow and alight at the next stop, Silecroft. The ride is a picturesque treat of 6 minutes.

**Best on an ebbing tide - more choice underfoot.**

**THE WALK:** Leave Silecroft station, cross the line and go south along the road towards the beach. Walk three-quarters of a mile, with Black Combe behind. When the gorse of Silecroft Heath is on the right, the surf heralds arrival at the beach car park. (Information panel). Turn R, go through the large car park (toilets at the far end) and onto the beach. As you stand on the sea wall the furthest point of cliff to the right is the end of our first section of beach walking. To the left, the lighthouse on the point is the Walney Island airfield building.

Go north-west along the beach where it can be bracing, even on a good sunny day, as the wind sweeps along the coast. The land terminates in low cliffs of boulder clay, left by the Irish Sea ice some 20,000 years ago. As you progress they gradually increase in height to defy the sea as rusty-coloured cliffs. T*he boulder clay contains multi-coloured cobbles of various sizes (see* **Annaside Battle**), *which the waves continually demand. The soft clay, together with its stones, soil and turf, submit to the winter storms which pound the coastline, causing a continual adjustment of the footpath.*

Pass gaps in the cliff, high bays with gorse and grazing sheep wandering the edge of the rich cliff-top meadows.

Gradually, after 2 miles Gutterby Banks is reached. The beach becomes littered with ever larger stones of grey granite. Look out for a deep valley with a CCW sign. Turn R up the valley to a gate, stile and signpost. **Inland route leaves here.**

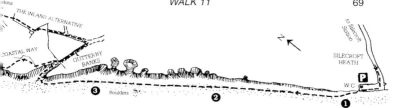

**The coast route and CCW continued.** Turn L up the bank before the gate, ignore a stile and, keeping an eye on the remains of the path, take a quick view of Black Combe. Thread your way carefully between the fence and the cliff edge to reach another stile. There are erosion problems but take to the safety of the field and keep ahead to meet a farm track and a cross fence. (Stile in the wrong place.) Go ahead joining the farm track, then over a brow which gives a fine view of the mountains surrounding Miterdale. Climb over a stile between gates, and keep on the track. Notice the trig point 35 yards to the left, while to the right is the village of Bootle and the railway viaduct over the River Annas. Far ahead rises the cluster of Sellafield chimneys, seen as you cross a stile by a gate with a huge bluestone gatepost. Continue by the right-hand wall/fence to another gate with stile. Still on the track go through another gateway and re-gain the cliff top. Pass a 'Private' sign.

The top of Annaside Bank allows us to scan the coast north to St Bees Head. Keep on past a wall/fence end. * The inland route joins here.

**Inland route Gutterby to Annaside**
Climb up left a few feet to cross the stile and return to the track. The track climbs and becomes enclosed with gates. As you move to the crest of the rise, a wonderful view of Black Combe unfolds, with Millergill Beck (L) and Townend Gill (R) biting deep into its flanks. At a junction turn L into a wider walled track. (This is **not a right of way** but its use is generously allowed by the farmer.)

Go along to enter a gateway signed 'Private Farmland'. Walk on facing a sweeping landscape showing the mountains surrounding Wasdale, and, out to sea, the Isle of Man reclines on the western horizon. Ignore a track right. You are now on a right of way.

Keep ahead through a gate and bend L on meeting the fence. Just before a sheep fold turn R. Do not be surprised to see gulls bathing in the rainwater ponds, which collect in the undulations of the meadows. Stay by the fence. Gradually the pyramid summit of Great Gable comes into sight away to the north. Climb over a stile with a yellow arrow waymark. Keep

ahead on the line of an old grassed-over
wall to a marker post in the pasture. At
the post turn L to reach a fence corner,
and keep on down the slope. The next
stile is closely guarded by a spring and
its attendant bog. Having made it over
the stile turn R. Follow the emerging
brook to its confluence with Millergill
Beck. Negotiate two more stiles and
cross a footbridge, still by the beck, and
come to another stile. Turn L up the

hill, the Hawes, to find a shy enclosed footpath which climbs to an upper
pasture. Turn R alongside windswept hawthorns. The height gained allows
a view over the fields to the east where a recent aerial photograph revealed
circles, resumed to be the wooden bases of ancient homesteads.

Go through the right-hand of two gates. The old, overgrown path forges
along through two more gates, then ahead by the fence as it develops into
a farm track. Follow it round to Annaside Farm. Go straight through the
yard, turn L then ahead (ignore the access lane to the road which turns
right) to a fork in the lane. The right-hand fork leads directly to the beach
but is **not a right of way**. To keep to the ROW fork L and go up the track
to find * at the offset ladder stile rejoining the coast route.

**The Inland Route and Coast route join here**. Leave the track to go over
the offset ladder stile. Turn L to go round the field edge, but not too near
as the cliff is unstable. Find a stile by a gate into a lane. Turn L along the
lane to the beach.

**Alternative 1:** Turn R along the beach for a short distance to double
gates. Now gain the ROW path in the field alongside the seaward fence. *The
barbed wire fence flies plastic 'flags', reminiscent of Himalayan mantras, yet without
their noble intent.*

An old look-out station is ahead. Go through a gate in a cross-fence
then ahead with the River Annas to the right. The ROW crosses the deep
river where a pair of stiles indicate the 'ford'. Either swim across with the
sea trout, or go downstream for 100 yards to an elegant wooden footbridge
placed by the National Park Authority.

**Alternative 2:** Turn R and crunch along the shingle beach until reaching
the footbridge.

Cross the river and trace a circle L between the flood ponds of Hyton
Marsh and a high bank of bright yellow spring gorse. The marsh gradually

*Hyton Marsh and the River Annas*

narrows to a stile. Go ahead on a path, which climbs the gorse bank to enjoy an unusual view back over the marsh to the river held captive by the pebble bank. Follow the CCW arrow sign ahead along the cliff top (erosion), and go along to the left of the farm, then through a signed gate. The old lookout is on the left. Keep ahead over a cattle grid and along the access track. The aspect is surprisingly good. Ignore the CCW sign, and gradually turn inland on the track-cum-lane, which passes Broad Water farm. The lane soon becomes surfaced yet retains its good view almost to the end, where we turn L to Bootle Station.

## Annaside Battle

The colourful cobble-stones of the coastline beach, brought and deposited by glaciers, were used in coastal wall building and as ballast in ships. The trade in cobbles gradually increased and the local population blamed an expansion of coastal erosion on the removal of the cobbles. In 1838 the crews of three ships, which had arrived to load cobblestones, were confronted by angry locals who drove them away. The practice of taking away the local stones was later banned.

*Oystercatchers*

# WALK 12 : Millom - Hodbarrow Iron Works Walk

*Hodbarrow Point and The Beacon*

**SUMMARY:** Millom seems an unlikely venue for a recommended walk, yet the old ironworks, now reverting to nature, provide a fascinating and very easy stroll with plenty of interest - a touch of industrial archeology in the old lighthouses and the mine site, an RSPB bird reserve, a fine rocky peninsula and bracing views over the Duddon Estuary and Irish Sea. A good filler for a poor day, or an outing for children on their bikes.

**HOW TO GET THERE AND PARKING:** On the A5093 at Millom pass the school then turn L at the station, signed 'Town Centre'. Pass the town square on the left and the park (toilets). Turn second R at Mainsgate, signed 'Nature Reserve' (telephone box), to the T-junction, then turn L to the parking opposite or over the cattle grid just beyond the gates of the recycling depot. There is a 'Wildlife Information' sign at the car park.

| | |
|---|---|
| *Distance:* | 3 miles |
| *Grade:* | Easy - children could cycle most of the way round |
| *Terrain:* | Flat walking mainly on broad paths. Some lane walking. |
| *Map:* | OL6 |

HODBARROW POINT

❶

*E S T U A R Y*

Old windmill

RSPB HIDE

*OUTER BARRIER built 1905*

THE BEACON

*INNER BARRIER built 1890*

HODBARROW

❷

Old mines now flooded

PORT HAVERIGG

CARAVAN SITE

**P START**

HAVERIGG

Stone wall

The Commodore

↓
N

MILLOM

to Town Centre

**THE WALK:** The first sight of the abandoned iron workings, now flooded to make a bizarre lagoon, conjures to mind a scene from the Everglades. It should arouse your curiosity for this unusual walk. Go through a gate by a cattle grid (additional parking on the left) and along the track with huge sandstone blocks, the bases for heavy machinery, lining the track. Ahead is the Beacon. Branch R on a red earthy track through gorse heathland. Facing right is the neat quarried red wall which was the first attempt to protect the delvings from the sea. The track diminishes to a path which rises towards the old Beacon giving a westward view over Millom to Black Combe. The heathland on the left has been colonised by a variety of plants, notably rare orchids flowering in early summer. If you wish to enjoy them please take care where you tread, as some species take many years to mature and seed. There is a surprise view a few yards ahead. We will pass to the R of the lighthouse, but not before climbing the mound for an extensive view of the Duddon Estuary.

Return to the track, go along (CCW sign) and up to the old windmill, built of limestone, where once more the panorama is superb (trig point). Descend - but **note,** if you use the path to the left of the trig point **take care of children** and dogs as you are on top of a quarry.

Now turn L to the headland where the rocks of Hodbarrow Point challenge the sea. *The low-lying shores of the estuary allow the tides to creep about undisturbed but, surprised by the zawned limestone of the point at high tide, the waves are forced into frenzied surges and sprays which prove hypnotic to watch. There are flat rocks with fossils and a sandy beach (**take care** - shelving beach), a grand place for supervised youngsters to enjoy themselves.*

Back on the path turn L along the sea wall. *The flooded* **Hodbarrow Mine** *workings on the right are now under the protection of the* RSPB *and form an important haven for wildlife.* Pass the massive sea defences and proceed to the metal lighthouse and Copeland Council danger notice.

Leave the track and turn R to a low concrete building. *This is the* RSPB *public hide. A report book shows the birds seen in the area, and a typical entry of daily sightings include Slavonian geese, ravens, tufted duck, grebe, goldeneye, many species of tit, goldfinch and goldcrest - not to mention the variety of ubiquitous seagulls. All indicate the reaffirmed importance of the old workings.*

Return to the track and carry on until, with the marina and dunes to the left and water ski centre to the right, you reach the end of the embankment. Pass the caravan site and at the road turn R. As you walk along the quiet road notice a neat wall constructed of large waterworn pebbles. Turn L at The Commodore and ahead through the car park. Turn R along a road, with a view across the fields to Millom and the fells of Black Combe, then fork R into a concrete lane. The lagoon is soon seen on the right and the hedged track will lead into the car park and start.

## Hodbarrow Mines

Veins of iron ore, exposed in the shore, were mined by the Earl of Lonsdale, but it was not until 1856, when the Hodbarrow Mining Company sunk a shaft that broke into deposits over 100 feet thick, that the importance of the site was realised. The deposits extended under the sea, but the overlaying rock was too thin to guarantee safety for underground mining, so opencast working, protected from the tides by a timber barrier, was excavated. In 1890 the first sea wall extended the potential, and finally the impressive outer sea barrier was built in 1905. Millom became a thriving community with the mines employing over 1000, but due to the decline in the price of ore the works closed in the 1920s.

A fine sculpture in tribute to the industry and the poet Norman Nicholson stands in the square.

The Folk Museum has a reproduction of an iron mine, made from genuine artefacts salvaged from Hodbarrow mine.

*The outer barrier, Hodbarrow*

CHAPTER 2
# Eskdale

Walkers in Eskale have a great choice - from the wild high scenery of Upper Eskdale to the beautiful woodland of the central dale or walks based upon the railway at its seaward end.

Ancient cairns, stone circles, forts and many old paths and roadways, once important for quarrying or peat cutting, remind us of people who lived and worked here many centuries ago.

The pink Eskdale granite is a feature of the middle and lower part of the dale, whilst gorse adds glorious colour in spring and early summer.

As in the Duddon Valley bracken can be a problem at the height of its growth and walkers must expect to encounter boggy patches on most routes.

*The upper part of Birker Force*

# WALK 13: Stainton Pike, Yoadcastle, White Pike and Barnscar Settlement

*Summit of White Pike*

**SUMMARY:** We usually include at least one challenging walk for the lover of wild country and this is it - wet and rough underfoot, relatively long and tiring. Allow a full day in good visibility. The rewards are many, including a lively waterfall, three fine rocky summits and views which encompass much of south-west Lakeland, and extend over the sea to the Isle of Man and Scotland. Add to that the atmosphere of walking where prehistoric man left his mark with ancient cairns and settlement remains. The terrain can be very wet, but our suggested route avoids the worst bogs. Both outward and return paths were once important bridleways from the Duddon Valley to Waberthwaite and Ravenglass, difficult to imagine now as many parts of the old track have vanished in the mire.

| | |
|---|---|
| *Distance:* | 8¾ miles (14km) |
| *Grade:* | Strenuous |
| *Terrain:* | Rough and wet |
| *Summits:* | Stainton Pike - 1634ft (498m) |
| | Yoadcastle - 1621ft (494m) |
| | White Pike - 1450ft (442m) |
| *Height gain:* | 1883ft (574m) |
| *Map:* | OL6 |

**HOW TO GET THERE AND PARKING:** One mile north-east of Waberthwaite on the A595, just north of the Corney Fell road junction, park on the left near the telephone box opposite Broad Oak Farm.

**THE WALK:** Turn R up the road and fork L at Corney Fell junction. Go straight up the fell road. Ignore a signed footpath on the right and as height is gained the attractive skyline of our walk is seen on the left (east), with the railway viaduct crossing the River Esk estuary to the west. Turn L on a public bridleway by an electricity pole, Fell Lane, where the road grind ends and the walk improves immediately.

The sweeping landscape from the track extends 180 degrees from Burn Moor in the south to the local landmark, Stainton Tower, and along the wooded ridge of Muncaster Fell to the Irish Sea.

As the track bends into Grange Farm keep through the gate ahead. (If the gate is tied fasten the band behind you; the farmer has gate-wise cows.) The track is decimated by the waters of the Whitrow Beck and the kneading hooves of livestock but soon is recognisable as it continues up

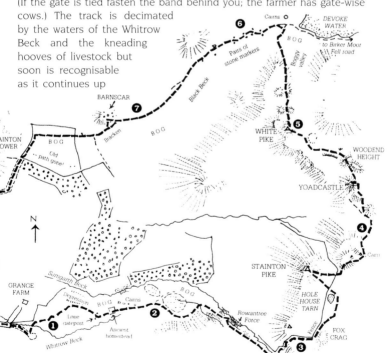

WHITE
PIKE

WOODEND
HEIGHT

YOAD CASTLE

STAINTON
PIKE

*Rowantree Force*

the moor. To the left are plantations, patches of lush pile on the sheepshorn moor. Cross Whitrow Beck and the track improves as it swings towards the forest then becomes a single trod between clumps of gorse. It bends gradually right to face a V-shaped streambed of Samgarth Beck and threads along a blind depression with a tiny stream which peters out. From here you can see the deep cleft with the waterfalls of Rowantree Gill descending the southern side of Stainton Fell to the forest corner, where it changes its name to Samgarth Beck. Ahead is a large area of bog, so ignore a path on the OS map by the beck which has fallen into disuse.

Scan ahead for remaining posts of an old gateway which indicates the ROW path rising onto drier ground. Steering towards the gill the path passes through the site of ancient homesteads and cairns. To the right the old bridleway can be seen slanting up Waberthwaite Fell. Pass a few old white-topped posts, and if the moor is fairly dry cross straight to the top corner of the forest and up the side of the gill. If wet (it usually is) circle well above the rushy area to strike the gill at a higher level and head up a spur to meet the ravine where the rowans peep from its bed.

The ravine is a different world. It contains a series of waterfalls and cascades with grassy platforms. The bright rowan berries of August overhang the only sheltered place for a stop on the bleak fellside. Do not fail to look back down the gill from above the falls. It is quite a picture.

Follow the gill up the moor until a faint line of the bridleway joins from the right. Ahead is Whitfell with its pimple cairn (Walk 8). When the left-hand fence bends left cross the stream and go along a trod near the fence. (Watch your step, I sank knee deep in a bog just here!) Bend L up a stone-strewn bank from which the bridleway can be seen running north of Whit fell towards the Duddon Valley.

Bend R with the fence and Stainton Pike looks much nearer. Turn L, passing Fox Crag on the right and along to Hole House Tarn, which rivals any tarn for the best mountain backdrop. Pass on either side; but we recommend the east side, where there is a splendid outlook over the Duddon Valley and the Coniston range of mountains.

Join the fence again, stride over it and make your way to the fine cairn on the summit of Stainton Pike. The view over the sea is breathtaking if you can stand against the full blast of the westerly wind, which carries the sound of the Eskmeals surf. After identifying the mountains from the south-east Pennines, north to Scotland and west to the Isle of Man take note of the onward route.

Our next task is to attain the rock cone of Yoadcastle (see sketch) by keeping to the highest intervening ground. Return to the fence at a reinforced bend, cross it and turn L. As the path diverges from the fence follow it round the right-hand side of a rocky knoll and keep to the highest ground passing a cairn on a rock. The line of the bridleway can be seen crossing Bigertmire Pasture - its east-west crossing of the fell almost complete. Gradually our path becomes easier to follow. Pass a large cairn before skirting L of a crag and a knoll. Divert L from the path to attack the bastion of Yoadcastle from the east side, where another grand panoramic view springs from its crowning rock.

Before leaving look at the onward route through a rock gateway on the west slope of Woodend Height. We are aiming for White Pike in a direct line with the towers of Sellafield.

*View from Stainton Pike*

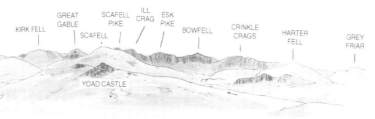

*Cyclists on the track between Devoke Water and Barnscar*

Return to the path and turn L to continue our direction and pass a pool well off to the right. Go through the rock gateway and ahead over the brow. Turn L down grassy shelves (parts steep) to meet a cross-trod and turn R along it above a red bog. Keep ahead, with Devoke Water showing down to the right, to the tall cairn on White Pike. *We can now look down over the site of Barnscar Settlement as later prehistoric man would have looked down on his home. This was the first time deforestation of the natural woodland and scrub took place to provide clearings for cultivation and grazing. We see today a boggy moorland valley which we must negotiate.*

Set off north, after skirting round the summit crag, towards the outlet of Devoke Water. Do not be tempted to make a short-cut west. Go down the grassy slopes between rock outcrops and down a broad ridge to the left of a boggy combe. Devoke Water has many faces but this aspect is surely its prime facet. As it appears closer do not descend towards it but stay on the drier ground now aiming ¼ mile below the lake. Make for a circle of bare rock on a low whaleback ridge. Go down to the edge of the bog under the circle, cross the lazy Black Beck and turn R round the right-hand side of the whaleback. Keep ahead by a pool and meet a cross-path. This is the old bridleway to Ravenglass guided by pairs of ancient stones then by cairns along the way.

Turn L following the stones over the remote moor. As we progress down the Black Beck valley White Pike presents a fine profile with Stainton

Pike behind. Pass an old sheepfold on the right and a couple of large cairns before the path runs through bracken gradually rising onto drier ground. The path splits and rejoins and seems to be heading for **Stainton Tower,** the prominent folly. When level with the distant great gash of Iron Groves to the south on Corney Fell arrive at a fork. Note this spot.

Fork R and in 100 yards reach the Barnscar Settlement. T*he banked circles of the huts are somewhat overgrown after 3000 years and a bit of imagination is needed to reconstruct the Bronze Age site. It was a thriving village with small fields growing grain, and the pollen, found when a burial cairn was excavated, showed the area was still forested at that time.*

Return to the fork and take the L-hand branch (or send someone else and cut across to meet them). At the edge of the bracken keep ahead to a signpost. Follow the yellow arrows through a gate and up a rising moor, now on a wet path where water seems to defy gravity. The worst sections have been gravelled. At the cross-wall ignore an old stile and turn L on the re-routed path alongside the wall.

At the forest corner go through the gate and negotiate the quagmire captured in a walled lane. Stainton Tower is accessible from here.

The going gradually improves as the lane bends R at wall gates with a lofty view over the estuary. Ignore a stile in a wall and keep L to a gate. Go ahead on the track to meet a better track and turn R, winding down the fell through the gorse to a lane. Turn L to a T-junction, then a R turn soon leads down to the road at Broad Oak Farm. Cross the road to the start.

## Stainton Tower

The tower was built in 1823 as a summer house by the benevolent grandfather of the present owner, who gave work to starving Irish labourers and paid their wages with food.

## Waberthwaite

Home of the world renowned Woodall's Cumberland sausages. You can buy them here or sample them at the local pub.

## Devoke Water (see p.97)

# WALK 14: Around Muncaster

*Woodland footpath in Muncaster Estate*

**SUMMARY:** A low-level walk, charming in all seasons and useful if the high fells are shrouded in mist. From Ravenglass the walk travels through woods above Muncaster Mill, and rises over a shoulder of Muncaster Fell to an imposing tower before descending to join the Cumbria Coastal Way. This is followed down the estuary to the Roman bath-house, which is but a short distance from Ravenglass.

| | |
|---|---|
| *Distance:* | 8 miles (12.9km) |
| *Grade:* | Moderate |
| *Terrain:* | Good paths through woodland and the Muncaster Estate but can be damp on the estuary |
| *High point:* | Shoulder of Muncaster Fell - 492ft (150m) |
| *Height gain:* | 721ft (220m) |
| *Map:* | OL6 |

**HOW TO GET THERE AND PARKING:** At Ravenglass, off the A595, park in the large car park in the village centre. For access by rail North West

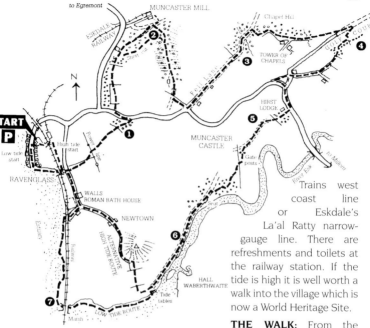

Trains west coast line or Eskdale's La'al Ratty narrow-gauge line. There are refreshments and toilets at the railway station. If the tide is high it is well worth a walk into the village which is now a World Heritage Site.

**THE WALK:** From the car park at Ravenglass go between the houses to the broad main village street. The street is built on medieval lines, narrow at each end to prevent the escape of cattle on market days.

**Low-Tide Start** The short stretch which follows is impassable at very high tides (see below and map for the high-tide start alternative). Turn L along the edge of the shore and go into an enclosed lane and under a railway bridge.

**High-Tide Start** From the car park turn L and cross over the railway footbridge, turn R through a field to an old enclosed lane from under a railway bridge, and turn L.

**High- and Low-Tide Starts merge here.**

The old enclosed lane soon meets a surfaced lane. Go straight ahead over a stile into a field. Keep on to two gates where we turn L through a kissing gate and bear over to an old abandoned stone gatepost. The field path is clearer now - gradually rising under the electric wires, under another set of wires and into woodland at a signed kissing gate. Go up the side of a stream to the main road. Turn L along the road for 100 yards to a R-pointing public footpath sign, somewhat hidden in the bushes. Cross the road and turn up the broad track to a kissing gate. The track has a fence on the left and gorse bushes to the right. Keep ahead by the fence when a more prominent track swings away right.

The path is now green and runs level. Keep ahead by the fence with extensive views over the sea to the Isle of Man. The path narrows, goes through a gate then descends through park-like pasture with a great bank of gorse above. Enter woodland at a gate. At the next path junction take one of two options.

## 1. Longer route via Muncaster Mill

The mill is now a private dwelling and is closed to the public. The restored water wheel cannot be seen from this path.

Go straight on the permissive path to Muncaster Mill. Pass above Barrows Cottage then the rising path becomes muddy but soon joins a forest road at a junction with a well-hidden multiway signpost. The roofs of the mill can be seen below but little satisfaction can be gained by casting about for a better view.

Turn sharp right up the hill, with banks of snowdrops to cheer a February day. At the top of the rise the Short route joins from the right.

## 2. Short route

Fork right on the forest track and climb to a T-junction with the 'mill' track, at the top of the rise. Turn R.

## To continue the route:

Keep ahead along a woodland dell where deer may be seen blending with the foliage.

*Branken Wall, the dell at right angles to the general line of the fell, was cut by water escaping from an upper lake dammed by the Irish Sea ice sheet. This Ice Age lake filled the whole of the seaward end of Miterdale and drained to a lake at a lower level around the Esk estuary. Other notches at a higher level along Muncaster Fell were formed in the same way.*

Keep straight on. To the left are examples of the exotic shrubs which adorn the Muncaster Estate.

At the forest gate turn L along the field edge to reach the road gate. Ignore the main road and turn sharp L on the public bridleway to Muncaster Fell via Fell Lane. The lane climbs steadily passing a covered reservoir. As you go notice the pink Eskdale granite of the walls and underfoot. Pass a gas 'artwork'

*Tower of Chapels*

(on left) unwittingly indicating a gateway (right) with a superb view right over Eskdale. Carry on up the lane.

At gates keep straight on over a brow. Ignore paths joining from both sides then cross over a culverted stream - the outlet from a small tarn to the left unseen through the dense rhododendrons which now hug the lane. Look carefully to turn R (sign 'Lower Eskdale') and escape through the dark pathway into a glade of silver birch and the open fellside. Meet an old wall and go through an iron gate, the path descending by a plantation, then through it to a farm. Behind the farm is the **Tower of Chapels.** This is an imposing monument reputed to mark the spot where King Henry VI was rescued in 1461.

Continue down the path to join a surfaced lane. After the untamed forest the sight of pristine turf comes as a surprise. Turn L and in 100 yards turn sharp R, signed 'to Main Road'. Follow the waymark arrows across the estate golf course and R at a belt of pines to stiles leading into woodland, then a field, followed by a muddy, hedged lane. Go over the stile at a gate and turn R on the farm lane for ¼ mile to Eskholme Lodge. The main road is seen to the left but keep straight along the ROW track to reach it on a bad corner.

Turn L until finding a place to cross the busy road and go about 200 yards to Hirst Lodge (note the coat of arms carved in red sandstone), where we join the Cumbria Coastal Way (CCW).

Turn R to a kissing gate then walk on in park-like pasture with beautiful mature cedar trees. Off to the left is the River Esk, its boisterous energy spent, wandering to and fro at the whim of the tide. Follow the CCW past old gateposts and spy the yellow waymark R to a kissing gate in the fence. Keep the fence on the left-hand side, cross stapled wooden footbridges, pass a break of bamboo into a sunken path then turn R up steps - the slight height gained allowing occasional views over the water. At a major path turn L to a viewpoint seat (local nature trail 8 view over the Esk). After a CCW designated sign the path descends to the water's edge. Across the river Broad Oak Beck, having changed its name several times since leaving its source on Stainton Pike, enters the Esk. Pass a crag with a neat inscription. An island splits the channel and just beyond the old right of way to Waberthwaite still crosses the estuary, but only on the map - any sign of the ford is long gone. Arrive at the tide table.

The CCW now runs along the beach, which is impassable 2 hours before and after high tide. Consult the tide table, and make your choice between the shore and an inland path. The ways join before reaching the Roman bath-house, so you will not be deprived whichever way you choose.

## VIA THE COAST (low-tide route)

Turn L, and in a few yards go through the wall gate and turn R. The flotsam and jetsam lie in a bank of rotting finality abandoned by the tide, but there is enjoyment. The seabirds call and an ever changing light and shade plays on the estuary as you make your way along to the railway embankment. Go under the bridge and over the stile. The path improves and gorse bushes seem to show a few golden flowers whatever the season, and pebbles and shells part to show the underlying red sandstone. Pass a No.3 stone and a sea defence of huge boulders then turn R under the railway bridge. At the lane turn L, pass Walls House. The inland route joins from the right at *.

## INLAND ALTERNATIVE (high-tide route)

Keep straight ahead for 50 yards then turn R (sign) to a kissing gate accessing a field. Aim straight up the hill towards a single pine tree and go through a wall-gate to its R. From here is a good view over the river to Stainton Tower (see Walk 13) and (L to R) Stainton Pike, Whitfell, Buckbarrow and Black Combe in the distance. Go ahead a few yards then bear L on a track between gorse, where the outlook is west to the Eskmeals viaduct carrying the main line over the estuary. The track now squeezes between the wall and a gorse-bank which retains rainwater, but a trod along the bank leads dry-shod to a muddy gateway. Negotiate the gateway and go on through fields and gates to Newtown House with its minute church by the track. Go down the access lane to join the coast route at the road. Turn R (join the coast low-tide route at *). To the left is the site of the Roman fort Glannoventa 'the town on the bank'. A short distance ahead is the Roman bath-house. *Information panels reveal its original layout and history.*

Continue along the lane to a signpost. Turn L and just before the railway bridge turn R. Cross the field to the footbridge over the railway. Go over and turn L to the start.

## Tower of Chapels

This is around 200 years old and was built on the spot where Henry VI was reputedly found exhausted after escaping from the battle of Towton in 1461. Shepherds took him to Muncaster Castle, where he recuperated. To show his gratitude he presented an enamelled glass bowl, 'The Luck of Muncaster', as a reward to the Pennington family. As long as it remains unbroken, the family will prosper.

## Muncaster Mill (See Walk 15 p.92)

## Ravenglass

Ravenglass is the most southerly part of the Hadrian's Wall World Heritage Site. It was a very important port in Roman, Norse and Saxon times but its traffic dwindled due to the continual silting of the estuary and the advance of the railway.

The Roman fort of Glannoventa and its surrounding civilian settlement was built nearby. A fine section of the bath-house remains, and the site of the fort and its surrounding earthworks are under development by the National Park Authority.

The attractive medieval village street narrows at each end, built to facilitate the recapture of runaway cattle on market day, and the seaward end is protected by floodgates at the launching ramp.

*Ravenglass*

# WALK 15:  **Muncaster Fell La'al Ratty Railway**

*'Northern Rock' on the Ravenglass to Eskdale railway*

**SUMMARY:** A classic day out which combines the famous narrow-gauge railway with a return walk to the car from Ravenglass over Muncaster Fell. The estuary is still attractive despite its proximity to Sellafield, as is the village port of Ravenglass.

The footpath through the exotic grounds of Muncaster Castle gives a glimpse of its tourist attractions. The traverse of Muncaster Fell, a bony granite ridge with numerous boggy

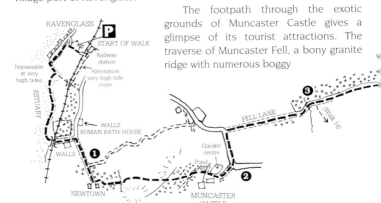

| | |
|---|---|
| *Distance:* | 6 miles (9.6km) |
| *Grade:* | Moderate |
| *Terrain:* | Woodland and low fell; rough and wet in parts |
| *Summit:* | Hooker Crag - 757ft (231m) |
| *Height gain:* | 1020ft (311m) |
| *Map:* | OL6 |

hollows, can be somewhat squelchy. If you walk this in May you will be rewarded with flora at its best: bluebells, rhododendrons and azaleas in the castle grounds, and gorse in full bloom elsewhere. Views up Eskdale and Miterdale to Scafell and Harter Fell are the reason for doing the walk in this direction.

A train mid-morning gives the advantage of a leisurely picnic on the beach at Ravenglass. Refreshments at the station, in the Ratty Arms.

**HOW TO GET THERE AND PARKING:** Park at the station car park, Eskdale Green. Railway timetables are available from the stations (tel: 01229 717171) or Tourist Information Offices. There are refreshments at Ravenglass station and family pub meals at the Ratty Arms.

**THE WALK:** Buy a ticket from Eskdale Green to Ravenglass and revel in the many facets of enjoyment the 4¾ mile (25 minutes) unique journey on La'al Ratty brings. Watch out on the left-hand side for Muncaster Mill as the best view of its restored water-wheel is from the railway.

**Ravenglass** is the terminus (toilets, cafè and shop), but can you leave the station without watching the gleaming little engine being lovingly coaxed onto the turntable and pushed round by its proud engineers?

Set off over the main railway line bridge towards the Ratty Arms. Pass the car park (toilets) and go straight on down a ginnel between red sandstone houses to the main street.

Turn L and walk along through the tidal defence gate to the beach. (See instructions on Walk 14 for a high-tide route which joins at the railway bridge.) Turn

L along the shore (ignore an enclosed pathway leading under the railway bridge) and follow the shoreline or walk in the same direction using a path on the grassy bank. *The extra 20 feet gives a lift to the estuary view, and in spring an assortment of celandine, stitchwort, milkmaids, pink campion and primroses add their bright colours until the path is forced back onto the beach and the flotsam. The line of posts out in the estuary is a salmon garth. Nets were strung along the stakes to ensnare the fish. The garth is occasionally used today.* Turn L under the main line railway bridge and up a shady lane past a Walls House and a lane on the right.

The Roman bath-house is a few yards further along the road and is well worth a visit. The site of the fort, Glannoventa, lies opposite. The name of the fort is Celtic in origin, comprises glan/glenn 'bank, shore or landing' and venta, 'market or trading station' (see Ravenglass p.87).

Turn R and continue to a junction near Newtown House and Knottview Cottage.

On the L signed Muncaster a broad estate road leads straight to the A595. However slightly longer but more interesting and rewarding is the footpath through the estate and castle grounds. This is recommended.

Keep ahead and look for a w/m footpath and National Park notice opposite the houses. Turn L through the gate and follow the path rising through silver birches. At a fork keep R uphill to the edge of the wood. Note carefully, before going over the stile, the direction of the waymark arrow, diagonally left, and follow it up through the pasture ahead. In the distance a walled woodland comes into sight. The height gained allows a retrospective view over the sea to the Isle of Man and north along the coast to Sellafield and St Bees head beyond. As the angle eases bear R and make for a white marker at the lowest R point of the wall. Pass a small erratic boulder and to the south the view across the dale shows a flat plateau area, the site of the late prehistoric Barnscar Settlement overlooked by White Pike.

Enter the Muncaster Estate and read the instruction notice. Follow the yellow waymarks straight on. This path must surely be shortlisted for the most beautiful woodland ROW path in early summer. At a junction read the 'Ramblers Please Note' sign to cross the lawn between the duckpond

BUCKBARROW   RED PIKE   YEWBARROW   KIRK FELL   LINGMELL   SCAFELL   BOWFELL

MITERDALE

and the playground. Cross the drive to go straight on past the church and reach the A595.

Turn L and cross the road to a Public Bridleway to Muncaster Fell via Fell Lane.

It is a steady climb onto the fell, the walls of the lane hung with pennywort (ground ivy). Go through a gate and continue the climb over the shoulder and onward. Ignore branching paths, and at a sign keep ahead to Eskdale and a kissing gate at the end of the Muncaster Estate land.

In front is the mini-fell of Hooker Crag. We are now in the Economic Forestry land and there are many vehicle tracks. Shadow the edge of the forest to its corner then strike ahead through the coarse granite bedrock to the cairn. If you have been expecting a superlative outlook you will not be disappointed. To the north the prow of St Bees Head juts into the sea with the Isle of Man to the west. The south displays patches of woodland, old and new, where once continuous native woodland grew, and to the east are the high mountains (see panorama).

Go over the summit and follow the path as it descends slightly to the R then down more steeply to a flatter area and path junction. Ignore the obvious path left and go straight ahead, not obvious at first as a path, along a line of rushes. Its line soon becomes clearer as it slants round the right-hand side of a bog then as it winds, undulates and crosses entertaining mires, old edging stones confirm that we have joined the ROW path. Go over another brow with a leaning stone and exactly suitable for sitting. A further brow and we arrive at an impressive stone table, Ross's Camp, not an ancient dolmen but merely a Victorian shooting party's lunch stop, erected in 1883. The enticing view is now up Miterdale to the Scafell range, but look to the path which goes straight into trouble across a bog (we advise to go round). Pass a rock hump to a gate in a cross wall.

Keep ahead down the wall-side with a view of Eskdale Green. Silver birches are scattered among bracken and heather as the path, lined with delicate waving grasses, gradually bends R. Sturdy stones mark the path, which becomes more solid - edged by a retaining wall as it rises over the final ridge and makes a traverse overlooking Eskdale and down the hill to become part of the view. Mature trees herald the approach of the valley. Go through a kissing gate at a wall and continue through head-

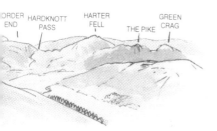

*Mountain panorama from Muncaster Fell*

high gorse long observed as a golden haze which becomes more sparse as we cross a pasture. Go over the stile in a cross-wall and turn L, on the bridleway to 'The Green and station'. Cross the field by following the wall to the left, passing under magnificent oaks (ignore a gate in the wall). Find a gap in the walls by the stream at the bottom of the field, cross the stream and go over a stile. Carry on along a walled path to meet a lane and level crossing. Turn R on the Eskdale Green station platform to the parking.

## La'al Ratty

The railway was opened in 1875 to bring iron ore from the Eskdale mines to the Furness Railway and, when this business waned, granite from the quarries. The original 36in.-gauge track was closed in 1913, but reopened in 1914 by a well-known model maker on a narrower gauge of 15in. It successfully carried passengers and goods until the quarries closed in 1953. In 1960 it was bought by a group of enthusiasts. A new company now operates the railway in conjunction with the Preservation Society and it is a major tourist attraction in the area. A railway museum at Ravenglass features the history of the line.

## Muncaster Mill

A flour mill has worked here since 1455, driven by water power from the River Mite. It has been restored. It is private and no longer open to the public.

## Muncaster Castle

Home of the Pennington family since the 13th century, the castle is now a popular tourist attraction. There are wonderful gardens, a lake with a heronry and exotic birds, a playground for children and a café. The castle houses many art treasures and the walled garden nursery is open to the public.

**Ravenglass** (See Walk 14 p.87)

# WALK 16: Devoke Water and Stanley Gill

*Bronze Age cairn guards the western end of Devoke Water*

**SUMMARY:** A good varied walk which contrasts the bleak fells around Devoke Water with a visit to the tourist honey pot of Stanley Gill and a pleasant riverside return.

The walking starts easily with the ascent of a well-graded pony track followed by trackless moorland over Water Crag, a fine viewpoint. Devoke Water shore can be squelchy in places where the peat has eroded. Across the Ulpha Fell road the character of the walk changes as you descend through farm pastures to reach the densely wooded ravine of Stanley Gill, now on well-trodden paths.

**HOW TO GET THERE AND PARKING:** Leave Eskdale Green on the Ulpha road, cross the bridge over the River Esk and park on the right immediately over the bridge. There are shops and toilets in Eskdale Green. King George IV pub is outside the village just before the bridge.

| | |
|---|---|
| Distance: | 8 miles (12.8km) |
| Grade: | Strenuous |
| Terrain: | Low fell and valley |
| Summits: | Water Crag - 1000ft (305m) |
| Height gain: | 1082ft (330m) |
| Map: | OL 6 |

**THE WALK:** Set off briskly towards Ulpha, pass Forge House farm and in 500 yards, just before Sword House Kennels, turn R disposing of the

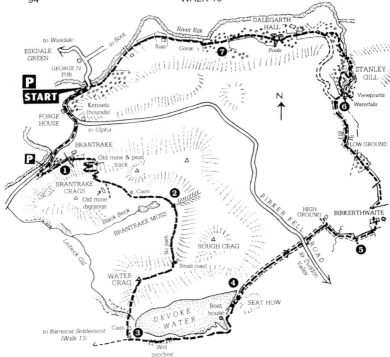

busy road walking for the day.

The lane is much quieter. On the left as you pass New Brantrake Cottage the old mine road can be seen zigzagging up the fell. Pass the confluence of a sidestream with the river then, 20 yards past the end of the sidewall, look carefully on the left for a path with a public bridleway sign leading to a stile in the set back wall.

Go over the stile and in a few yards find the old peat road and turn L along it. Although the surface has succumbed to nature the steady gradient remains. When the road levels above the woodland go through a gap in the broken cross-wall. *From here you can look down on the farmhouse and adjoining bank barn, so typical of the old Lakeland farms, now a prestige dwelling.* Turn R up the broken wallside and you are on the first zigzag of the old green track meeting with a track from the gate. Some of the stone edgings are still in place, and as height is gained the northern scene is of Muncaster Fell with the forests of Miterdale behind. It is easy walking up the green road, the only break in the craggy hillside. Pass a ruined fold and a cross-wall. Just before a bend to the next cross-wall keep L heading towards a gap in the skyline. (The old road has now gone ahead to the diggings by some sheepfolds but there is little of interest to see there. The promising iron ore deposit was never worked because the price of ore fell.) Go through a wall gap to pass a small cairn and arrive on the widespread moor by some glaciated granite rocks. Ahead is the extensive, lonely Brantrake Moss, silent and atmospheric, with the infant Black Beck oozing from its miry cradle. Beyond rise the peaks of Rough Crag (left) and Water Crag (right).

Spy out the onward route round the left-hand (east) side of the moss and a rising traverse path to the col between the two crags. Continue using a narrow trod which bends L then abandons you to find a pioneering way round the east side of the bog with the sheep your best allies. Gain the rising traverse and head for an outcrop of rock on the col. From here look back to a Bronze Age settlement, the two ancient enclosures like a pair of spectacles looking out over the moss.

A few yards above the outcrop turn R towards Water Crag. Follow the broad ridge passing old cairns to join a broad path for the final climb to the summit. The panorama is splendid in every direction and even on a mediocre day Snaefell and North Barrule on the Isle of Man can be seen west across the Irish Sea.

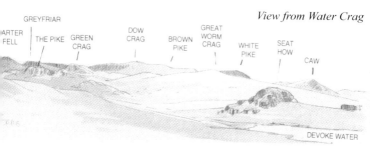

*View from Water Crag*

GREYFRIAR
ARTER FELL   THE PIKE   GREEN CRAG   DOW CRAG   BROWN PIKE   GREAT WORM CRAG   WHITE PIKE   SEAT HOW   CAW

DEVOKE WATER

Overlooked by its little guardian knoll Seat How **Devoke Water** is to the south. It is a private fishing tarn. We aim to cross its outlet stream Linbeck Gill. Keep along the ridge until you can see a path running south-south-west down and across the boggy moor to the gill. It can be a bit squelchy but the grass carpet will keep your boots clean despite the water of the tarn which seems to be rippling in the wind at eye-level. Cross the gill above a pretty cascade (there are plenty of stones) and go up the bank to a Bronze Age hollow cairn with a pole. Keep ahead for a further 50 yards to meet a major path.

The bridle-path alongside Devoke Water is now favoured by mountain bikers as an adventurous route over the bleak moorland. *It was once an avenue through native oak forest, lined by pairs of stones and leading west to the ancient settlement of Barnscar* (see Walk 13 p.80/81). Turn L and make your way along the cairned path, avoiding the occasional cyclists extracting themselves and their machines from the embrace of the peat. The wild aspect is mellowed by the songs of skylarks and the migrating geese riding the ripples on the far side of the water. Even the boat-house lends elegance to the scene, but on approach its ruined posterior is a bit of a let down. Turn R up the track curving from the boat-house and, with Seat How to the right and Rough Crag left, go through the gap to the Ulpha road, ½ mile. (Note the old peat diggings on the right.)

Cross the road and go down the lane facing a new scene over the rocky topped hills of Crook Crag, The Pike and Green Crag beyond a spread of walled pastures. On the left of the track is a boulder worn smooth and stained with oil, a rubbing stone for many generations of sheep.

At the junction turn R (sign for public footpaths to Birkerthwaite and Stanley Gill). Over the intake wall Slight Side and Sca Fell lie on the horizon. Go through the Birkerthwaite gate. *Birkerthwaite was the site of a Norse shieling with field wall patterns earlier than the present walls.*

*Two-tone volcanic bands make an interesting feature seen ahead on the north end of the Great Whinscale ridge.*

Keep on the farm track to Ganny House. Follow the footpath signs through the yard and walled enclosure to go through the gate ahead into a walled green lane. The next gate leads into a field where the Smallstone Beck chatters on its way to Stanley Gill. Keep by the left-hand wall to angle L, sign through a gate (ignore the bridge). The wall on the right has waymark white spots. Notice the thickness of the wall. Are the stones from the opposite wall now stored in its vast girth? The green path sinks down to a gate and a stone-arched bridge. Go through the plantation to join a gravel track (yellow waymark). Turn R and along to Low Ground. Go behind

Burnmoor Lodge stands guard over Burnmoor Tarn (Walk 21)

The granite knoll of Latterbarrow with Wastwater and its high fells behind (Walk 22)

Great Gable, with the Napes ridges, dominates the walk up Wasdale Head (Walks 27/28)

Ancient field clearances have left enormous walls
and stone piles at Wasdale Head (Walks 27/28)

the house and turn R into a green bridleway with views over Eskdale to the central mountains. The plantation to the right ends and the track crosses open fell with the wind carrying the song of the gill from the cluster of trees below.

When level with a footbridge over the gill fork diagonally R over the grass to a stile where the fence meets the wall. T*he rich vegetation emphasises the change that a descent of* 400 *feet has wrought. The russets of the starved weather-bleached grasses have dramatically given way to the shining green glow of the rhododendrons, sheltered by the gorge, misted by the falls and enjoyed for their spring blooms by the steady stream of admirers who visit the walkways.* Read the warning notice then go over the stile and peer over the viewpoint. Make your way down the path, cross two sidestreams and choose the lower path R down the steps into the gorge. Keep downstream and just enjoy it. At the end of the ravine follow the main path up L to a gate. Go through to rejoin the bridleway. Turn R for 200 yards then go L and over a stile towards Forge Bridge. At once the sightseers are left behind. On reaching the next gate look right where there is a set of typical Lakeland round chimneys on Dalegarth Hall, then go through. Keep on the gated bridleway ignoring tracks branching right then left. Pass through 'the everglades' which are replaced by delightful woodland and a glade of redwoods. Meet the River Esk and now walk the riverside to pass an old ruin, the set pebbles of its yard still underfoot. N*otice over the valley the line of an old tramway up the hillside, a remnant of the iron mines above* Boot. Ignore a footbridge right over the river. Keep ahead over the stile to the road bridge and the start.

## Devoke Water

In Bronze Age times Devoke Water was surrounded by native oak forest. Pollen samples have revealed that grain was grown in forest clearings. Many stone tools have been found around its shores. In medieval times monks introduced golden trout. It is now a private fishing water stocked with brown trout, but it is still possible to catch a golden trout today.

# WALK 17:     Green Crag and The Pike

*Peat scale on the old Birker peat road*

**SUMMARY:** To the east of the Ulpha Fell road a line of dark, rocky but lowly peaks, like a miniature Cuillin ridge, attracts the eye. The rocky ridge is a sham as the other side is less dramatic, nevertheless these modest peaks lie in some of the roughest terrain in Lakeland; a wilderness of rock, heather and bog. Our walk explores these lonely fells and surprisingly follows paths for almost all the way; indeed the broad green track of the old peat road which climbs out of Eskdale is a pleasure to walk. Thereafter a narrow but adequate trod, with numerous tiny cairns, skirts the bogs to gain the tops and runs back close to the rocky summit ridge. Route finding can be tricky especially if the vegetation masks the narrow trod. It makes a satisfying circuit with a fine panorama of the multitude of high fells which surround upper Eskdale.

| | |
|---|---|
| *Distance:* | 6¼ miles (10km) |
| *Grade:* | Strenuous |
| *Terrain:* | Medium fell. Rough walking but on paths almost all of the way. |
| *Summits:* | Green Crag - 1604ft (489m) |
| | The Pike - 1492ft (455m) |
| | Crook Crag - 1538ft (469m) |
| *Height gain:* | 1444ft (440m) |
| *Map:* | OL6 |

**HOW TO GET THERE AND PARKING:** At Eskdale Green, by the King George IV pub (refreshments), turn up the valley on the Hardknott road.

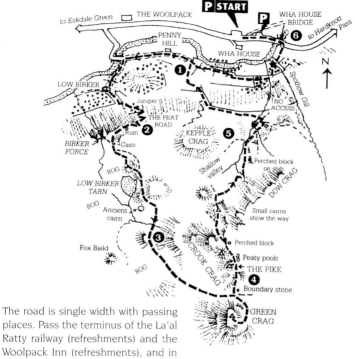

The road is single width with passing places. Pass the terminus of the La'al Ratty railway (refreshments) and the Woolpack Inn (refreshments), and in ½ mile the parking is on the left opposite Wha House Farm, with more parking 400 yards further on if needed.

**THE WALK:** Set off along the road towards Hardknott Pass and cross the River Esk at Wha House bridge. Turn R downstream on a signed public bridleway through the waterside pasture. *Already the valley's charms - rich green water-meadows, wooded slopes and rugged fells - catch the eye, with Harter Fell (2142ft/653m) towering above, its height exaggerated by the isolated pyramidal shape.*

Cross a footbridge over Spothow Gill and go through a gate on the right of the stream. Walk up through the oak wood past old mine workings to a gap in the wall ahead. Turn R to Penny Hill, cross the ford and walk along the park-like pastures, crossing stiles, with views over the valley. Above on the left rises the plateau we intend to visit, and on approaching a shapely pine an old peat road can be seen, a green zigzag up the rough plateau side. (Note: the return route rejoins here.) At a pathside signpost keep straight on through a gate to Penny Hill Farm. This was once an inn on the old packhorse route up the valley. Continue on the cobble-set track through the farm. Just before a bridge take the L track signed 'Public bridleway Dalegarth and Low Birker'. The track runs beside the River Esk, crosses a cattle grid then rises to Low Birker.

Pass the buildings and in 25 yards turn sharp L on the Birker peat road, in reality a delightful green path, up the side of the larch plantation, over a cross-path (ignore a gate in the wall on the right) and, casting an eye on the original hollow way in the trough on the right, go up the green peat road. The road rises in a steady gradient (made as a sledge track) through juniper, where you may see as well as hear a variety of finches. The scene north is to Scafell, Bowfell and Crinkle Crags. Go through a kissing gate and continue, facing a contrasting view down Eskdale. *Across the valley the levels of the Nab Gill haematite (iron ore) mines (1875-1912) above Boot appear as a square-cut gash in the fellside and further up the valley a cluster of 16th-century* **peat scales** *(peat storage huts) remain on the moor.*

Pass an old roofless peat scale and amble along the road, now a level scenic balcony, to a little crag with pathside boulders. The road bends left to a cairn.

**Diversion to Birker Force** (careful supervision of children required) Turn sharp R and down through a broken wall, and beyond a slight path bends L through a rock gap to several viewpoints overlooking the series of beautiful waterfalls in the ravine. (The narrow path into the ravine is the scrambler's exit and leads to steep rock.) Return to the cairn.

Just beyond the cairn the path forks. Take the right-hand one, but before striding off look ahead. The plateau is heather-clad with rock outcrops, wide boggy hollows and a jagged skyline ridge, reminiscent of the Cuillins yet deceptive in scale. It appears a trackless wilderness but there are ways to be revealed. We are heading to the right-hand end of the skyline ridge. Go round the boggy hollow on its left leaving the peat road to bend away westward. The path rises and Low Birker Tarn appears to the west. In a south-west direction a wart of rock, named Fox Bield, protrudes from the bog, but signs of an actual bield seem to have gone. Descend and cross the next hollow. The path has small cairns, one standing proud on a triad of rocks as the path steepens to pass through a gap at the foot of the Whinscale Ridge. Make a slight descent into a shallow valley and follow the path as it bends L heading for the col. Green Crag is to the right, Crook Crag to the left, with The Pike the most prominent of its knobbly summits. If the light is hazy the peaks take on alpine proportions and although the path

HARTER
FELL

CROOK    CRAG

THE
PIKE

GREEN
CRAG

*Profile of the route behind Birkerthwaite from Walk 16*

becomes vague at a boggy bit it emerges clear, dry and cairned and it is only a few minutes to the cairn at the col. Go ahead to a cross-path just beyond the highest point. A parish boundary stone stands off to the left.

## Ascent of Green Crag

Turn R (south) and follow the path along grassy rakes to the south-east side for the easy way to the summit. (The north and west faces of the crag are steep rock used by scramblers.) The captivating landscape of Lakeland mountains and over the Irish Sea to the Isle of Man demands a lengthy stay with your spread map at the summit. Return by the ascent way to the col.

## The return via The Pike

*To the summit*: Turn L and up to the highest point of the path halting just before two small peaty pools. Turn L on a narrow path which leads to a short, easy scramble (note the point of descent) to the summit. The slight effort expended is richly rewarded with a superb panorama.

*To continue the route*: Make your own exploratory way over the remaining rocky summits of Crook Crag

**or** follow the given directions which are in close detail as no path can be seen far ahead.

Pass the pools (heading north) on the narrow path. Pass a boggy area, a perched block and go through a gap. Keep ahead to the next brow and descend gently. A scene of virgin moorland stretches eerie in mist, shimmering in heat, a waving carpet of russets and browns flowing into the distance. The descent becomes steeper, the path winding as it skirts the right-hand side of some rocks. At a cairn turn L for 100 yards then R at an insignificant path junction. Pass a cairn 20 yards further on and from here the path is more straightforward along a wide heather and bilberry shelf. (Ignore a trod descending left.)

Cross a rock rib and keep a sharp eye for the guiding cairns on the left as you make a steep descent over a rock bar which puts the rocky territory behind.

Bend R on a narrow path leading round the gathering ground of a stream with a glance right to a ruined sheepfold and barely a blade of grass. Shortly after fork R on a narrow path at a cairn. Look carefully for cairns as the path bends round the rim of the bowl. Cross a stream and find the path again tracking north. Craggy walls bound the eastern horizon and a few yards behind the path has dissolved into the rough terrain. Keep on to the narrowing of the valley at the plateau edge.

Look out for a rock slab with split boulders on top, one hanging over its edge. About 20 yards beyond ignore an old cross-path, used by the farmer's quad-bikes. Keep ahead on a bit of a trod, with the stream valley ever deepening on the left, to a pathside boulder split into four geometrical shapes. Halt a moment to survey the onward route. To avoid difficult streamside terrain, yet still descend the valley, we will divert slightly taking a diagonal line right (about 45 degrees) down the bracken slope to a rock outcrop with a tree sprouting from its left-hand wall. Go for it. At the tree continue the direction over a tributary stream to an old path (cairn), and turn left along it.

Pass the remnants of an old wall and at a fork turn L to cross the stream above a small cascade. Climb up the bank to a cairn and signpost then bend L to follow the wall on a rough path. At the wall corner turn R and descend to join a green peat path (signed 'Harter Fell'). Keep on down the path, through a gate and by the right-hand wall until the path develops into a farm track winding L down rough pasture to a gate. Go through and the pine and outward path are seen ahead. At the pine turn R and retrace the outward route to the ford, turning L at the mine and, on reaching the road L over the river bridge to the start.

## Peat Scales

Thirty-five small dry-stone huts known as 'peat scales', are to be found in Eskdale up the valley from Eskdale Green. They are situated on the edge of a peat-yielding moor above the intake wall at a height of approximately 985 feet (300m) and adjacent to a carefully graded sledge track.

In the 16th century each tenant had 'Common of Turbary' (the right to dig peat for fuel on the manorial waste). In 1795 lawsuit documents concerning the illegal enclosure of fellside states - "*As places for Turbary lay upon the Tops of the Hills and it is often difficult to win their peats in Summer, every Tenant has a House or Peat Scale in some suitable place where he can conveniently go in Winter and fetch his peats.*"

The peat storage ceased between the First and Second World Wars.

# WALK 18:

## Border End via Hardknott Roman Fort

*Border End, Hardknott Fort and the line of the Roman road over Hardknott Pass*

**SUMMARY:** One of the finest views in the Lake District must be from Border End over the wild expanse of upper Eskdale to the full spread of the Scafell range. Climb in the steps of Roman legionaries past Hardknott Fort to gain the knobbly top. Hard Knott is another rocky summit visited before an easy stroll down a broad ridge which drops into Lingcove Beck. Return pleasantly down Eskdale with the lively river as companion.

**HOW TO GET THERE AND PARKING:** Park 200 yards above the foot of Hardknott Pass in Eskdale. Alternatively there is parking on the verge of the valley bottom lane.

| | |
|---|---|
| *Distance:* | 6 miles (9.6km) |
| *Grade:* | Moderate |
| *Terrain:* | Medium fell. Some rough walking |
| *Summits:* | Border End - 1712ft (522m), |
| | Hard Knott - 1801ft (549m) |
| *Height gain:* | 1565ft (477m) |
| *Map:* | OL6 |

**THE WALK:** Set off up the steep road keeping to the right and using a grass short-cut to take out the hairpin bend. It is worth a peer into the defile where Hardknott Gill leaps in an attractive fall and coal tits flit amongst an unexpected variety of trees lining the gorge.

When opposite the left-hand wall corner cross the road, turn L (signpost) and ignoring other paths go up the wallside until seeing a stile (to be ignored). Climb diagonally R to **Hardknott Fort** south-west gateway. *Allow time to read the excellent information panels, which give so vivid a compressed history of the site that you can image the hustle and bustle.* Take a historic ramble through the fort to emerge at the north-east gate. March straight ahead to the parade ground, its construction an amazing feat considering the toil needed to tame the hostile terrain. Go across and up the ensuing slope using the onward Roman road, now buried beneath the oozing grass of Border End. In a few yards, just below some scree, bend R on a hint of the road which runs behind rocky knolls. The crags of Border End rise impressively ahead but we reach the summit by an easy circuitous route. Cross the remains of a wall behind the first knoll. Descend slightly and, as the road is under bog, fork L on a dry diverging path which runs above the Roman road climbing steadily. (The Roman road meets the surfaced road above a big hairpin bend, joins it for 100 yards, then forks right to go over the pass to Black Hall Farm in Dunnerdale then over Wrynose Pass to the Galava fort near Ambleside.) Keep on the path as it bends, running

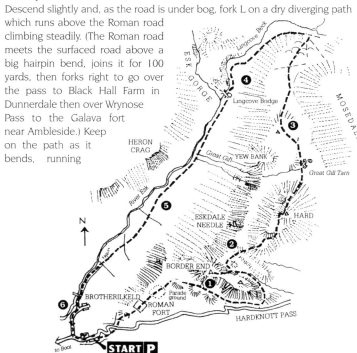

below the scree to the top of the pass. Various stones provide grandstand seats for a view across the valley to Harter Fell and down the valley, for amusement, as would-be rally drivers struggle with the 1-in-3 gradient.

Cross the remains of an old wall and when opposite the large cairn at the pass top keep ahead until the scree ends. Turn L up the side of the scree on a trace of a path which climbs steep grass. A retrospective view shows the wooded valley of the River Duddon with the Coniston range beyond (L to R: Swirl How, Old Man of Coniston, Grey Friar, Dow Crag, the line of the Walna Scar road with Caw and the knob of Stickle Pike merging into the distance). As you climb higher walkers' wanderings merge into a definite path. Pass through an old wall and keep climbing up the side of a lively little stream to its source in a corridor of red bog. As the corridor widens, just before a pool, the main summit cairn can be seen above.

**To Border End.** Turn diagonally L up the fell and make your way to the summit. The grand view of upper Eskdale and its cordon of mountains merits an extended study, but don't miss the more gentle pastoral aspect of lower Eskdale (see panorama p. 106/107).

**Note:** there are three cairns on Border End. Having made a mental note of your summit approach and the direction (NE) to Hard Knott - our next summit - amble past peaty pools to the north-west cairn for an unrestricted view of Eskdale and the coastal hills. Return to the summit cairn. Retrace your way down to the red bog.

**To Hard Knott.** Turn L to continue the original direction, pass a small tarn and squeeze between the red bog and stones shrugged from Border End. Just beyond turn R, circling on drier ground to an extended finger of bog. (Short diversion - for an unusual view of the Eskdale Needle carry on down the side of the bog for 50 yards.)

**HARD KNOTT FROM BORDER END**

Cross the narrow bog and go on the path up the rise ahead. Keep straight on towards a rock face on Hard Knott, dipping down to cross another boggy area. Approach the rock face and bend R on a rising path which circles L to merge with another path. Keep ahead past a rock outcrop to an upper bog which has stepping stones, some sunk below the surface. Go straight on up through a rock gateway to a false summit. Spy out the cairn as the path descends, crosses a flat area then climbs to the left of lying stones onto a shelf. As it narrows turn sharp R up an earthy cleft to the summit cairn. From this higher vantage point Border End is now an

insignificant foreground to Harter Fell, and
to its left the full length of the Duddon from
Wrynose Pass to Morecambe Bay can be seen.

Set off northward by either going back down the earthy
cleft and turning R along the shelf or cutting straight from
the summit. A broad nondescript ridge leads down towards
the valley of Lingcove Beck. We aim to reach this avoiding
losing any height towards Mosedale, the deep valley on the
right. There are various paths and trods. Keep on the highest
ground aiming for a knoll with a great slab of rock on its side.
Ahead is Great Gill Tarn; work your way to it. The little path, a
flattened furrow across the rosy hue of the bog grass, goes down the slope
to track round the left-hand side of the bog-tarn complex. Cross the outlet
stream and keep on the path. (**Take care here** not to veer off to the right
and gradually find you are dropping into Mosedale.)

Proceed slightly L onto the crest of Yew Bank. In front is a knoll-top
with a cairn. Keep on over the moor to its right-hand side. A clear path now
leads down over the moor, leaving the head of Mosedale away right and
Lingcove Beck with Bowfell dominating its valley head. Smooth heaps of
moraine lie ahead. Ignore a cross-path, if it is seen, and keep straight down
the ridge. Then head slightly L on a greener swaithe which merges with a
better-used path from Mosedale valley head. Pass boulders and bend L,
beginning the descent of the Lingcove valley.

The path runs well above the beck and is eroded in places, but gradually
becomes more user-friendly; by way of compensation the gorge scenery
becomes more spectacular. Arrive at the beautiful **Lingcove Bridge** and the
confluence of the beck with the River Esk. If you need a break have it here.

RAG

GREAT END                            ESK PIKE                              BOWFELL

Set off down the valley on a broad path with the cascading river to hand and the Needle on the left-hand skyline. It is 2 miles down the valley, but gradually green meadows beckon as we pass Heron Crag to the right and arrive at the intake wall. Cross the ladder stile and follow the vehicle track. Pass through a cross-wall and along to the next gateway by the riverside. Go through the small gate into an enclosed footpath above the river. Ignore the footbridge and keep ahead to a kissing gate and the Brotherilkeld Farm (see Brotherilkeld Walk 19 p. 111) access lane. Turn R and go along to the road (telephone box). At the surfaced road turn L and climb the 200 yards of the Hardknott Pass road to the start.

**Hardknott Fort** The Roman fort of Mediobogdum, built between the reign of Emperor Trajan (AD 98-117) and Hadrian (AD 117-138), occupies a commanding position on the road between Glannaventa (Ravenglass) and Galava (Ambleside). The fort was only briefly occupied. The bare fells of today would then have been covered by scrub, which would have compensated for its bleakness.

**Lingcove Bridge** The original bridge was built by the monks of Furness Abbey. It is an old packhorse bridge built without parapets to allow laden ponies to pass unhindered.

# WALK 19: The Great Moss and Cam Spout

*Lingcove Bridge*

**SUMMARY:** The remote head of Eskdale is a good objective, being in the heart of Lakeland's highest peaks. It is reached by a varied walk up the roadless valley. Upper Eskdale was once owned by the monks of Furness

| | |
|---|---|
| *Distance:* | 7½ miles (12km) |
| *Grade:* | Moderate |
| *Terrain:* | Rough valley on stony paths with bogs to negotiate |
| *High Point:* | Foot of Cam Spout - 1312ft (400m) |
| *Height gain:* | 1115ft (340m) |
| *Map:* | OL 6 |

Abbey who pastured sheep here and left their mark in the much admired packhorse bridge and remnants of their boundary walls on the Great Moss. Our approach benefits from a sudden view of the high peaks as we leave the Esk Gorge

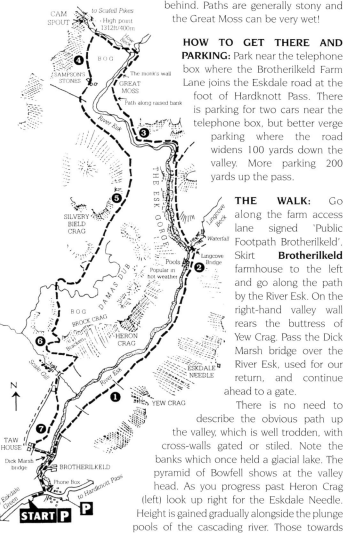

behind. Paths are generally stony and the Great Moss can be very wet!

**HOW TO GET THERE AND PARKING:** Park near the telephone box where the Brotherilkeld Farm Lane joins the Eskdale road at the foot of Hardknott Pass. There is parking for two cars near the telephone box, but better verge parking where the road widens 100 yards down the valley. More parking 200 yards up the pass.

**THE WALK:** Go along the farm access lane signed 'Public Footpath Brotherilkeld'. Skirt **Brotherilkeld** farmhouse to the left and go along the path by the River Esk. On the right-hand valley wall rears the buttress of Yew Crag. Pass the Dick Marsh bridge over the River Esk, used for our return, and continue ahead to a gate.

There is no need to describe the obvious path up the valley, which is well trodden, with cross-walls gated or stiled. Note the banks which once held a glacial lake. The pyramid of Bowfell shows at the valley head. As you progress past Heron Crag (left) look up right for the Eskdale Needle. Height is gained gradually alongside the plunge pools of the cascading river. Those towards the river junction with Lingcove Beck, its waterfall seen ahead, are especially popular with bathers on a hot summer's day. Ill Crag now shows above the interlacing spurs up the valley with the little rocky cone of Pen catching the light in front of it. The grassy bank by the sheep-folds is a perfect place for a scenic stop. Lingcove Beck pours into the River Esk under Lingcove Bridge (see Walk 18 p. 107), just below where the river emerges from the Esk Gorge, a classic Lakeland scramble after a long dry spell.

*In 1242 David de Mulcaster gave the monks a "great part of Upper Eskdale" allowing them to enclose pastures. We will be grateful for one of their walls later in the walk.*

Cross the bridge and climb more steeply up the broad path. A retrospective view down the valley shows its U-shaped glaciated section and the Needle protruding from the skyline. Eventually the gradient relents and the spectacular rock scenery of Upper Eskdale is ahead with the feeling you have penetrated into the heart of Lakeland.

When the path diverges keep by the river and cross a sidestream on a slab by a remnant of a wall. Continue under the dark, dripping crags of Scar Lathing, with each bend of the path bringing fresh mountain views until the valley floor flattens and they completely surround the Great Moss. At a short length of wall keep ahead for 50 yards then turn L along an embankment into the moss. This is all part of the monks' wall, now covered with grass but giving a firm footing to the narrow path. (Do not be tempted to turn left by the river bank.) A very nasty but short section, where the wall has sunk, leads ahead to higher firmer ground. Look for a pointed boulder to the left where the river bank devotees will have a far longer, wetter crossing to join the path. Across the river are Sampson's Stones, huge blocks which have trundled down from Cam Crag at some time, the falls of Cam Spout and the outstanding face of Esk Buttress. Keep on up the valley and cross a wettish channel draining the moss. The wall appears again and, although part has been washed away by a bend in the river, continues on its way. Go as far as the confluence of the river and How Beck (cairn on the wall) then turn L and wade the river. There are shallow diagonal pebble banks and, even after rain, make a quick, running splash and you can cross fairly dry. Walk up the right-hand bank of the beck and cross where it goes underground. Make for the foot of the waterfalls of Cam Spout and sit on a convenient stone to soak in the splendour of the wild combe, at the apex of our walk.

Turn your back on the falls and set off again down the path continuing its descent down from the side of the spout from Mickledore. In 100 yards bend R on a path keeping to drier ground along the foot of stone slopes to go between the Sampson's Stones. Notice the lush vegetation which crowns one of the stones safe from the sheep. The next feature we pass is a cluster of sheep-folds, then the path climbs slightly giving a balcony view of the spread moss and upper Eskdale.

Gradually tracking right the path leads away from Eskdale, a corner acting as a vantage point to our outward route as we turn into a side valley. Go over a low, wide col leading to the valley drained by Damas Dubs.

Pass a cairn indicating the brow and go along the flat top with Silvery Bield Crag to the right. Descend into Damas Dubs, and as the moor becomes monotonous a cairn confirms the way. Look out for a boulder with one split and a tree and for one with two splits and a tree to the left. Descend passing the two-split stone (ignore a small cairn off to the right) and on reaching the foot of smooth rocks pass a cairn and cross the bog by keeping round and well up the rock and firm ground to its right-hand side. Cross a plank bridge over the outlet stream and now, having escaped the clutches of the bog, we can admire the improving scenery. The descent becomes more determined as the green meadows of the valley floor come into sight.

The path is clear and makes an easy descent of the very steep fellside in sweeping zigzags. Look for peregrine falcons above Brock Crag on the left; they nest here. At the intake wall keep down the valley of Scale Gill which is bridged just below a series of falls and cascades. Keep L by the wall and fork L on the public footpath to Taw House. Follow the path left of a large ash tree and by a broken wall through gateways and a stand of mature oak trees. A gate gives access to an enclosed track. At Taw House go into the yard then turn L over a ladder stile and down the enclosed path with stiles and nettles. Cross the memorial bridge over the River Esk and turn R to Brotherilkeld and the start.

**Brotherilkeld** This was acquired by the monks of Furness Abbey in 1242 for its importance as a centre of wool products. Trails linked Eskdale with Borrowdale, where the monks had other sheep farming interests. Wool was an important part of the abbey's economy, together with iron.

Centuries ago the area had a covering of scrub. The wall on the Great Moss was built by the monks to enclose their grazing sheep, yet was low enough to allow deer from the adjoining deer park to cross.

# WALK 20:

## Whin Crag, Eel Tarn and Stony Tarn

*The stepping stones and St Catherine's Church*

**SUMMARY:** This walk combines a gentle riverside stroll with an exploration of the knobbly little hills which bound Eskdale on its north-west. There is some rough, wet walking on the hills, but the reward is a fine sharp summit and a visit to two isolated tarns. The ubiquitous bracken poses no real problems, although route finding requires care.

| | |
|---|---|
| *Distance:* | 6½ miles (10.5km); Short version from the Woolpack Inn 3 miles |
| *Grade:* | Moderate |
| *Terrain:* | Low fell. Wet in parts. |
| *Summits:* | Whin Crag - 1181ft (360m) |
| *Height gain:* | 1017ft (310m) |
| *Map:* | OL 6 |

A shorter version, starting at and returning to the Woolpack Inn is given (start B).

**HOW TO GET THERE AND PARKING:** From Eskdale Green turn up the valley at the King George IV for 1½

STA

to Eskdale
Sta
Ho
Cl

miles towards Hardknott Pass. 200 yards beyond Stanley House and opposite the old school turn R on a narrow surfaced lane to Stanley Gill. Cross the River Esk, and Trough House Bridge car park is on the left.

**To the Woolpack Inn** (short version start) - continue 1¼ mile along the valley road. The Woolpack is on the left (refreshments). Ask for permission to park; a fee is charged.

### THE WALK - START A: Trough House Bridge car park

At the car park entrance turn L towards Stanley Gill. Fork L to 'Waterfalls' on a track. *Across the field is Dalegarth Hall, known for its typical Lakeland cylindrical chimneys and occupied by the Stanley family, hence the name Stanley Gill, and the waterfall in the gill is also known as Dalegarth Force.* Go through a gate and in 100 yards turn L at a signpost 'Bridleway Boot and Upper Eskdale'. The path leads through a field then to woodland bordering Stanley Gill. Cross the footbridge and exit the wood at the next gate. Go straight ahead, leaving the bridleway to a more circuitous route. The open view right shows the Eskdale granite of Gait Crag above the old mixed woodland.

Go along by the River Esk until opposite St Catherine's Church. Two gates access the stepping stones.

**If the water level is low** cross the

stones to St Catherine's Church on the opposite bank to visit the church then carry on upriver on a path made suitable for the disabled as far as Gill Force bridge. Do not cross the river.

**If the water level is too high** proceed along the river bank to the gorge of Gill Force, a place to look down on brilliant dragonflies. The path drops into an old cutting and approaches Gill Force bridge. Cross the river here.

*The supporting girders look rather substantial for a footbridge, but it originally carried a railway line to mines and later quarries up the valley.* (To visit the church return along the path.)

**To continue the route** climb up through a gap in a wall and follow the right-hand wall round, joining the old bridleway. Go through a gate where the way becomes walled, then pass through gorse and broom overhung with rowan amidst an air of isolation. Two gates further on and Birker Force appears on the right.

At the spot where the path becomes walled again stop and let your eyes follow the wall right, over the river, and where the wall continues is an **archeological site** of old bloomeries. Keep along the path to a junction then straight on to Doctor Bridge. *So named because it was widened in 1734 by a local doctor Dr. E. Tyson of Penny Hill.*

Turn L along the lane to the road. Turn R and continue for 150 yards then turn L on the public footpath to Burn Moor just before the Woolpack Inn.

**START B: The Woolpack Inn** The shorter version joins here.
From the post box the old peat road can be seen winding down the opposite side of the valley (see Walk 17).

Go ahead on the track behind the inn, climbing the soggy path to a gate through which the path improves. Keep ahead on a rising curve to run parallel to a wall, then by a stream. When the stone-edged path begins to bend back towards the wall (the short return joins here), keep ahead on a lesser path up a bracken slope to a col on the right of a domed knoll. Harter Fell is majestic ahead, but only briefly, as the spreading valley and the tiered triangles of Hare Crag slabs steal the scene. Cross a small stream and, carefully keeping to the path, bend L uphill to the left of rocks and round the right-hand edge of a bog. Make your way up into a watery gap towards a scree tongue and at its top continue your same direction on the right of the bog. The old path seems temporarily to have disappeared so rejoin it at a higher level. (The scouts among you can discover the old path slyly sneaking off R just before a large boulder and running high and dry to meet the bog-trotters.) Go through the trench and look ahead to the next gap for a small holly. Go to it and through the gap.

*Stony Tarn and Whin Crag*

Ahead are twin peaks. The 'highest', on the right, is merely a shoulder of our objective, Whin Crag, the left-hand peak.

Keep ahead on the improved contouring path. The little waterfalls of Blea Beck zigzag down the rocky slope descending from Stony Tarn. Go through another gap and along the left of a flat area. Ignore a rising path left (which leads to Stony Tarn) and keep along the valley - first on the left of Blea Beck then stride across to the other bank avoiding the bracken. There is no path now, but the grass-floored combe offers easy walking. (Stony Tarn is over the hill on the left - north.) The beck turns away left. Keep ahead using a trod on the fringe of the bracken which climbs passing a fine upstanding rowan. Looking back on the left of the tumbling beck is the humpy hilltop of Peelplace Noddle. Prominent ahead and slightly left is Whin Crag (view A). Hold a straight line to the broad ridge. Turn L and make your way to the summit cairn to savour the excellent view.

Use the vantage point to spy out the onward route to Stony Tarn and Eel Tarn (just showing to the south-west). We go down the ridge, past the fenced area, to the tarn outlet. Beyond the outlet the line of a cross-path can be seen traversing the bracken slope. We aim for this path (view B).

Set off from the cairn by retracing your steps a few yards to avoid crags beneath the protruding summit then descend left over steep grass to pass the fenced area, a haven of lush vegetation protected from the nibbling sheep. Continue ahead then bear R and down to the outlet of Stony Tarn. Complete silence pervades the lone tarn, natural, unfrequented and unspoilt.

Jump the outlet and go straight up the grass to meet an old path coming from a ruined sheepfold on the right. Turn L to reach ice-scored slabs. (Alternatively short-cut L below the bracken to the ice-scored slabs.)

A glance back left shows the tarn in its setting.

Continue the traverse, cross a boggy wallow and go ahead towards a perched block (view C). The gill now turns away to the left. Pass right of the boulder and through a rocky "gateway". A glance back gives an unfamiliar view of Scafell. Keep below rocks as you veer R, skirting the edge of a nasty quagmire, then on through a wider gap revealing a view out to sea (view D).

Drop into a green hollow with clusters of mossy Turk's Heads (view E), then turn away R along the edge of the hollow past a waymark cairn to a small, perky, pointed block. Turn L between the rock and a boulder in a pool. Descend passing a cairn to the right. Keep ahead and descend as the path hugs left-hand rocks on a shelf with a cairn right. To the north is Scafell and Slight Side.

Pass another cairn on a rock and a perched boulder. Keep a sharp eye on the path (view F), holding a straight line (ignore a fork left) to gain the path on the drier ground between the bogs, where Yewbarrow and Pillar fill the northern horizon. Move rapidly across a wet section, the best way you can, to the path below a rock on the other side.

Drop through a gap with small stones on its right, also cairns and two trees, a holly and an ash. Below, Eel Tarn, defended by its swamp, is now visible. Keep down the right-hand side of the trench (cairn), until below the ash tree. Go ahead to descend along the bracken edge, where the old path has stone edges, before crossing the swamp. Drier ground gives easier walking now to pass shapely boulders (right) to the outlet of Eel Tarn.

**Short return to Woolpack Inn** leaves here (see below).

**To continue A - Trough House car park:** Follow the stream down to join a major cross-path from Scafell and turn L along it. Across the Whillan Beck is the bare slope of Brat Moss, once busy with iron ore mines. Freewheel down the broad path to the intake wall and on past a ruin until the path becomes walled. When near a monkey puzzle tree look over to the valley to see stone buildings - old peat storage huts spread on the fellside.

When the right-hand wall bends away go R with it to a signpost. (If you miss it, at sheep-folds turn back sharp right.) Go through a gate then turn L down a surfaced lane. The cascades of Whillan Beck accompany the lane. As you arrive at Boot look out for the twin waterwheels of the old Corn Mill.

Turn L past the shop (telephone), Burnmoor Inn and Brook House Inn (refreshments at both). Notice the worked-out vein and spoil heaps above the hamlet, the reason for its existence, and the extra thick walls containing stones cleared from the fields.

At the main road turn R along the road for ⅓ mile to the old school, turn L to Stanley Gill and go over the river bridge to the car park.

**To continue B - Short Return to the Woolpack Inn:** Cross the tiny three-stone outlet bridge and go along the pleasant green path overlooking the tarn. Rise over a low shoulder and continue down the right-hand side of the emerging valley. The path bends right to a gap. Do not go through but turn L using stones to relocate the path which becomes clearer and drier again. Just before a ruined barn turn L, pass a waymark and go over a stone-slab bridge. There are rich views of Eskdale as you descend to the intake wall with a stile, which is ignored. Turn L above the wall (waymark) and follow it downhill towards a larch plantation, where the outward route is joined and the roof of the Woolpack seen a few minutes below.

## Archaeological Site

Despite hopeful claims that it dates back to Saxon times, local experts think it is the site of a medieval bloomery (for processing iron ore).

*The old corn mill, Boot*

# WALK 21: Miterdale and Burnmoor Tarn

*Brat Moss Stone Circle*

**SUMMARY:** The walk up Miterdale imperceptibly changes from a forested lowland valley to a lonely mountain stream. Its rugged valley head where waterfalls cascade into a fine miniature cirque is well worth seeing. Burnmoor Tarn lies on a broad moor once crossed by the corpse road from Wasdale to Eskdale. We return along an easy airy path to the atmospheric stone circles on Eskdale Moor, whence a more intricate route twists between rocky knolls, tarns and bogs to reach the road in Miterdale close to the start.

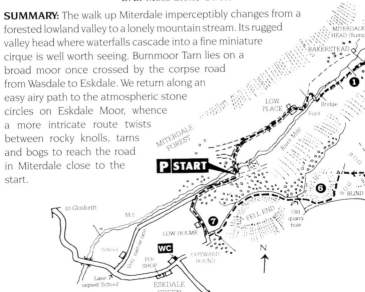

**HOW TO GET THERE AND PARKING:** From the western end of Eskdale Green village, turn up the lane at the 'school' sign (if approaching from the east it is the second 'school' sign). There is no other sign on the main road. Drive up the lane to the Forest Enterprise parking area at the end of the surfaced road.

**THE WALK:** Set off over the bridge on the public bridleway to Wasdale Head. The beauty of this hidden valley gives a feeling of serenity as you ignore paths to the left and make your way up the valley to Low Place Farm. The sides of the fells are covered with forest, its random patches of larch, fir, spruce and pine enhancing the low granite fells.

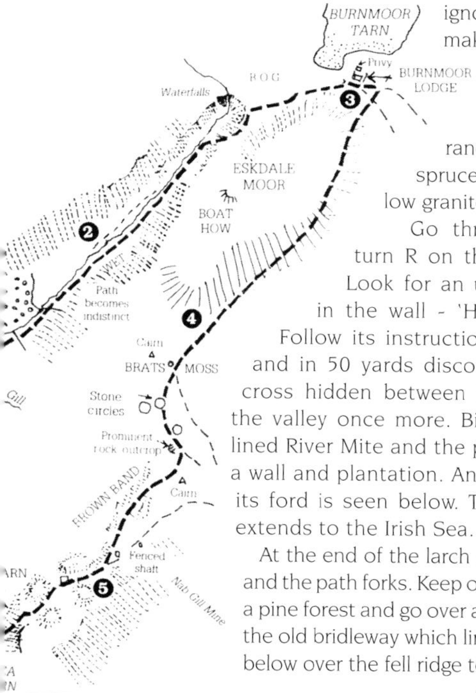

Go through the farmyard and turn R on the bridleway to Wasdale. Look for an unusual wooden sign set in the wall - 'HOD REET FUR ESHDEL'. Follow its instructions as you pass the ford and in 50 yards discover a little footbridge to cross hidden between holly bushes. Turn L up the valley once more. Birds flit about the gorse-lined River Mite and the path rises gently between a wall and plantation. An old farm, Bakerstead, by its ford is seen below. The view down the valley extends to the Irish Sea.

At the end of the larch planting the wall descends and the path forks. Keep on the higher level alongside a pine forest and go over a stile by a cross-wall. Cross the old bridleway which linked ruined Miterdale Farm below over the fell ridge to Boot in Eskdale.

Carry on up the narrowing valley, and cross Black Gill to glimpse Scafell above the valley head. The plantation on the north ends at the intake wall. Cross its ladder stile and go ahead into the wild upper valley.

| | |
|---|---|
| Distance: | 7¾ miles (12.5 km) |
| Grade: | Moderate |
| Terrain: | Valley and low fell. Some wet paths. |
| High point: | Eskdale Moor - 984ft (300m) |
| Height gain: | 820ft (250m) |
| Map: | OL6 |

### Waterfall at Miterdale Head

Where the river-meanders end, cross to the north bank for a better, drier path by the tumbling water. The stream is captured between interlocking spurs as it leaves the crag-encircled head of Miterdale. Recross to the south bank near a struggling holly. Listen as you go, for the chattering water is hushed and footfall is muffled by the green path, adding to a solemn aura of peace issuing from the impressive cirque. At a path fork (just before a pointed stone up right) take the R upper fork, which rises to give splendid view of the waterfalls spilling over the crags to form the River Mite.

Our way now tracks along the edge of the cirque with a few birch trees sprouting over the void. After the last tree take to the moor, branching R on an evasive trod north-east - the direction soon confirmed by the appearance of Burnmoor Tarn. Head for three privies with tree, on the right-hand side of the tarn. The scene is now extensive. Above Miterdale rises Illgill Head, with Pillar and Kirk Fell seen through the gap.

Go round the back of Burnmoor Lodge, built as a fishing lodge, desolate except for a quote from the Scriptures on the gable end. Ignore the obvious level pony path and angle R on a lesser upper path to a brow and path junction. Turn R towards the flat summit of Boat How (1106ft/337m) on the easy green path, with Eel Tarn glinting below and the dark pyramid of Harter Fell on the horizon beyond Eskdale. The path lies clear ahead for ¼ mile. Note the dark triangular rock outcrop in the moor ahead. Pass a cairn hollowed to form a wind shelter and various ancient stones and cairns.

When opposite the triangular rock outcrop the path forks. Go ahead to Brat Moss stone circle. *This Scheduled Ancient Monument is the remains of a Bronze Age settlement some 2500 years ago. It was also used for ritual and burial purposes.*

*The Bronze Age farmers cleared the oak scrubland. They preferred the upland locations where the vegetation was more easily cleared than in the dense valleys. In those days the climate is thought to have been warmer and drier than today.*

From the stone circle turn L to the rock outcrop and go between the rock and another stone circle. Ignore paths branching down left and keep ahead on a path roughly holding to the high ground passing a cairn (20 yards away on the left). Pass a rocky knoll on the improving path which runs below the ridge of Brown Band. Keep at this height and soon a wider green hollow way which can be seen below is met. (It is an old mine path rising from Boot. The fenced area below guards the workings of **Nab Gill iron mine.**) From here is a wonderful view of the mountains surrounding the head of Eskdale.

Progress about 50 yards to a cairn then fork L through the gap now ahead. Go round a red bog on a cairned path, pass an unsuccessful wind shelter and go through an upper gap to a cairn, where the view from our highest point is west down Eskdale to the sea and, floating as if in a silver mist, the mountains of the Isle of Man. Blea Tarn Hill summit is off to the right.

Freewheel ahead down the shallow valley, which becomes steeper, to lonely Blea Tarn. Follow the path round the left-hand shore and stride over the outlet stream. Rise up the bank and through the gap in a broken wall. Ignore the path left and go ahead passing to the right of a perched boulder to the reedy basin of Siney Tarn, ideally situated to catch the afternoon sun.

Branch L on the narrow trod by angular stones, between Blind Tarn and Siney Tarn. Shadow the tarn at first then pass through a tussocky gap and head L down towards the forest for 200 yards to a cairned path junction. Turn L and go past a flat boggy area with a high stone wall/fence beyond. Gradually draw nearer to the wall as you progress round the bog, until you can look over it to the rich green meadows of lower Eskdale with Muncaster Fell piercing the seascaped horizon.

Ignore the ladder stile in the wall and cut R on a rising trod below rocks for 100 yards, then descend L towards the forest to find a stile in a cross-fence. Go over and along by the forest edge. Follow the edge of the beautiful

*View over upper Eskdale from Brat Moss*

HARTER
FELL

CROOK
CRAG

THE
PIKE

GREEN
CRAG

BIRKER
FORCE

spruce forest for a while down towards Miterdale. Keep by the wall for ½ mile past a ruined sheepfold until approaching another plantation which bars the way. (Ignore the stile ahead into the forest which gives access to the Eskdale Outward Bound grounds.) Make a short cut across R to a gate and enter a walled pathway which leads to a bridleway and turn R along it. At Low Holme notice the foul weather gallery connecting the farmhouse with the bank barn and the fine weather-vane on the roof.

On reaching the surfaced road turn R for ¼ mile to the start.

## Nab Gill Iron Mine

Nab Gill Mine 1845 was worked for haematite (iron ore) in a series of five adits. The ore was transported down an inclined plane to the valley. Here the mine offices and railhead sidings were located - the line being opened in 1875. The railway outlived the mine which closed in 1912.

*Kestrel*

CHAPTER 3
# Wasdale

One of Lakeland's most famous scenes is up Wastwater and The Screes to the distinctive cone of Great Gable. Sometimes bare and gaunt, or tree-framed from the foot of the lake, despite its familiarity it never fails to impress.

The higher fells around the head of the dale are a magnet for those walkers who enjoy strenuous days, but the lesser hills lower down the dale offer easier walks to attractive summits with wonderful views.

We have selected a couple of walks which explore the rocky recesses of Scafell Pike and Great Gable, a valley walk to Scoat Tarn, and walks on the shapely minor fells.

*Yewbarrow and Great Gable from Wastwater shore*

# WALK 22: Whin Rigg and Irton Pike

*Whin Rigg and The Screes*

**SUMMARY:** Whin Rigg is the most westerly summit of The Screes, a fine vantage point, reached by a steep but interesting ascent. Our walk then chooses to explore the lower seaward prolongation of the ridge to another good viewpoint, Irton Pike, whence a return is made on forest paths. Some of the forest paths may be dense in the peak vegetation of summer when the **Short Return B** may be preferable.

If the steep ascent to Whin Rigg is too daunting when seen, an alternative **Short Return A** provides a pleasing ramble in its own right visiting the lake and Woodhow Tarn.

**HOW TO GET THERE AND PARKING:** At Forest Bridge, Nether Wasdale. Park on wide grass verges near Forest Bridge over the River Irt. Hotels with bar meals, and camping at Nether Wasdale (1 mile).

| Distance: | 7 miles (11.25km) |
| | Short Return A 3 miles (4.75km) |
| | Short Return B 5 miles (8km) |
| Grade: | Strenuous |
| Terrain: | Medium fell and forest paths |
| Summits: | Whin Rigg - 1755ft (535m) |
| | Irton Pike - 738ft (225m) |
| Height gain: | 1722ft (525m) |
| Map: | OL 6 |

**THE WALK:** Cross the bridge and turn along the public footpath to Lake Foot and Easthwaite Farm. Note the white house right, The Flass, as its sight heralds our return across the fields. The view ahead from the farm lane shows Wasdale's renowned gullies and screes, their eroded rocks escalading down to settle peacefully at the lake-filled valley floor. The highest point above this western end of the Screes is Whin Rigg, our first objective. The farm sits in the crook of the intake wall which rises up the fellside beyond, enclosing a green pasture, from which our path can be seen climbing the fell - but don't be put off, it isn't as bad as it looks. Great Gable blocks the valley head with Scafell right and Kirk Fell left.

Go through the farmyard, signed 'footpath Wasdale Head', and in 100 yards, where the main track swings left, go straight on over a stile

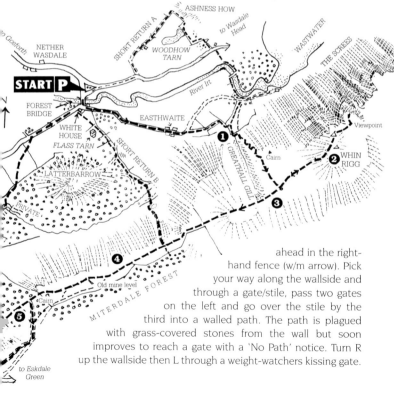

ahead in the right-hand fence (w/m arrow). Pick your way along the wallside and through a gate/stile, pass two gates on the left and go over the stile by the third into a walled path. The path is plagued with grass-covered stones from the wall but soon improves to reach a gate with a 'No Path' notice. Turn R up the wallside then L through a weight-watchers kissing gate.

Turn R up Greathall Gill for a few yards to discover a pink granite slab where you can sit and absorb a most wonderful view of the lake (see p. 136). Across the valley is Middle Fell, identified by a band of pale pink quartz intruded into its rocky face, a reminder of the volcanic nature of the rock containing mineral veins. On seeing the steep path left (which is not as bad as it looks) you may wish to abort, escaping along the **Short Return A.**

**TO WHIN RIGG:** Go up to a stile in the intake wall, step over onto crunchy granite sand, turn L over the gill washout and mount the far bank. Ignore a stile left and turn R up a very steep path which winds its way reasonably with the tree-lined gill to the right and a view down the valley to the Isle of Man. The path gradually moves further from the gill and becomes grassy. Two pointed teeth on the skyline above gradually draw closer and Sellafield Nuclear Power Station spreads its weird towers along the western shore. Pass a cairn, and as the teeth lose their bite, a large cairn heralds that the steepest part of the climb is conquered. Keep straight ahead up the brow, maybe muttering that effort is still required to reach the broad ridge which continually moves away ahead. Note a broken wall across the gill. A view south over lower Eskdale to the Stainton Pike fells shows briefly, and at last you reach a large cairn on the ridge path. Note this point for the return.

Turn L along the wider path. The first rock outcrop shows that the granite has been replaced by the volcanic rock which makes up the core of central Lakeland. The path is well cairned and rises steadily to pass just left of the right-hand summit cairn on Whin Rigg. It is hardly worth a visit for the view which is cut off by the lie of the land, but it is an easy tick-off for the summit bagger. Go on a few yards instead to the left-hand summit with a low windshelter and an excellent outlook. (Take a moment to look back to the noted cairn, the gill and wall beyond as cloud can easily form with little warning on this exposed ridge.)

A little further on and two rocky viewpoints enhance the scene with a thrill. Continue past the left-hand summit on the path for 50 yards for a breath-taking peer of some 720 feet (220m) down Great Gully.

Now move along the path to viewpoint number two, a protruding rock where your gaze dives straight down into dark Wastwater then surfaces to

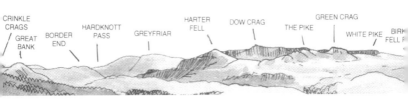

see Wasdale Hall. *It is now a Youth Hostel in an idyllic setting surrounded by a remarkable collection of trees planted by Stansfeld Rawson in the early 19th century. Look north-west to the more mundane chemical works at Whitehaven with St Bees Head behind on the coast, the Solway Estuary and Galloway Hills on the northern horizon. The tiny island in Wastwater is the seasonal raucous gullery seen at close quarters from Walk 21.*

Return between the summits of Whin Rigg and down (west) to the previously noted cairn then straight on the broad green path above the head of Greathall Gill and through a gap in the wall. The path rises, to show briefly Harter Fell and Hardknott Pass climbing out of Eskdale (south-east), and as it begins to descend again our next objective, Irton Pike, just protrudes from the forest at the ridge end. Beyond Irton Pike the River Irt from Wastwater meanders over the plain to join the Rivers Mite and Esk to enter the sea at Ravenglass. *They return up Eskdale as gleaming nameplates on the sides of the steam engines of the Eskdale railway.* You may hear the hoot of the train as you go over a stile near a wall corner and ahead through heather moorland on a wallside path. When the wall swings left to enclose the forest keep straight on, cutting over the moor to a cairn. This marks the junction with an old bridleway from Nether Wasdale to Eskdale Green. **SHORT RETURN B turns R here (see note below).**

**To IRTON PIKE:** Go ahead until reaching the forest corner to the left and along by the trees until crossing a small stream (alias rushy bog). Bend R and keep to the main green path which passes an old mine level, identified by a pile of stones and overgrown cutting on the left. Advance until opposite a huge pile of stones to the left. *The stones are now out of situ, piled roughly after an excavation in 1950. This was the site of early Bronze Age hut circles, where a superb jet necklace and other artefacts were found.* (The path beyond the pile runs down the hillside to the road.) Divert right to a solitary viewpoint where the length of Wasdale is magnificently spread before you. Return to the path and enter the forest at a stile. Go along to where a broader track merges from the left and ahead on a slender path which dips and rises to

*View from Irton Pike*

BRANT RAKE — HESK PIKE — WATER CRAG — WHITE PIKE — WHIT FELL — STAINTON PIKE — BLACK COMBE

MUNCASTER FELL

the summit of Irton Pike. There is a splendid panorama and there are plans to keep this part of the forest more open. Felling around the summit makes a direct descent impracticable so until a path is reinstated you will need to retrace steps to the broader track and descend R. A fork R leads to a forest road near the base of the hill where the direct descent joins. Turn R on this which traverses just above the Eskdale Green to Santon Bridge road. The track bends gradually R away from the road, becomes narrower and descends through mixed woodland passing above London Heath Farm to be joined by a path slanting up from the farm. Keep ahead on the rising path to a gate in a fence then along by the wall to another gate (footpath sign). Cross a track and still follow the wall to a gate in a cross wall. Enter a plantation where you may see pheasants well camouflaged against a background of birch leaves. Pass through a gap in a broken wall, go on to cross a stream then mount a rise which brings open sky above and Shepherd Crags, the end of Latterbarrow, on the right.

The way bends leftwards and descends on a wider track with a wall on the right. Ignore an old stile over the wall and a track joining from sharp left. Go on until a rock slab is underfoot and a ford seen several yards ahead. Turn R into the bushes on a secretive and meagre waymarked path, go over a stile and along the ensuing forest road. Cross a stream and in 25 yards turn L (w/m) on a path hugging the forest wall and brushing aside rhododendrons as you pass. Go through a young larch plantation (white pole w/m) and over a stile L into a field.

Scan the far wall for a signpost and set off across the field diagonally R. The white house, The Flass, seen beyond the far field corner is near the start. Go through a gate in a cross-wall, and turn L to a ladder stile accessing the road. The wide verge indicates that this was once a **drovers' road**. Turn R and in ¼ mile pass over the bridge to the start.

## SHORT RETURN A via the lake and Woodhow Tarn

At the kissing gate turn L down the pasture to a stile in the fence at the riverside track. Turn R and follow the track along the woodland edge where the narrowing outlet of the lake, aroused as the River Irt, gurgles its way to the estuary at Ravenglass. Go through a kissing gate and just before the track passes through a shallow cutting (opposite a PO stone) notice a circular bowl with cinders on the left of the track. This is an old bloomery where iron ore was once smelted. Carry on past the pumping station for a wonderful view up the lake to Great Gable and the famous Screes Path, a white, flimsy line threading across the screes and leading to the head of the lake three miles away.

The laid stone path gives an easy descent from Hollow Stones,
Scafell crags behind (Walk 28)

Entering the Lowther Park Forest. Dent is the hill behind (Walk 30)

Ennerdale from Crag Fell iron mines (Walk 32)

Return through the kissing gate and branch R onto the riverside path. Cross a concrete bridge and go through kissing gates and fields to turn R over Lund Bridge. *You are now in Low Coppice Wood (or the Peninsula) which was originally covered by 'old shrog wood' (scrubby undergrowth). In 1811 Stansfeld Rawson of Wasdale Hall planted 71,000 trees which have matured to our benefit.* Bend L along the riverbank, go through a gate then ahead up the field aiming to the left of the farm buildings. On arriving at the iron kissing gate at the road look back for a stunning view of the Wasdale gullies.

Turn L, cross the road and climb up by a retaining wall signed to Buckbarrow and Greendale. Go through a kissing gate into woodland and over the brow to a gate in a fence. Turn L on a track towards Woodhow Tarn which smiles shyly in its green dale. At the next wall turn R and go through the rushy meadow towards a gate with the tarn to your left. This gate and prominent signpost beyond is not for us. Find a kissing gate 25 yards to the R and turn L through it. Go between the wall and the gorse-decked knoll then turn L at the fence corner. Now you can proceed to the signpost. Keep ahead on the bridleway to Gatesyke, a gated and stiled old green bridleway which bends to meet the road. Turn R, pass Gatesyke and go over the brow to a junction. Turn L to Santon Bridge and the start.

## SHORT RETURN B

Turn R down the fell, tiptoe across a boggy hollow then go ahead to find a small gate into the woodland with pine on its right and birch to its left. Go down a path with side-rails, cross a track, go over a footbridge and emerge from the wood at a wallside track. Turn L, signed 'Nether Wasdale' (ignore a track sharp back left), and on the top of the brow fork R, to Nether Wasdale. There are good views of the dale as you descend to meet a forest track. Keep ahead over a stile signed 'Nether Wasdale' and through parkland pasture with stately oaks and beautiful old pines. Cross a stream, pass Flass Tarn, and straight on over a stile to the road near Flass House. Turn R over the river bridge to the start.

## The Drove Road

In the 17th century West Cumberland farmers fattened Scottish black cattle over the winter months then sold them on in spring. A drove route was established and is still visible from Eskdale Green to Santon Bridge, Nether Wasdale then over the moors to Blengdale and the lower fells of West Cumberland.

The walls enclosing the drove road were set well back with wide grass verges to allow the cattle to graze as they travelled.

# WALK 23: Circuit of Nether Wasdale

*Bridge over Cinderdale Beck*

**SUMMARY:** A gentle low-level walk among charming scenery through heathland, pastures and wooded knolls in the heart of lower Wasdale. A brief visit to the lakeshore gives wonderful views to the mountains and screes before returning along the River Irt.

Mainly on paths (one boggy section at the camp site) and tracks with a short road stretch at the beginning and end.

**HOW TO GET THERE AND PARKING:** Forest Bridge, Nether Wasdale. Park on the grass verges by the bridge. Hotels with bar meals, and camping at Nether Wasdale.

**THE WALK:** The signpost at Forest Bridge indicates the direction we take to Nether Wasdale, ¼ mile. Go along the road for 100 yards then turn L, signed 'Gosforth'. At Nether Wasdale, before we turn R to Church Stile Camp Site, go a little further ahead to the stone drinking fountain on the green between the two

| | |
|---|---|
| *Distance:* | 4½ miles (7.5km) |
| *Grade:* | Easy |
| *Terrain:* | Valley |
| *Height gain:* | Less than 100m |
| *Map:* | OLM 6 |

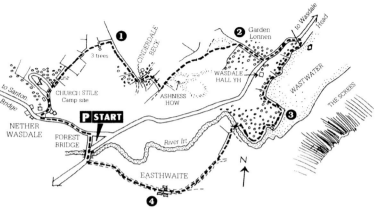

hotels. *It was donated by Lady Irton in 1880; she will be remembered as a caring lady as the fountain provided water for people, horses and dogs.* Go towards the camp site, pass the farm using the left-hand track and go into the camping field happily situated among wooded knolls. Pass the toilet block and fork R, keeping on the track alongside the fence and over a ladder stile into heathland. In 50 yards the path leaves the track and goes straight on up a quagmire of a slope. Advance the best way you can until the path improves and, as a bonus, gives a face-on view of Buckbarrow (Walk 24). Go over a ladder stile in a cross-wall and straight on using the stepping stones to reach drier pasture over a brow then make for a gate by a wall corner. Through the gate is spread a pastoral scene stretching up Wasdale. Accompany the left-hand wall until it bends away left to Buckbarrow then keep straight on towards a wall-end with three trees to its right. Go between the trees and find a footpath sign. Now look across the heath diagonally to spy out the next signpost and go for it. Turn R towards Mill Place. Cinderdale is the neat gorse-lined vale on the left, lending a picturesque foreground to the view up the valley.

Go through a gate into old woodland where the dark side of the valley, The Screes, stand in contrast to the gentle floor. Go through a gate to a signpost and turn sharp L on the gated bridleway to Buckbarrow. Cross a field, go over Scale Bridge ('scale' is Norse for 'shieling') and ahead for 100 yards to a stone bridleway sign. Turn R along the old way between walls to go through a gate and along the fence with the little knott of Ashness How on the left. At multiple stiles turn L to Greendale. The aspect is now wide to the north. Ignore a path right to Woodhow and carry on over a stile

*The peaks at the head of Wasdale*

at a cross-wall, walking ahead into an eye-catching spread of peaks at the head of the dale. Do not miss a solitary key signpost but take heed of the direction R to the lake. Wind round a rise or, better still, leave the path briefly, go on top of it and spend a few minutes identifying the mountains (see diagram).

Go over a ladder stile in the field corner into a walled track, Garden Lonnen. You are now in the woodlands of **Wasdale Hall**. The track leads through woods where native trees and imported trees mingle to give a spread of shape and colour. To the left is High Scale Wood and to the right High Birkhow. The garden was once the kitchen garden of the Hall. At the road turn L (ignore a gate

right to the Youth Hostel) and roadwalk a short distance to just beyond a cattle grid. The sudden open view up the lake urges you to stop, but better awaits. Go down R out of the way of the traffic, over a stile near the wall-end and onto the shore path.

*You cannot fail to have noticed the gull colony where black-headed gulls quarrel in full squawk on their tiny island. From the path The Screes appear in their full splendour, the gullies of Illgill Head spilling chutes of stones resting at 40 degree angles and renowned by their reproduction on calendars and*

*Great Gully seen from the lakeside path, Wastwater*

chocolate boxes throughout the world. *Go through a kissing gate into woodland and a viewpoint seat. Wastwater is 258 feet deep and plunges well below sea level.* The shore path continues through the grounds of the Youth Hostel, a most attractive building so well situated that you feel like joining the Y.H.A. on the spot. Pass a gate and a memorial seat, then carry on until you can see the chasm of the Great Gully. *The gullies were numbered A B C and the Great Gully by climbers early this century, who tested their prowess by scaling them.*

Pass a boathouse and circle the inlet in a bluebell wood. The great crested grebe favours this stretch of sheltered water. The building across the water is the Northwest Water pumping station.

Gradually the lake stirs itself into action and wanders off as the River Irt towards the sea at Ravenglass. The path now rises to run amongst the slender trunks of a beech and birch wood to its edge. Go through a kissing gate and over Lund Bridge, where the river is now livelier.

Take a line diagonally L across the field and through the left-hand of two gates. Turn R by the fenced hedge to meet a farm track. Turn R along the gated track up the hill and through the yard at Easthwaite Farm.

Keep on to reach the road, turn R, and over Forest Bridge is the parking at **the start.**

## Wasdale Hall Woodland

When Stansfeld Rawson, a wealthy Yorkshire banker, came to Wasdale Hall, Birch How (High Birkhow) was treeless with 'not a stick on the Ground', and High Scale and Low Coppice hosted 'old shrog wood' (low scrub). He set about planting trees, some native and some introduced species, probably influenced by his connections with the East India Company. Between 1811 and 1813 he had planted over 307,000 trees, the beautiful mature woodland we see today. He did not have total success however. He tried an apple and pear orchard but the fruit trees all died. It was blamed on the inhospitable weather.

*Old tractor at Easthwaite*

# WALK 24: Buckbarrow and Middle Fell

*Buckbarrow from Walk 23*

**SUMMARY:** The shapely, craggy fells above Wastwater to the north-west are interesting objectives, with worthwhile views of the higher fells at the head of the dale. Buckbarrow, our first summit, which appears so dominant from below, is a minor top of a higher fell. It is well worth the short diversion to the crag edge for a bird's-eye view of Wastwater. With hardly any height loss we cross to Greendale Tarn in its secluded hollow, whence a traverse over Middle Fell completes a fine mountain walk.

**HOW TO GET THERE AND PARKING:** Go along the Wasdale road to Wastwater. 300 yards past the viewpoint windshelter turn L to Gosforth. Park on the common just before Greendale, the first group of buildings on the right at the foot of Greendale Gill. The return path can be seen descending Greendale.

| | |
|---|---|
| *Distance:* | 5 miles (8km) |
| *Grade:* | Moderate |
| *Terrain:* | Low fell with some rough, wet walking |
| *Summits:* | Buckbarrow - 1394ft (425m) |
| | Middle Fell - 1909ft (582m) |
| *Height gain:* | 1739ft (530m) |
| *Map:* | OL 6 |

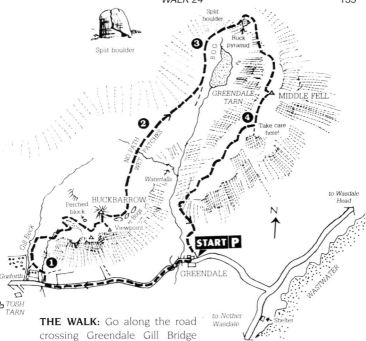

**THE WALK:** Go along the road crossing Greendale Gill Bridge and along the ribbon of tarmac rising over the common. On the right tower the crags of Buckbarrow, a volcanic rock inlaid with bands of quartz. On the other hand lie the lush meadows and woodlands of the valley floor bounded by Whin Rigg and the ridge pushing west to terminate in the wooded knoll Irton Pike (Walk 22).

Just before reaching an enclosed young plantation of pines turn R on a green path up the fell. Bear L to cross a stream by the wall corner and follow a diagonally rising path to meet a major path coming from the road up the side of Gill Beck. Turn R up the gill which is lined with ash, holly, and larch and bordered with gorse. It is a gill for all seasons with promising glances up and down the main valley. Reach a pretty cascade where a grassy shelf allows open views down to Tosh Tarn and out to the coast.

The path now bends R away from the gill. Cross a small stream and turn up L to pass through a few stones of an old wall and up by the stream, bubbling in its cleft, to a flatter moor.

BUCKBARROW            SEATALLAN                        MIDDLE FELL

The path, now a slightly worn swath through the grass, runs straight and parallel to, though well away from, the climbing crag of Buckbarrow. The atmosphere changes to a wilderness with rocky summits thrusting from the rough moorland grasses. The cairn on Buckbarrow's highest crag is ahead. Pass alongside an inclined slab of rock and climb up R to the ridge. *To the south the distant Black Combe stands in profile, its steep lower slope produced by the action of a south-thrusting ice-sheet.*

On coming face to face with the edge of the climbing crag swing L to a fork in the path where the crag diminishes. In a hollow down left is a cloverleaf sheepfold. Fork R and go up behind the rock, passing a perched block, and along a grassy trough to a flat area. The higher of various summits with cairns is ahead. Carry on past a pointed rock and up to the ridge and a red bog. There is a small fenced area (plastic bags store) to the left. Note this spot.

A very pleasant diversion can now be made. Turn R for about 100 yards to an eminence with a cairn on the mountain's edge for an impressive view of Wasdale and Scafell.

Return to the noted spot, then carry on past the fenced area and up to the summit. The bulky fells provide a desolate, wild outlook over rolling slopes of tussock grass, but it offers a bird's-eye scan of the onward route. Look NE across the deep valley of Greendale Gill to Middle Fell. In the overlapping folds of the valley Greendale Tarn can just be distinguished. We aim to cross the intervening trackless moor to the tarn without losing height and without getting wet, for this moor is the gathering ground of Tongue Gills. It is not the dreadful challenge it appears.

Set off from the summit a few degrees L of your arrival (E). A path leads down and follows across the top of the red bog pools then gradually disappears. Hold your height and keep bending L on solid ground to face in the direction of Greendale Tarn (NNE). There may be signs of quad bike tracks but they are of no significance and just rove about to a fenced area

YEWBARROW  KIRK FELL  GREAT GABLE

*View from Greathall Gill, Walk 22 to Buckbarrow and Middle Fell*

down on the right. Cross over a carpet of moss then **beware** of drainage ditches, narrow, overgrown, deep and wet. Trek on until you go over a rocky shoulder and Greendale Tarn is ahead. Aim to walk below rocks to gain the left-hand side of the tarn.

**SHORT RETURN:** Turn R and go down to the tarn's outlet stream. Cross it and turn R down the valley path to join the path from Middle Fell at *.

**TO MIDDLE FELL** Follow the left side of the tarn taking the opportunity to examine the scallop patterns, formed by scree rolling down former snow patches, on the slope of Middle Fell. To the left is the dome of Seatallan.

As you approach the col between Seatallan and Middle Fell look for a split boulder. 50 yards below the boulder bend R across a boggy spring and work your way up L to a line of small cairns and on to where the ridge of Middle Fell ends in a rocky pyramid. Skirt left below it where there is a view of the Nether Beck valley and (R to L) Red Pike, Haycock, and Seatallan. Discover also a path from the col and turn R along it as it gradually climbs the shoulder of the mountain and gains a broad ridge with expanding views all the way. The path passes pools, then levels and wanders along easily to the summit of Middle Fell. It is well worth allowing time to do justice to the mountain panorama.

Go over the fell top, drop R a few yards from the summit dome, then regain the original direction keeping to the right side of the broad ridge. It soon becomes obvious that the path is making towards the Greendale valley. Keep a careful eye on the path as it turns R at a flat, boggy area. (Do not go straight across the narrow top of the bog this leads to a steep rocky drop-off further down.) The descent becomes steeper but easy, passing two fenced areas and a large cairn. *We join our short route here.

The plunging valley on the right reveals the tributary twin chasms of Tongues Gills, their impressive falls would have warranted individual descriptive names if nearer civilisation.

The path now veers L away from the gill and descends a more gentle slope to the start.

# WALK 25: Scoat Tarn via Nether Beck

*Scoat Tarn*

**SUMMARY:** A popular walk up the valley of Nether Beck to a secluded glacially formed mountain tarn of unusually sunny aspect is followed by a virtually pathless return. After the enclosed stony valley approach, the views from the ridge are breathtaking, spreading over Low Tarn to Scafell and Burnmoor and the shapely cone of Harter Fell.

Route finding is straightforward and grass underfoot is welcome for the descent. You will see ant-like columns of people on the Red Pike ridge and the Overbeck path, but here you will savour one of Lakeland's rarely visited gems.

| | |
|---|---|
| *Distance:* | 6 miles (9.6km) |
| *Grade:* | Strenuous |
| *Terrain:* | Valley and medium fell. Some rough stony paths and pathless fell. |
| *Summit:* | Unnamed peak on ridge at 2132ft (650m) |
| *Height gain:* | 1968ft (600m) |
| *Map:* | OL 6 |

**HOW TO GET THERE AND PARKING:** Park at Nether Beck Bridge, near Wastwater shore, 1 mile past the Gosforth road junction either:
**1)** in a small roadside quarry just before the cattle grid sign or
**2)** in a larger parking area ¼ mile beyond the bridge on the left.

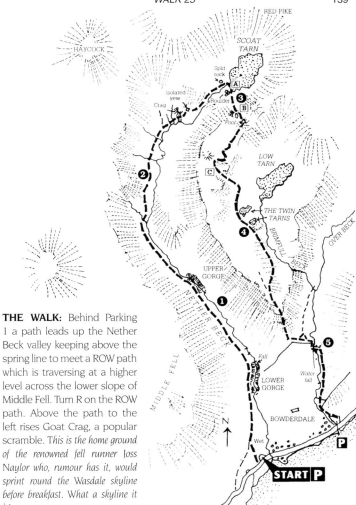

**THE WALK:** Behind Parking 1 a path leads up the Nether Beck valley keeping above the spring line to meet a ROW path which is traversing at a higher level across the lower slope of Middle Fell. Turn R on the ROW path. Above the path to the left rises Goat Crag, a popular scramble. *This is the home ground of the renowned fell runner Joss Naylor who, rumour has it, would sprint round the Wasdale skyline before breakfast. What a skyline it is!*

Pass a hump of ice-scoured rock where there are sounds of the beck surging in its gorge. The path levels and gradually approaches the gorge.

At its nearest point, immediately below where the water in the beck is first visible, take a careful stroll down the grass bank and peer in at the waterfall: a sudden surge setting rainbows dancing around the chasm before plunging into its deep transparent pool. Pass a cairn and an old cross-wall where the beck offers another cascade and a pool, looking so inviting in summer that willpower may have to be used to make progress up the valley. Pass the upper gorge. To the right rise the flanks of Blackbeck Knotts and Knott Ends with the ridge of Yewbarrow poking up behind. We trek along the Knotts' ridge on our return. *On the left fellside a scalloped string of stones left by a retreating ice forms a necklace to the dome of Seatallan.*

The path climbs more steeply with the tops of hardy trees - holly, ash, rowan and yew - stretching for sunlight above the deep sheltering walls of the upper gorge. Carry on up the valley, which continually bends to the right (N), until reaching the flatter upper valley. Our path keeps on the left-hand side above a boggy area. Carefully identify a path junction. A square-cut crag stands in the valley between two tributary streams and the junction is roughly level with the last old fence pole over the stream. Fork R and cross the stream from the left arm of the valley. (The left fork goes up to the Haycock/Red Pike ridge.) There are old sheepfold ruins to the right. Keep a sharp eye out for cairns and make to the right of the square-cut crag, climbing steeply now, to a solitary yew bowed by the prevailing wind (may its seedlings evade the nibbling sheep). Now well above the square-cut crag we can see an erratic boulder perched on its top.

From the yew tree bear R towards the stream then turn uphill again on the sparsely cairned path to pass a distinctive split boulder at Scoat Tarn.

Scoat Tarn occupies a lonely ice-scooped combe below the inhospitable slopes of Red Pike, yet it is not unfriendly. Allow time to enjoy its unspoilt proximity and, after crossing R over the outlet stream, bask in its suntrap and eye the onward route - for it is a pioneering endeavour, there is no path.

From the outlet head R to a group of large boulders and hold that direction (S) to a grassy col on the skyline (see point A on map). Once on the

col the steaming towers of Sellafield and the mountains of the Isle of Man line the seascape viewed through the col between Seatallan and Haycock. Just over the col is a small pool. Pass to its left

and go ahead onto the highest ground, an unnamed summit (see point B on map), insignificant in itself but wow - what a view (see panorama)!; and there is a bonus of three lakes, Low Tarn, Wastwater and Burnmoor Tarn.

Spy out the way down before setting off. We aim to walk down the broad ridge ahead. There is a good view down left (east) to Low Tarn but we do not visit it. Set off south winding round the little pools and rocky outcrops using sheep trods to avoid wet patches but generally holding to the ridge (see point C on map). A glance east shows lofty Great Gable looming up. Now watch out for a bit of a crag on the ridge. It looks worse from above than from below so bypass it on the R. Leave the ridge for a  while and keep down L of the next knoll aiming briefly towards Low Tarn and down a steeper grass gap with chunky stones on its right. Turn R away from the tarn aiming now for two small tarns set in the peat, although only one of them is seen at this stage. When the second tarn shows its face move along the R side of the further one. Go to the lip ahead, where the valley of Brimfull Beck, which drains Low Water, can be seen forming over to the left.

Keep rightwards towards two rocky knobbles and work your way down the ridge again until it comes to a sudden end. (Ignore the Brimfull Beck valley to the east which drops over crags into Overbeck. Ignore any temptations to the west for there lie the crags of Knott Ends.) Walk ahead on grassy bands which wind easily down the steep ridge end, and as it narrows keep on the crest. An old zigzag path suddenly appears underfoot but it is fleeting. A rock step is easily negotiated, or bypassed R through sparse bracken. Go down to the wall.

Turn L and follow the wall down about 30 feet, then the path veers left

*View from rocky summit above Scoat Tarn*

away from the wall to join a more major cross-path. Turn R to a gate in the wall but do not go through, turn L down the wallside to a gated gap and cross the footbridge on Over Beck.

Turn R down the pretty valley, taking care at an earthslide and on a high traverse along the narrow path look down to a fine waterfall. Go over the stile in a fence then on to a kissing gate. Go through and along to Parking 2 and the road. Turn R and along to the bridge and to Parking 1 just beyond.

# WALK 26:     Yewbarrow and Over Beck

*Yewbarrow*

**SUMMARY:** The steep pyramid of Yewbarrow is a magnet which draws walkers irresistably to its summit. It is all the more attractive as it is somewhat easily attained, in spite of the ascent being steep with rock scrambling, compared with its higher neighbours. Of course the pyramid is a sham, but the extensive summit ridge provides a prolonged, high-level viewpoint. On reaching the top of Stirrup Crag the way seems to end, but with care the steep rocks can be descended without too much difficulty, and this is followed by a gentle stroll down the valley to the start.

| | |
|---|---|
| *Distance:* | 4 miles (6.4km) |
| *Grade:* | Strenuous, some scrambling and exposed path. Unsuitable for small children or dogs. |
| *Terrain:* | Medium fell |
| *Summit:* | Yewbarrow south summit - 2021ft (616m) |
| | north summit - 2040ft (622m) |
| *Height gain:* | 1961ft (597m) |
| *Map:* | OL6 |

**HOW TO GET THERE AND PARKING:** Go towards Wasdale Head and cross Overbeck Bridge approximately three-quarters of the way along the lake. Car park immediately left.

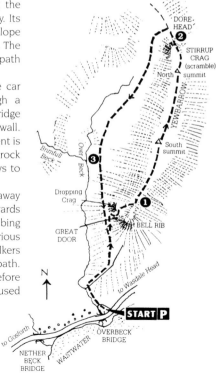

**THE WALK:** Yewbarrow is seen as a pyramidical slope dominating the scene a little further up the valley. Its steep grass, bracken and rocky slope threatens a formidable challenge. The slope is cut by a prominent green path line which is our route.

Set off from the back of the car park by Over Beck, go through a kissing gate and along the rising ridge to a gate in a fence mounted on a wall. Go through and turn R. The gradient is steep but steady and, at the first rock outcrop, offers retrospective views to the lake and down the valley.

The path bends leftwards away from the wall now heading towards Dropping Crag, a rock climbing venue, and quickly splits into various branches formed by sheep and walkers staggering back along the return path. Keep to the upper branch. Just before the crag is a scree chute which used to be the path. Turn R on a new-laid path which snakes up towards the Great Door. The path becomes rougher turning into a gully scramble and, about

30 feet above a section of old wall off left, it is easier to turn into a steeper part of the gully on the left then return to the gully for the final scramble. The gully widens and emerges onto grass and heather slopes. The view below into the Over Beck and Nether Beck valleys recedes as the outlook over Wasdale is enhanced, with Whin Rigg standing proud at the end of the Screes Ridge before it stretches to the forested pimple of Irton Pike and the coastal plain.

Abandon the gully and ascend diagonally L, which takes us above the height of the top, seen from the valley, which now stands isolated off to the right.

Emerge onto a narrow ridge with an airy view into space scanning over the head of the lake to Burnmoor Tarn, with Great How on its left, and beyond to Harter Fell, Green Crag and Caw crouching on the far horizon.

Turn L and carry on up the ridge, a beautiful array of purple shades as the bell heather and ling flower in late summer. Follow the ridge to the cairn, which, sadly, after all the hard work it is not the summit but a false one. However, earn one get one free; go easily along the scenic path to the south summit cairn. There is a magnificent view of the central Lakeland mountains.

Continue along the summit ridge descending to a gap. The path leads round a knob and undulates. Pass a cairn on a rock right and carry on to reach the north summit cairn.

**Do not allow children to run ahead.** Keep straight on down rocky steps where we begin the descent of Stirrup Crag overlooking Dore Head, the pass between Over Beck and Nether Beck. Climb down carefully. There are plenty of hand and footholds, and bottoms also come in useful. Be aware of dislodging loose stones as other walkers may be coming up. Above the final step watch out for a cairn indicating a L turn for the less exposed way.

Descend to the pass with Red Pike ahead and Black Sail Pass opening into Ennerdale on the right. Raise your eyebrows at the impressive buttress you have just descended and turn L to freewheel down the Over Beck path.

There are views down the valley all the way and across the valley to Brimfull Beck falling in a series of lively cascades from Low Tarn, hidden on its isolated shelf.

Pass a wall-end under Dropping Crag. This heralds the junction with the outward path. Turn R down the wallside and retrace the outward route to the start.

# WALK 27: The Napes of Great Gable

*Sty Head Pass with Great End*

**SUMMARY:** Great Gable dominates Wasdale, with the rocks of the Napes Ridges prominent high on its scree-covered slopes. That a walker's path traverses the mountainside seems improbable, yet the Gable traverse gives a close-up

| | |
|---|---|
| *Distance:* | 5¼ miles (8.4km) |
| *Grade:* | Strenuous with some scrambling, exposed path |
| *Terrain:* | Valley, fell and pass. Scree slopes and rock ridges. The roughest walk in the book. |
| *Highest points:* | Sty Head Pass - 1558ft (475m) |
| | Napes path - 2132ft (650m) |
| *Height gain:* | 1886ft (575m) |
| *Map:* | OL6 |

experience of climbers' terrain. Sty Head Pass is the first objective, most pleasantly reached by the easy zigzags of the old pony trail rather than the stony direct path. If you have dogs or small children retreat from here; if you don't mind a rough adventure carry on. The contouring path climbs around crags, crosses scree gullies, scrambles over the foot of rocky ridges and enjoys an aerial view of patchwork fields in Wasdale Head. Emerge on the blunt shoulder of the mountain and endure the steep, seemingly endless descent to the valley.

**HOW TO GET THERE AND PARKING:** Park at Wasdale Head car park, Wasdale.

**THE WALK:** Set off along the public bridleway to Sty Head. A copse of yew trees shelters the tiny church of St Olaf. *It is a church respected and loved by climbers, poets, walkers, writers and visitors worldwide in addition to its own small parish. Go into the churchyard where one headstone tells of a tragic accident in 1903 and others mark the resting places of those famous in climbing circles, who came to grief in the surrounding mountains. Visit the church, which is usually open, if only to admire its remarkable timber roof trusses.*

Carry on along the bridle-path between massive walls punctuated by mounds of stones gathered to improve the fields before 1795. Great Gable, frilled by the Napes Ridges, soars ahead, with Sty Head Pass to its right and Beck Head leading to Ennerdale on its left. The slopes of Lingmell form the right-hand valley wall with Kirk Fell on the left.

Go through Burnthwaite Farm, signed path L, and through a gate to join the path from the Wasdale Head Inn. Turn R and progress up the valley, where Great End is gradually revealed from behind the shoulder of Lingmell. Cross the footbridge over Gable Beck (ignore the path left which is our return route) and keep on up the valley. As the fence on the right angles away go R with it, cross a small stream and follow the fence/wall, exchanging the stony way for an old green pony path. Look up left to identify the Napes Ridges pricking the skyline and the pink screes from Great Hell Gate and Little Hell Gate invading the fellside. Just before a cross-wall notice how the beck, prone to violent changes of water level, has changed its course and cut new channels leaving raised banks along its course.

Go through a gate and along the beck, now in a gorge where it is joined by Piers Gill. Keep up the left bank until the gorge peters out. Some 65 feet (20m) beyond the confluence look for a large arrow R scratched on a flat rock. Cross the beck

here to two small cairns indicating the path on the opposite bank. The path zigzags up the hillside following the line of the pony path mounting the spur between the streams. To the right (south) is a fine arena of mountains riven by deep chasms. The stream right is Piers Gill, but the actual gill is hidden round the corner. Just above the bracken stands a boulder with a few stones on top.

**\* Walk 28 to Lingmell via Piers Gill turns R here.**

**To Sty Head** The pony path climbs steadily to a large cairn. This is the start of the connection with the Corridor Route to Scafell which will veer away rightwards. Keep on to the next cairn where **Sty Head** comes into sight. Our path forks L to cross a stream, but the bank has eroded and it is easier to go on to the third cairn then turn L over the stream issuing from Skew Gill, the deep chasm on the right. Reach the path and go up the set rock steps and continuing path. Look ahead for a huge cairn and join the main path. Turn R and find the First Aid stretcher box behind the first big boulder.

Sty Head has long been a major crossroads of paths. The view east over Styhead Tarn looks into Borrowdale. The path right (south-west) is to Langdale via Rossett Gill and Eskdale via Esk Hause. It was always a major packhorse route from the coast to Keswick. (To return to Wasdale from the box go west to the huge cairn and down the main path.)

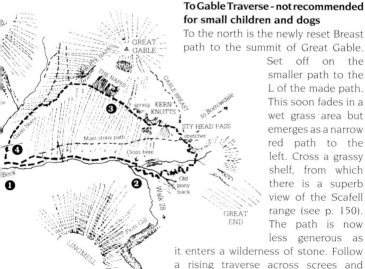

**To Gable Traverse - not recommended for small children and dogs**

To the north is the newly reset Breast path to the summit of Great Gable. Set off on the smaller path to the L of the made path. This soon fades in a wet grass area but emerges as a narrow red path to the left. Cross a grassy shelf, from which there is a superb view of the Scafell range (see p. 150). The path is now less generous as it enters a wilderness of stone. Follow a rising traverse across screes and

*The Gable Traverse*

go through a rock slit then round a corner. The approaching mountain face becoming more exciting where Kern Knotts Crag, looming above its shattered boulders, bars the way. *Two cracks split the rockface, the wider, Kern Knotts Crack, was popular with Victorian climbers, who thrust their way up in tricouni nailed boots. The narrow crack, Innominate Crack, is popular with modern Stealth shod climbers. Kern Knotts suffered slight damage in the earthquake of the 1970s.* Go to the boulders below the face and scramble through the gap 20 feet below the foot of the climbs (hands and bottoms very useful). Stay close under the crag until it bends right and the grass reappears. Strike away from the crag on a slightly rising traverse the path now heading for the Napes screes. Cross a boulder slope to a cairn. Keep below the rocks. Some 25 feet above the path is a small square-shaped cave and inside is a spring - cool, fresh and flowing even in a drought. Cross the pink screes of Great Hell Gate as the path makes a rising traverse, levels, then rises again. Above the Gate is Tophet Wall, usually strung with climbers on a dry day. Pass round the foot of a rock rib and **Napes Needle** comes into view. *It was first climbed in 1886 by Haskett-Smith. The hand and footholds are now so worn and polished as to be conquered nowadays only by a skilled rock gymnast*

*The Cat Rock*

with all the necessary equipment. Many of the occupants of the graveyard below fell from these cliffs. Photographers are unlikely to get the famous picture postcard profile from the path. These shots are usually taken from the 'Dress Circle' at a higher level than our path. However, when underneath the Needle enjoy the classic view of Wasdale before moving on.

Mount the next step in the path to be overlooked by the Sphinx Rock (sometimes referred to as the Cat Rock because of its prominent tail). Ignore a cairn on a rock 50 feet below the path. Our path threads on more or less level crossing Needle Gully and running below Eagle's Nest Ridge. Turn and look back for a better view of the Needle, then keep on traversing until the path is barred by pinnacles.

The continuing path is barred by a rock step **(1)** the 'sting in the tail'. It proves easier than it looks. For the more cautious take the alternative way round **(2)**.

**(1)** Go behind the pinnacles, descend a few feet then progress across the top of a slab. (If tall, there are handholds on the siderock; if small go on hands and knees.) Next scramble down the 6 foot rock step. (Launch from a sitting position, face into the rock and use the large footholds and handholds.)

**(2)** From the far end of the hands and knees ledge scramble down a short cleft on the left to grassy ledges descending diagonally left. Join a traversing path. (It is the old one which has gone out of use.) Turn R and go under the rocks to meet the path from the scramble.

Cross the next scree slope, Little Hell Gate, towards the White Napes. There is a good retro view of the Sphinx from here. The path traverses until meeting the ridge path from the summit of Great Gable.

Turn L down the nasty steep and stony path which soon turns into a better one descending a grassy ridge. (If you are thinking of continuing the traverse and turning left on the Moses Trod path from Beck Head it is not worth the extra distance and effort, as the Moses Trod path is almost as steep and stony.)

Merge with the Moses Trod path and, with good views into the Ill Gill chasm, go through the intake wall and down to the bridge over Gable Beck. Turn R and along to the farm. Keep straight on by the beck, cross a footbridge, and go through a gate. Stay by the beck crossing a series of bridges. The path from Mosedale joins in from the right and you can now relax on a seat or dash past a beautiful old packhorse bridge to the pub and toilets.

The start is 500 yards down the road.

## Napes Needle

The Needle was first climbed solo by W.P. Haskett-Smith in 1886. Descending from the top of Great Gable he discovered the top of the then unclimbed Needle Ridge. He climbed down the ridge to Needle Gap and proceeded to climb the Needle - in those days a daring feat of mountaineering. On a subsequent ascent he celebrated by doing a headstand on the point of the Needle.

## Sty Head

Sty Head (sty meaning 'ladder') has always been an important route from the coast to Keswick. It was used in the 17th century by smugglers who transported goods from the west Cumbrian coast ports. The pass had a well-engineered track and in 1896 plans were put forward for a coach road, but these were never implemented. It was still maintained as a pack-horse route in 1930.

*Walk 27 - View from the traverse to the Scafell Range*
*Walk 28 - can be seen alongside Piers Gill, the deep cleft on the right*

# WALK 28:  Lingmell via Piers Gill

*The twin summits of Lingmell*

**SUMMARY:** The northern flank of the Scafell range is riven by deep-cut gills and guarded by tumultuous crags. The walk penetrates the heart of this striking rock scenery to culminate at the summit of Lingmell, an isolated peak with a splendid view far better than that from its higher neighbours. The descent enters the impressive combe of Hollow Stones, then joins the modern stone pathway down the side of Brown Tongue.

**HOW TO GET THERE AND PARKING:** Park at Wasdale Head car park, Wasdale.

**THE WALK:** Start as for Walk 27 Napes of Great Gable (see p. 145) and continue to * just beyond the junction of Lingmell Beck and Piers Gill Beck.

There is little sign of a path, but stay above the bracken and gradually a trod develops into a path. The gill in its grey boulder bed becomes more lively and

| | |
|---|---|
| *Distance:* | 6 miles (9.65km) |
| *Grade:* | Strenuous with some scrambling |
| *Terrain:* | High fell |
| *Summit:* | Lingmell - 2641ft (805m) |
| *Height gain:* | 2395ft (730m) |
| *Map:* | OL6 |

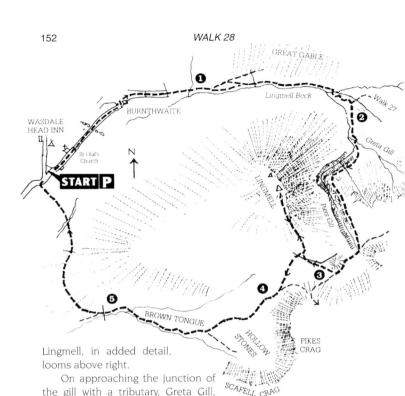

Lingmell, in added detail, looms above right.

On approaching the junction of the gill with a tributary, Greta Gill, from the left you will find that a path has consolidated. *Select a place to sit and study the scenery; at hand is the deep cleft of* **Piers Gill,** *across the valley stands Great Gable with the Napes Ridges and screes; and to its left Kirk Fell lanced by a deep gully.*

Bend R and cross Greta Gill above a cascade. The path gradually bends right as the gill turns a sharp right angle and continues to ascend into awesome rock scenery which keeps you guessing where it will lead next. The path becomes more exposed, yet sound underfoot, as it moves closer to the deep chasm. Never close enough to peer into the gill but giving a view ahead of the Bridge Rock - a chockstone wedged across the cleft at a crazy angle.

The path now turns up above a side gully, crosses it and continues on grassy slopes once more. From here is a lengthening outlook north-east over Borrowdale to Blencathra (Saddleback). The path is now cairned and leads to a rock barrier.

Scramble up (plenty of hand and footholds) and reach the ensuing path. Keep on to cross a cleft (do not turn left up its bed in mistake for the path) and go along to another short scramble. Traverse the cunning path with the bare ribs of Lingmell ahead. Piers Gill now turns left. Carefully follow the path, now on its brink, until the gradient eases. Meet a major cross-path, the Corridor Route to Scafell Pike.

Briefly turn R on the Corridor Route and cross the streamlet of Piers Gill. The left-hand skyline dips into Little Narrow Cove and a procession of minute silhouette figures in summit pilgrimage toil up the final slope of Scafell Pike. In 50 yards branch R round the back of a little knoll and cross over to a wall. Go up the wall side and at the top of the rise stride over the wall and wander to a cairn on the col. (Note: another cairn can be seen a little further up the col.) Turn R up the slope of Lingmell. As you climb look back and observe the broad, light-coloured path tracking down Scafell Pike and veering off to the right. We will use this path for the return.

Gain the summit. Lingmell stands apart from the Scafell mass thrusting into the Wasdale valley. Its position makes it a wonderful viewpoint and time spent at the summit cairn, wandering over to the second (lower summit) or other positions of vantage nearby, are more than amply rewarded.

Return to the col and as you go down spy out a short-cut over to the Scafell Pike path. At the col cross the old wall and make a diagonal right traverse to the cairned Pike path. Turn R and in a short distance encounter a spectacular view of Pikes Crag and Scafell Crag with the gap of Mickledore between. The path now gives a rough stony descent to Hollow Stones and gradually falls to merge with the newly laid path from Mickledore. Tread the steep slope comfortably down the laid way to cross the valley stream and go through a gate in the intake wall.

Fork R on a narrow traversing path which leads round the foot of Brown Tongue to a cross-wall with kissing gate. There are good views down the valley and the parking is already in sight. Descend to the beck, cross the footbridge, signed to Wasdale Head, and go straight across the meadow. At the road turn R to the start. Keep on the road for facilities at Wasdale Head.

## Piers Gill

The deep dog-leg of Piers Gill is rarely climbed, for a long dry spell is needed to make its pools and waterfalls passable. Climbers prospecting the climb by descending the unclimbed gill in 1921 were surprised to find a walker who had fallen in and had lain there, with a broken ankle, for eighteen days. A fortuitous rescue!

CHAPTER 4

# Ennerdale and the coast

Deep and heavily forested with conifer plantations, Ennerdale is relatively inaccessible and at times appears a sombre place. However, the lower fells around Ennerdale Water provide some more easily reached walks with memorable views up the dale to Pillar with its famous Pillar Rock. The forest contains some walking trails, but we have only chosen the one which follows the river, a good choice for a wild weather day.

We also suggest a walk which explores the remote valley head in spectacular surroundings.

The Coast-to-Coast walkers abound here, for Britain's most popular long-distance route traverses the dale. We include several walks which use parts of this trail. The choice starts with Cumbria's most impressive coastal scenery.

*Crag Fell and Ennerdale Water (Walk 32)*

# WALK 29:  St Bees Head

*The Smuggler's Cave, Fleswick Bay*

**SUMMARY:** The most popular coastal walk in Cumbria, with a constant procession of Coast-to-Coast walkers starting their journey and families on a short excursion from St Bees. Much of the spectacular red sandstone cliffs is an RSPB reserve, where fulmar, kittiwakes, puffins, black guillemots as well as the ubiquitous gulls can be seen. Take binoculars to benefit from the well-sited and stoutly fenced observation points.

With well-supervised young children a family walk as far as Fleswick Bay is a rewarding outing.

**HOW TO GET THERE AND PARKING:** From the B5345 on the north-west edge of St Bees village a turning signed 'To Beach' leads to a pay and display car park with toilets and refreshments and children's playground.

**THE WALK:** Go past the playground and down to the beach. Just beyond the lifeboat station is an information sign about the Coast-to-Coast walk which starts here and ends at Robin Hood's Bay on the Yorkshire coast. other information is

| Distance: | 7½ miles (12km) |
|---|---|
| Grade: | Moderate |
| Terrain: | Cliff-top path, lane and field |
| Highest point: | St Bees Head - 466ft (142m) |
| Map: | PF593 or Landranger 89 |

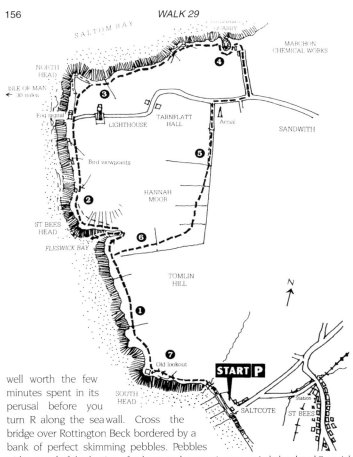

well worth the few
minutes spent in its
perusal before you
turn R along the sea wall. Cross the
bridge over Rottington Beck bordered by a
bank of perfect skimming pebbles. Pebbles
with a wonderful selection of colours and romantic names, Lakeland and Scottish
granites, granodiorites, andesites, tuffs, greywackes and quartz, were collected,
shaped and deposited by glaciers, and lie ready to skim if the tide is up.

Follow the C to C signs and mount the cliff-edge path leaving the
caravan site behind. *The seawashed platform below is of new red sandstone of the
Triassic period, probably laid down in a shallow sea, similar to the Persian Gulf today,
and topped by red boulder clay with the consistency of toffee when wet. Notice the wide
stone walls topped by gorse, typical of Pembroke, Cornwall and the Isle of Man. Pass*

*the old lookout post on South Head. Keep alert for goldfinches (a small bird with a red face, black and white neck, and yellow wing bars) which flit around the gorse.* The next stile leads into a field then leaves at a ladder stile ahead.

Fleswick Bay, a steeply cut valley, is now ahead. Descend into the gulch and turn L to visit the cove.

*The action of the waves has undercut the base of the cliffs giving spectacular rock scenery, a cave (smugglers' of course) to peer into, small semi-precious pebbles of agate, jasper and carnelian to search for and a fluted wave-cut platform to picnic on at low tide (take extra care on slippery rocks).*

Return to the stile (ignore footholds cut in the left wall), cross the stream and go over the second stile still - on the C to C stepped path. An information board is on the path and over to the right is a seat with view. Carry on along the path, where you will pass four protected viewing stations teetering on the very cliff edge as you go along. *It is awesome, yet intimate, to look down on the nesting seabirds. Take your binoculars, as each station is well worth a stop but the second is most definitely not to be missed.*

*St Bees Head from one of the RSPB observation points*

Cross another stile and the lighthouse appears. Pass by the viewing stations where meadow and rock pipits swoop about and meet a concrete path. Pass the foghorn post and go over a waymarked stile by a stone wall. (Ignore the next stile left which is a steep and dangerous path down the cliff used by rock climbers and fishermen. Also from this stile a narrow vegetated path runs round the headland and returns at the next stile.) Cut across the field to the next stile as the path swings to face the chemical factory at Workington.

Press on past a waymark pole and stile at a wall's end, the path now hugging the clifftop. Pass a RSPB welcome notice and some ornate graffiti to a series of old quarries cut into the upper section of the high cliff. Take to the cultivated field at a stile, as the clifftop path is insecure, and look back out along the coastline for a glorious view.

Birkhams quarry, now working, is quite a sight with huge blocks of high-quality stones cut and individually numbered, laid out on the dressing floor. *Stone from these quarries was used for building locally but was also exported to America in the 18th century as ballast in ships.* Go through gates by the quarry cottages to a lane end.

Turn R w/m, leaving the coast. Prominent throughout the Workington district the chimney of the Marchon chemical factory cannot be missed. *The factory is one of the main employers of the area. A drift mine under the sea provided anhydrite, used for the production of sulphuric acid, but this has long gone and at present the works manufacture ingredients for detergents.*

Reach a surfaced road and turn R, saying 'bon voyage' to the C to C, and walk up the hill towards a large aerial which has been a landmark tantalising from a distance. At the crest turn L, signed to Fleswick Bay.

Follow the lane until its end with views to the Lakeland hills to the east. A series of stiles leads ahead through fields to the top of a brow. Go over a bridged ladder stile, noting the direction indicated by the waymark on the bridge, then fork diagonally R across the pasture to the far side and turn R down through a gateway to the bottom of the field. Fleswick Bay is below on the right. Turn L and traverse across the field to merge with the outward route. Retrace the way back to the start.

# WALK 30:     **Uldale and Dent**

*Looking over Uldale to Flat Fell*

**SUMMARY:** Popular with local walkers, and the first taste of Lakeland for Coast-to-Coast walkers, this little corner of Cumbria deserves attention. Dent is a modest fell but its isolated position makes it a splendid viewpoint, whilst the trench of Uldale and Nannycatch, formed by an ice-dammed overflow channel in glacial times, is quite charming. Our starting point is on the high fell road (Cold Fell) which neccessitates some effort on the return, but is worthwhile for the views through the forest into Uldale. An easier, shorter version of the walk could be achieved from the parking at the end of Nannycatch Road (see map).

**HOW TO GET THERE AND PARKING:** The Cold Fell road crosses the moorland between Calder Bridge and Ennerdale Bridge. Park near its highest point by the Lowther Park forest gate. (For an alternative starting point park at the forest gate at the end of Nannycatch Road gained from Cleator Moor.)

| | |
|---|---|
| *Distance:* | 5½ miles (8.8km) |
| *Grade:* | Moderate |
| *Terrain:* | Forest, valley and low fell |
| *Summit* | Dent - 1155ft (352m) |
| *Height gain:* | 1500ft (457m) |
| *Map:* | OL4 |

**THE WALK:** Go over the stile to the forest road where a fringe of gaunt trees shelters the forest for this is a windy spot. Walk the short distance to a junction in a dip. Turn R down a steep path and emerge onto a forest road at

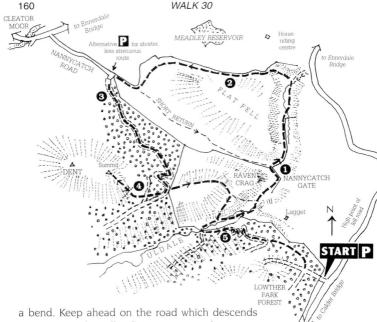

a bend. Keep ahead on the road which descends
in zigzags to the valley floor. Our onward route up
the valley is tantalisingly close but a deer fence bars access and we must
continue the short distance down the road to a junction, where a gate in
the fence gives access to a footbridge over the stream.

Make your way up the charming green valley on a path which has several
footbridges where the stream meanders. You may notice the 'C to C' joins and
the path becomes more well used. The Coast-to-Coast long distance footpath
from St Bees to Robin Hoods Bay is the most popular in the country. Make
your way through the narrow defile of Nannycatch Gate. These valleys were
ice overflow channels. Pass an overhung crag and go over a stile* at a merging
of two valleys. **Short return joins
here\*.**

Fork up the R valley, which
becomes narrower with a more
active stream. On the left Flatfell
Screes inch down their grey-blue
and rusty rocks of Skiddaw slate.

The well-maintained path is edged with stones of granophyre, a smooth pinkish rock. Ford a stream at the next valley junction and branch L. (The C to C leaves to the right.) Follow the rush-lined path round a bend then slant up L to a wall/fence with hawthorns. The little valley dwindles to a dip in a pasture. Turn L up the side of the wall/fence where views now extend - on the left the fell road, with Grike peering above the forest beyond, over the wall right, the west Cumbrian plain with Frizington Salterhall limestone quarries and Meadley Reservoir.

At the highest point divert from the ROW path (somewhat disused as it follows the wall into a boggy hollow) and fork L on one of the traversing paths to avoid losing height. Keep one eye on the wayward traversing path and the other to scan Dent, now ahead. A valley separates Dent from Flat Fell on our left. Team up with the ROW path by the wall again and go down into the valley.

**SHORT RETURN** Turn L along the valley and join the outward route at the Nannycatch Gate stile* at the merging of the two valleys. Turn R and go over the stile to retrace the outward route down the valley to a bridge and gate ***.

**TO DENT** Follow the wall right on a track to the roadhead at Nannycatch road by the forest corner. Go through the fell gate onto the tarmac, turn L and climb over the forest gate stile. The steady climb up the forest road soon makes light of the height gain. Though views are nil there are tadpoles swarming in the roadside rainpools and continual birdsong to entertain. Keep on the main forest road.

Where the road climbs in a zigzag the forest has been cleared and note a tall ladder stile on the left. **Note this spot.** This is our continuation after the ascent of Dent which is so close that it would be a shame to miss. A short distance past the stile, take a path on the R. At a signpost, go straight across following the C-C up the hill. Climb up the domed summit of Dent. The first eminence is the highest but the second has a

*View from Flat Fell*

GRASMOOR    CRAG    HERDUS    GREAT                    GRIKE
            HILL              BORNE

*View from Dent*

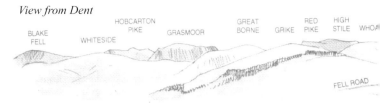

fine cairn. Both have wonderful views due to Dent's position thrusting into the west Cumbria plain. You can see High Stile (east), the Isle of Man (west), and the seaboard of the Cumbrian coast from Black Combe to the Solway and Galloway beyond.

Retrace your steps to the ladder stile and climb over it. A green path leads down the slope of a spur. The path steepens as it drops into Uldale. Across the valley Lagget Farm is the prominent white house and to its right our initial route the Lowther Park forest can be seen. Go down as far as a lone rowan tree then branch R on a narrow path, as though heading for a forest road. The path steepens to reach the valley floor and the outward route. Join the **Short Return**.*** Cross the bridge, go through the gate into the forest, turn L along the road and prepare for the gruelling climb back the way we came, up the zigzags then the path L at a bend. It is satisfying to emerge onto the forest road and see the entrance gate.

# WALK 31:          Whoap and Grike

*Grike and Crag Fell*

**SUMMARY:** If you want to escape the crowds and enjoy a day of easy walking on grassy hills, then this may suit. The high starting point from the unfenced Cold Fell road reduces the amount of ascent, although there is an initial drop into the head of the Calder valley, reminiscent of the Scottish southern uplands.

The walk gains the broad grass ridge of Whoap at the valley head, still graced with the song of the skylark, then crosses a forested depression to reach Grike and views to the Ennerdale peaks. A short-cut over a minor top takes you easily back to the start.

**HOW TO GET THERE AND PARKING:** The Cold Fell road crosses the moorland between Calder Bridge and Ennerdale Bridge. Near its highest point, just north of the forest plantations and ¾ mile south of the stone circle on Kinniside Common at a sharp bend a signed bridleway goes east. Parking is limited but spaces can be found on the verges of the unfenced road. There is a large parking area opposite the Kinniside Stone Circle but it involves a ¾ mile walk up the road to the start of the route.

**THE WALK:** Set off along a signed public bridleway over a watershed which looks out over the Calder valley. *It flows through a landscape of high domed hills attractive in their shapeliness. Behind, in contrast, lies the vale of Uldale, its forested sides hiding the coast and its flat emerald floor a token of the glacial overflow channels which shaped this region.* Follow the main track into the Calder valley ignoring the many other paths branching in various directions.

As you descend, forested Grike is to the north-east and the long ridge of Whoap stretches across the head of the valley. Skylarks sing, breaking the silence of isolation which pervades the mottled fellsides and the only trace of civilization is the odd section of stone wall tottering in the valley bottom.

Reach the River Calder, meandering on its way to Calder Bridge and the sea at Sellafield, then

| | |
|---|---|
| *Distance:* | 6 miles (9.5km) |
| *Grade:* | Moderate |
| *Terrain:* | Low fell |
| *Summits:* | Whoap - 1676ft (511m) |
| | Grike - 1601ft (488m) |
| | Blakeley Raise - 1276ft (389m) |
| *Height gain:* | 1506ft (459m) |
| *Map:* | OL4 |

carry on to cross Stinking Gill, still on the left-hand side of the valley. The path gradually gains height and across the valley is a textbook example of soil-creep with a patch of bare earth undercut by the meandering river, its waters swollen a few yards upstream by Whoap Beck. A circular sheepfold stands in the angle of the junction and to the left the slopes of Lank Rigg rise, their only feature being streaks of recent erosion.

Cross the River Calder at a ford with dubious stones to step on or find others more suitable upstream. Go up the track, round a bend and as the track bends left keep ahead, with a side-step a yard down the slope, on a minor path up the Whoap valley. A series of trods run parallel but as you approach a seven-pole enclosure make sure that you are using the better path about 50 feet above it. The U-shape of the valley tells of its glacial origin, seen to perfection as the path mounts to run a rising traverse across the valley head to arrive at a col between the ridge from Whoap and Lank Rigg.

When the path levels turn L on a narrow path leading up and along a broad ridge. To the right lie the lonely hills surrounding Worm Gill, with Haycock protruding above the far horizon. In 500 yards a section of wall to the right may afford a scenic shelter according to the wind direction, but look up left to Whoap, where a triangular 'cairn' appears to be the summit. Walk on, gradually rising round the valley head and cutting below the ridge to reach the triangular 'cairn', which proves to be a boulder and is neither on the summit nor the ridge. Go straight up the slope a few yards to a track along the ridge top. Turn L to a rounded stone which we will call the summit of Whoap, a low plain dome on a drab ridge of windswept grasses yet the focal point for a diverse variety of landscapes from sea to coastal plain up valleys to mountains.

Turn 180 degrees and retrace your way back along the ridge and over a rise which to the eye appears to be higher (but is not) than the 'summit' we visited.

Scan ahead for a prominent wall travelling along the fell. As the track takes a slightly curving descent look carefully for a gate in the wall which will quickly disappear from sight. The track levels and as soon as it starts to rise turn L

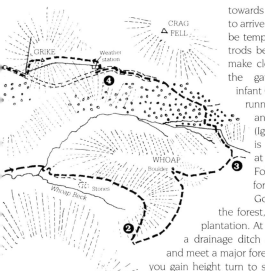

towards the immaculate wall to arrive near the gate. (Do not be tempted to shortcut down trods before this or you may make close aquaintance with the gathering grounds of infant Calder.) Meet the path running down the wallside and turn L along it. (Ignore the gate.) Ahead is Crag Fell with Grike at the end of the ridge. Follow the wall to the forest fence.

Go over the stile into the forest, turn L and enter the plantation. At a clearing turn R over a drainage ditch and up a broad ride and meet a major forest road. Turn L and as you gain height turn to see the distant profile of Pillar Mountain rising above the young spruce. The road gradient under the slope of Crag Fell is so gentle as to pass almost unnoticed, and the summit of Grike is soon ahead with the apparatus of a fenced weather station close enough to identify. Just before the weather station turn R, go through a gate in a fence and ahead for 10 yards to reach the path from Crag Fell. Turn L and climb the final rise to the summit with both cairn and windshelter. *From here is a fine overview of the route, the Isle of Man with Snaefell and North Barrule floating in the sea mist, the Galloway coast and the intricacies of nearby valleys formed by ice-overflow chanels.*

Go straight over the summit and descend to a fence. Turn L and follow it down to a cross-fence. Stride over to find the forest road once more. Turn R and keep on for ½ mile to a junction.

## A: Direct route over Blakeley Raise

Turn L and go up by a pond to a locked gate. Turn R up along the forest fence-side which terminates at a corner on the top. Stride over and, using the corner post, an iron post and a rock in line to point the direction, head for Sellafield and the fell road. Descend the moor veering left towards green-floored Uldale and arrive at the road and the start.

*View from Grike*

## B: Descent to the Kinniside Stone Circle

Turn R on an old green forest track (not the main forest road which is sharp right) and follow it down to the fell road. Turn R for the stone circle which is worth the short diversion to visit. Turn L up the road to the start.

## Kinniside Stone Circle

This fine monument stands near the roadside yet is not quite what it seems. The stones have been reset in concrete. Experts, however, are of the opinion that originally it was a genuine prehistoric circle similar in age to that at Castlerigg near Keswick.

# WALK 32: Crag Fell and Ennerdale Water Shore

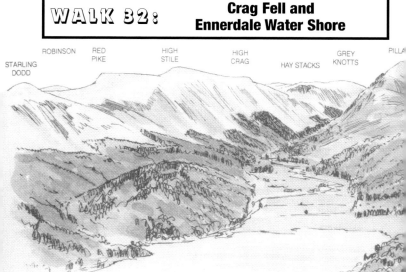

| | |
|---|---|
| *Distance:* | 5 miles (8km) |
| *Grade:* | Moderate |
| *Terrain:* | Low fell and lakeshore. Some rough walking and a steep descent. |
| *Summits:* | Crag Fell - 1715ft (523m) |
| *Height gain:* | 1378ft (420m) |
| *Map:* | OL4 |

**SUMMARY:** Ennerdale Water is dominated by the steep rocky slopes of Crag Fell, which is a splendid objective for a short walk. The summit is easily gained on a pleasingly graded path and the views are breathtaking. Bracken can be a hindrance on the steep descent, but the lakeside path is ample recompense, enlivened by a rocky passage of Anglers' Crag (see p.168/9).

**HOW TO GET THERE AND PARKING:** At Ennerdale Bridge turn east to Ennerdale Water. After ½ mile branch right at the forest and in ¾ mile find two large car parks on the left.

**THE WALK:** Cross the bridge over the River Ehen if parked in the first woodland parking area, where the fenced river banks are decked in delicate shades of pink, orchid and ragged robin, mixed with deep rich ruby of the clover. Crag Fell rises ahead, its summit fringed with crags and its slope cut by the yawning gash of Ben Gill.

Fork R passing the entrance to the Ennerdale Treatment Works (noting the blue slate name plaque set in the first huge sandstone block) then ahead towards Crag Farm House. To the left is the first view of Ennerdale Water with the wooded knoll of Bowness Knott and (L to R) Herdus Great Borne and Starling Dodd rising behind. Ignore the fork and keep straight on to the 'Welcome' stiles over the forest fence. Advance to a track and turn R along it. Continue to a track and plantation corner on the right.

Turn sharp L on the trace of a path which improves as it rises steadily between old and new trees to join a cross-path which has mounted direct. Turn R and climb more steeply now to the stile at the edge of the plantation. Pass a fine old iron fence pole, complete with

BLACK CRAG   STEEPLE   SCOAT FELL

*Ennerdale from Crag Fell*

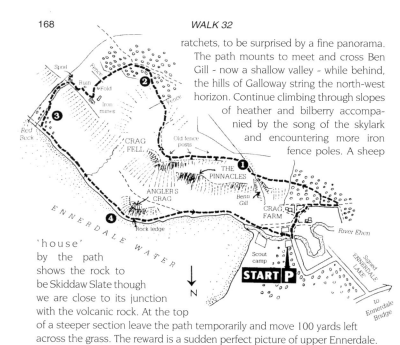

ratchets, to be surprised by a fine panorama. The path mounts to meet and cross Ben Gill - now a shallow valley - while behind, the hills of Galloway string the north-west horizon. Continue climbing through slopes of heather and bilberry accompanied by the song of the skylark and encountering more iron fence poles. A sheep 'house' by the path shows the rock to be Skiddaw Slate though we are close to its junction with the volcanic rock. At the top of a steeper section leave the path temporarily and move 100 yards left across the grass. The reward is a sudden perfect picture of upper Ennerdale.

Return to the path and on to the summit cairn. The view south-west shows the towers of Sellafield nuclear power station framed in a fold of the hills. Keep on the same direction over the summit to a small cairn at a path junction. Go ahead to a stile in a fence at a plantation. The path now runs through lush grasses where swifts skim for insects at knee level. Pass between a few stray trees and go down the slope to meet a track at a cairn.

Turn L along the track soon leaving the trees behind. Go over a stile in a fence. Keep an eye open left for a small stone fold. It is of little importance as a shelter but not so for the wheatear family who nest here. Carry on for a few hundred yards and the old iron mine can be seen to the left *The pink spoil is being colonised by carpets of wild thyme.* An iron sheet covers the adit. From the top of the spoil heap survey the onward route. The cross-wall below has a wooden gate, which is not for access, and the stile which we cross is in the far right-hand corner below the lower mine. A rough heathery section has to be crossed to arrive at this stile.

Back on the path turn R and keep level with the mine where the heather is shorter, and patches of grass hint at an old path to a ruined building.

Either turn left down to the wall and R along a bit of a trod to the stile or continue level with the ruin on the imaginary path from the ruin to the lower mine. **DANGER** Keep away from the rotting poles over the shaft, and turn L between the mine and the wall to the stile in the cross-wall.

Over the stile Red Beck begins its long descent to the lake first through bright turf and rowans, later through bracken and birch. Go down the wallside path and, after an exciting step where the path squeezes between the beck and the wall, continue comfortably for a while. Do not let the path evade you as it crosses L over the beck, or the rest of the descent to the lakeside path will turn from a jolly ramble into a botanical expedition.

At the lake turn L and ahead the bluff of Anglers' Crag rises from the lake with the Pinnacles of Crag Fell against the sky. *In 1900 keen climbers would make the expedition from Wasdale to climb the rocks. Today the traffic is in the opposite direction as laden Coast-to-Coast walkers trudge up Ennerdale on their way to the Yorkshire coast at Robin Hood's Bay.*

The lakeside path is a pleasure, lined with birdsfoot trefoil, thyme and tormentil. Be careful the weighted kissing gate does not bite you. The path now climbs to cross a rocky section below Anglers' Crag. On approaching the highest point notice the green and wine colours in the boulders of the Skiddaw Slates. Scramble over the top or take the exilharating ledge round on the right, from either the view is excellent. The path now descends a user friendly cleft and makes its way to the waterside where the Pinnacles appear huge and spectacular up to the left.

Go through the gate at the boundary of the National Trust land. To the left is a floral bog, cross its outlet on a footbridge, and on the right the lake dam and outflow of the River Ehen. At a stone cairn fork R to the car parks at the start.

*Skylark*

# WALK 33: Great Borne and Floutern Pass

*The fox bield, Great Borne*

**SUMMARY:** This corner of west Cumbria has gained a reputation for being distinctly hostile to walkers. A proliferation of signs along the Floutern Pass pony track and blockage of the ROW linking path to the lakeshore serves to emphasize the problem. It is hoped that the National Park's legal department will be successful in dealing with this. There should be no problem in following the route described.

Whilst the ascent of Great Borne is steep, the path is good and the way is split into interesting sections, first to a small col with good views, then the climb past the fox bield passing cascades in the beck, to finish on a path through a bouldery dome to the top. The descent is quite varied, at first steep to a crossing of the mire to reach the drier bridle-path to give an easy return. In 1999 the final stretch along the road was enlivened at Routen Farm by numerous llamas being reared for their fine alpaca wool.

| | |
|---|---|
| Distance: | 4½ miles (7.25km) |
| Grade: | Strenuous |
| Terrain: | Steep path, moor, medium fell and lane (or lakeshore path) |
| Summit: | Great Borne - 2021 ft (616m) |
| Height gain: | 1660ft (506m) |
| Map: | OL4 |

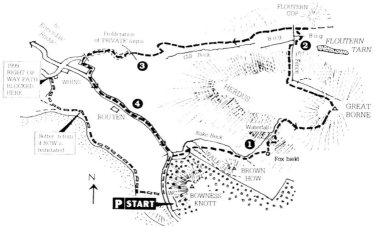

**HOW TO GET THERE AND PARKING:** From Ennerdale Bridge take the road up the dale. Ignore two right turns signed 'Ennerdale Lake'. Follow 'Roughton, Ennerdale only'. Parking and toilets (may be closed in winter) at Bowness Knott car park.

**THE WALK:** Set off back down the road for under ½ mile, with the forest-clad Bowness Knott to the right and, across Ennerdale Water, the rocky face of Crag Fell. *Ennerdale Water, its level raised by a dam to provide water for the industrial west Cumbria plain, was formed by glacial action. It is now 45 metres deep and is occupied by minnows and sticklebacks, of interest to small fishermen, and brown trout, char and salmon for the big boys.*

Pass the end of the plantation and turn R over a stile. A winding path now leads up a bracken slope with Rake Beck to the left. *If you hear a weird wailing sound issuing from the treetops it is only the resident buzzard warning you off its territory.* At the forest corner the path forks*. (Walk 34 to Bowness Knott keeps ahead.)

Fork L, cross a tributary stream and follow the path, now somewhat narrower and rougher. When the path widens with the rock outcrops of Brown How right and ahead turn and look back for a fine outlook over the plain to the coast and, on a clear day, to the Galloway mountains beyond. The path swings L then R, climbing beside gurgling Rake Beck to a large boulder at the col between the grass dome of Brown How and the pink granophyre scree and crag slopes of Herdus. The scene is impressive, but is enhanced if you care to climb a few metres up Brown How.

Fork L at the boulder following the beck up a steepening narrow path heading alarmingly straight for a rock-girt skyline waterfall. The path ahead is invisible, but it is there, sound underfoot and surprisingly easy to negotiate. Reach an old fox bield, one of the remaining few in the Lake District, enjoy the view, then attack the upward path once more as the waterfall beckons. Conquer a rock step and continue closer to the ravine. Above the fall the gradient begins to ease. Look downstream across Ennerdale to see an old mixed deciduous forest, a remaining example of the original woodland which once covered vast areas of Lakeland. Take care where the path is eroding into the cascading beck. Now leave Rake Beck as it goes off left and angle slightly R up a mossy tributary to the moor. Keep ahead with the path. The summit of Herdus is over the untracked moor to the left. On we go up a rock-strewn dome until the stones become organised into a wind shelter and built into a triangulation point on the summit of Great Borne.

The entrance to the windshelter faces east and looks out over Crummock Water to Whiteless Pike and Robinson but the bulk of the surrounding moorland retricts the view. (Ignore the subsidiary summit cairn to the north-west.)

From the wind shelter set off north past the triangulation point on a good path shadowing a fence. The fence is the boundary of the National Trust land. Descend to a peat-and-pool shelf. (Ignore a stile right which takes a path towards Starling Dodd.) Keep on until the ground drops away dramatically with a line of lesser fells ahead (L to R: Knock Murton, Blake Fell, separated by Whiteoak Moss from Hen Comb and Mellbreak, with Grasmoor behind).

Before starting what looks like a formidable fence-side descent, which is easy, prepare for the rare sighting of Floutern Tarn on the right. Blink and you will have missed it. Also, much lower down, it is necessary to stride over the fence before reaching the cross-fence, the limit of the NT land, in the valley bottom. Do so when the gradient eases but well before the boggy floor.

The fence is now on your left. On reaching the bog divert R round a fenced mire, stride a cross-fence and go ahead to the bridleway. Turn L to a gate.

(If Floutern Tarn eluded you turn R and walk along the bridleway until the tarn is visible. Return to the gate.)

Go through into private land. Stay strictly on the bridleway.

*The bridleway was a pony route for transporting snuff and tobacco from the port of Whitehaven to Keswick. A proposal to build a light railway to link the iron mine by Floutern Tarn to those at Knock Murton over the grassy fells fortunately came to nothing as the price of the ore fell.*

Pass an old sheepfold and, as the valley of Gill Beck narrows, Bowness Knott comes into view to the left. Keep strictly to the bridleway as it winds down passing stiled gateways with numerous instructions and becoming sandwiched between banks of wild flowers. Pass an old stone gatepost just before a junction.

*Llama at Routen Farm*

### Return via the lake shore path (not possible at the time of writing)

Turn R along the ferny way to a gate at the road. Cross over to a lane (offset L) by the side of Whins Farm. At the first bend turn L into the field on the ROW path to the lakeshore. *At the time of writing the ROW path was blocked at this point. Action is being taken by the National Park authorities to restore access. In 2009 the situation remains unresolved.

### Return via the road

At the junction turn L to the road. Turn L and walk the 1½ miles to the start.

### Fox Bield

The fox bield was a trap. The bell-shaped thick walled structure was baited with a dead goose. The fox, attracted by the prey, walked along a plank which tipped the fox into the bield from which it could not escape.

# WALK 34:  Bowness Knott, Ennerdale

HIGH STILE          GREEN  GREAT  PILLAR  PILLAR
                    GABLE  GABLE  ROCK
                                                    STEEPLE

*View from Brown How*

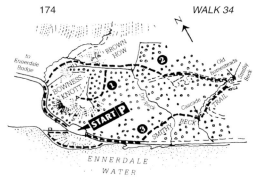

**SUMMARY:** This insignificant forested knoll, rising from the east shore of Ennerdale Water, gives a walk with an atmosphere of the unknown which children will enjoy. A path up rough pasture leads to a pass behind the Knott. (A diversion left [east] over Brown How and part way up the path towards Great Borne is worthwhile to visit the fox bield, see Walk 33.) Forest rides (fire breaks) make an easy passage to a summit clearing with fine views. Return via forest road and lakeshore paths.

**HOW TO GET THERE AND PARKING:** See Walk 33 p. 171

**THE WALK:** Follow Walk 33 Great Borne until you reach reach a path junction before a stream crossing indicated by *.

Leave Walk 33 and continue straight up between the shallow valley, now dry, and the forest edge. Hug the fence-side and sidle between the fence and rocks emerging near the summit of Brown How. It is well worth a short diversion left to capture the splendid view up the dale from Brown How, then for the stronger children to continue east to the path rising steeply towards Great Borne and visit the fox bield (see map p. 171).

Return to the forest fence at a stile which leads over into a forest ride (fire break). It may not look inviting but it is certainly an adventure as you progress along the ride path through a carpet of bilberry, mosses and exotic ungrazed grasses. The ride now takes a more definite climb. Look for the remains of an old sheepfold in the trees to the right as you pass. Forge ahead to an old metal fence pole and in a few yards turn R (north) up an intersecting ride. Pass moss-covered stones, and with an occasional glint from the lake far below left (west) and carry on brushing branches which reach for the sunlight.

On emerging from the trees stand and identify your position for the return before leaving the ride. Notice a group of rowans at the ride entrance. Turn R shadowing the forest edge and forge up towards a pine with an occasional glance back to memorise the return.

| | |
|---|---|
| *Distance:* | 3½ miles (5.5km) |
| *Grade:* | Easy to moderate |
| *Terrain:* | Low fell, forest ride and road, lakeshore path |
| *Map:* | OL4 |

When 25 yards short of the pine go diagonally L to the summit cairn on its little plateau. The summit is seldom visited, and for its best views over Ennerdale and the Solway go a few yards away to the plateau edge.

Return towards the pine and follow the forest edge down to the first break (previously noted) and turn L into it. Decend to the cross-break and turn L. Pass the old metal fence pole and arrive, surprisingly quickly, at the exit stile.

Turn R on the open moor with the U-shaped upper Ennerdale valley displaying ahead. The block of forest takes a bend. Aim for a gate to the left of the corner.

Go over the gateside stile and down the wide ride. Pass a young plantation which allows views west to Woundel Beck and Cawfell. At the new road turn L and at a junction keep ahead on an older road. The road now curves to cross Smithy Beck. In a few yards divert L (information board), to see a settlement of **medieval homesteads.** Return to the road and a few yards further brings you to a clearing and another track on the left. *Here you can walk among the stone bases of the ancient dwellings and imagine their lives.* Back on the forest road it is a refreshing change to enjoy the wayside flowers and walk by the birch, holly, oak and rowan which grow along the beck. Red-topped poles by the roadside indicate that we have joined the Smithy Beck Trail. At a left bend go ahead on a footpath to pole 31/QF, where we turn R. Cross a footbridge which has been carefully placed to gain maximum pleasure from the cascades.

Follow the red poles to the footbridge over Dry Beck and eventually arrive at the lakeside road. Turn R along it.

At the start of the surfaced road fork L along the shore path (green and red poles). (The road leads directly to the parking area but the distance saved is minimal.) We recommend you take the shore path which gives a beautiful walk, passing a picnic table and skirting round a small rocky knoll. At a wall/fence turn R on a path which becomes an old walled lane. Cross open ground to the parking.

*Forest clearance near Smithy Beck has revealed remains of a medieval homestead*

# WALK 35:

## Ennerdale Valley Walk along the River Liza

*The end of the Liza path*

**SUMMARY:** The parking at the end of the public road at Bowness Knott attracts many families content to stroll around the nearby knoll above the lake. Our walk strides out along the forest road to explore the Liza Trail, which is reminiscent of walking in a Scottish glen. Although the walk is rather long, much of it is rapid, easy going along forest roads, apart from the riverside path which is narrow and tortuous, rough and heathery. We chose this walk on a poor day after a spell of exceptional rain. The bridges

Bowness Knott, Ennerdale, with Pillar in the background (Walk 34)

Ennerdale Water is a place to enjoy in all seasons (Walk 35)

On the Loweswater balcony path, with views to Whiteside and Grasmoor (Walk 38)

Low Fell south summit looks over Crummock Water
to the head of Buttermere (Walks 39 and 40)

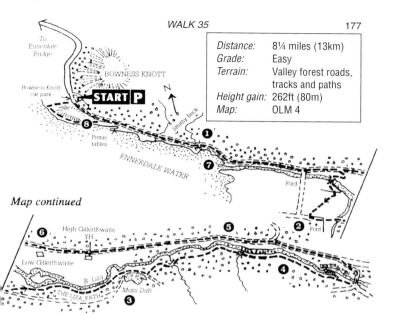

| | |
|---|---|
| *Distance:* | 8¼ miles (13km) |
| *Grade:* | Easy |
| *Terrain:* | Valley forest roads, tracks and paths |
| *Height gain:* | 262ft (80m) |
| *Map:* | OLM 4 |

*Map continued*

on the side-streams had been displaced and the normally dry ford was a wade. It was relief to find that the bridge over the River Liza at the head of the walk was substantial and well above the flood level! Dense forest masks views apart from the stretches along Ennerdale's shore.

**HOW TO GET THERE AND PARKING:** From Ennerdale Bridge take the road up the dale. Ignore two right turns signed 'Ennerdale Lake'. Follow 'Roughton, Ennerdale only'. Parking and toilets at Bowness Knott.

**THE WALK:** First visit the car park information board for a fine view of the lake. We are walking the Liza Trail. Green waymarks on poles show the way and route description is unnecessary. The brief comments as you progress may help towards the enjoyment of the area, so turn L on the road and off you go.

Pass a promontory with picnic tables and fine views up and down the valley. The ***forest*** *bordering the way is edged with silver birch and rowan and is never overbearing. Watch for clean rock on the left, an example of pink granophyre. Look out for Smithy Beck where there is an important old bloomery site close to the road.* If you prefer, a path runs parallel to the road near the end of the lake. At the head of the lake meet the River Liza and across the meadows the side valley of

Woundell Beck twists into the hills. Ignore the ford at Irish Bridge.

Branch down R on the Liza Path, pass a yellow waymark and cross the footbridge. Note the high level of the flood debris on the fencing, the valley crossing giving but a limited idea of the extensive valley head drained by the stream.

The track through the pine forest leads to a vehicle bridge which had extensive damage from a cloudburst. We had to paddle across the top even when the floods had subsided.

The riverside path is pretty in all weathers, running along the edge of the forest, and the outlook over the heathland of the valley floor aglow with gorse and heather is a fair rival to any Scottish glen. A little further across the valley you see High Gillerthwaite youth hostel. As early as 1322 Lower Gillerthwaite was a medieval vaccary.

Stands of horse chestnut and beech surround Moss Dub, its sheltered position honing the beauty of the reflections, and a few tree stumps supply seats from which to enjoy a break. Turn L up the wide path and look L for a hidden waymark pole and narrow path running down to the river again.

Step over the stones of an old wall and bridges over a beck. This is the site of an old homestead.

At an old sheepfold the path leaves from its far left-hand corner. Cross a footbridge over a sidestream. Pass the bare concrete footings of a river bridge. Don't worry - there is a very substantial road bridge to cross further upstream spanning a colourful gorge.

Return down the pleasant valley road with views to the surrounding mountains to the start.

If you tire of the road walking it is possible to take advantage of the Smithy Beck Trail and the shore path on the return.

## Ennerdale Forest

Planting began in 1926, in such an intensive way that it quickly drew criticism from lovers of the fells. Objections were so strong that in 1935 further planned forests in Eskdale and Duddon were modified. As felling and replanting alters the character of the forest Ennerdale is gradually changing to a more aesthetically pleasing place.

# WALK 36: Moses Trod and the Head of Ennerdale

*Black Sail youth hostel*

**SUMMARY:** Moses Trod, the reputed bootleg route of the moonshiner quarryman from Honister, provides a traversing path into the dank atmospheric craggy combe on Great Gable's northern flank. Our traverse continues below Kirk Fell's equally impressive crags to join the Black Sail path and a pleasant descent into the isolated head of Ennerdale. At this point Honister seems distant and considerable effort is needed to effect the return by the popular Coast-to-Coast walk path. Quite a tough round mainly on stony paths.

**HOW TO GET THERE AND PARKING:** Park at the Honister Slate Quarry (small parking fee, pay at the shop, refreshments available) at the top of Honister Pass between the head of Borrowdale and Buttermere. Additional parking in the National Trust car park behind the youth hostel (pay and display).

| | |
|---|---|
| *Distance:* | 7 miles (11.2km) |
| *Grade:* | Strenuous |
| *Terrain:* | Rough paths in high fell country |
| *Highest point:* | 2198ft (670m) above Beck Head |
| *Height gain:* | 1115ft (340m) ascent to Beck Head |
| | 1017ft (310m) on return from Black Sail |
| *Map:* | OL 4 |

**THE WALK:** From the quarry gate signed 'public bridleway' turn R through the dressing floor and onto the working quarry road. A pair of sharp eyes scanning the valley can take in a quick history lesson before branching L at the Cockermouth Mountain Rescue box on a more steeply rising footpath signed to Great Gable and Dubs. A deal of work has been done to make this once gruelling ascent a pleasant stone-set path leading up through a rock cutting, part of the old incline with samples of the wooden sleepers still surviving. *This was a tramway, built to replace a sled run.* The top keeps receding but eventually you catch it and emerge at the stone-built loading platform and an impressive view of Lakeland's central mountains.

Turn L on a wide cairned path. You won't be lonely on this path as there is a continuous stream of walkers heading for the Gables and, via **Moses Trod** and Beck Head, to Wasdale. The path climbs and levels as it circles above Warnscale Bottoms. A lovely view down the valley shows Buttermere and Crummock Water separated by a bright green swath of watermeadow. Go through a rock nick ignoring a cairned path on the right (our return route*).

The path gains height again to reach a broad ridge with old iron fencing poles. The path splits as it goes over the ridge, becoming vague and grassy. Do not go to the left which climbs to Green Gable. Follow the cairns over the brow through the line of poles and, as the dramatic north faces of the Gables confront you, the path becomes clearer. This is Moses Trod taking a tour, yet losing little height, round the headwaters of the River Liza which flows into forest-clad Ennerdale. Enter Stone Cove and pass a path on the left rising up red screes to the perfectly U-shaped, and aptly named, Windy Gap separating Green Gable from Great Gable. Carry on, climbing now, under the grim, forbidding face of Great Gable. *In winter its dripping crags are transformed by the magic of ice and snow into a sporting pleasure ground for ice-climbers. Two-thirds of the way up the face is a ledge, with the remains of a stone building where Moses is*

*View west from Moses Trod*

LOOKING STEAD    PILLAR     HAY STACKS    SCARTH GAP    HIGH CRAG    HIGH STILE    GREEN CRAG

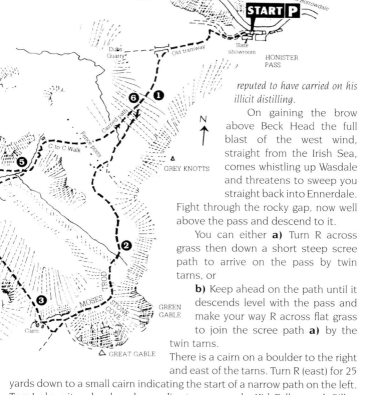

*reputed to have carried on his illicit distilling.*

On gaining the brow above Beck Head the full blast of the west wind, straight from the Irish Sea, comes whistling up Wasdale and threatens to sweep you straight back into Ennerdale. Fight through the rocky gap, now well above the pass and descend to it.

You can either **a)** Turn R across grass then down a short steep scree path to arrive on the pass by twin tarns, or

**b)** Keep ahead on the path until it descends level with the pass and make your way R across flat grass to join the scree path **a)** by the twin tarns.

There is a cairn on a boulder to the right and east of the tarns. Turn R (east) for 25 yards down to a small cairn indicating the start of a narrow path on the left. Turn L along it and make a descending traverse under Kirk Fell towards Pillar. Cross the rock bed of a gully and carry on, keeping an observant eye on the path as you pass under Boat How Crag and scan the vast expanse of hill and vale, north-east across Ennerdale to the far peaks of Skiddaw. On the left-hand skyline three square-based chunks seem to be missing. When under the middle one the path suddenly becomes indistinct among rocks. Look for a cairn on a boulder which indicates the line of the way at this level. Go straight ahead and the path reappears. Keep on passing old cairns and gradually the path approaches Sail Beck.

Spy out the onward route on the opposite side of the gill by identifying the path from Black Sail pass, between Kirk Fell and Pillar, to the valley floor which we aim to use.

Follow the path into the chasm, an awe-inspiring sight, cross the gill and escape up the opposite side. Go forward on the path until grass slopes make it safe to turn R down the side of the ravine to join the Black Sail path and go with it down to the valley. Take care descending a rock step by an ash tree with a section of set stones by way of compensation below. Cross the bridge over the River Liza, our lowest point, and turn L along the side of the forest to **Black Sail youth hostel** where a friendly wooden bench offers a welcome break.

The climb over Loft Beck pass starts from the back right-hand corner of the hostel where a narrow trod, a splinter path of the Coast-to-Coast, turns up the valley rising gradually to Loft Beck. (** An alternative is to return to the bridge then continue along the valley floor until the path begins a steep ascent on a moraine ridge bearing left to Loft Beck.) From the trod it is fascinating to look down on the perfect domes of the moraine heaps which decorate the valley floor.

Cross the beck and turn L on the path * from the valley. Now for the sting in the tail. The climb is steep, so just knuckle down to it. When you think the top is in sight ignore a path branching left and carry on crossing a sidestream, and continue climbing on the cairned path, which turns to grass and eases in angle. Pass a fence line and, with the climb over, enjoy the level, well-cairned path to join our outward route at **.

Turn L and retrace the outward route to the incline where a turn R leads down to the start at Honister below.

## Black Sail youth hostel

A former shepherd's hut and for many years unwardened, it is the goal of many hostellers who think it is the epitome of what a youth hostel should be - simple accommodation only accessible by foot or bike.

## Moses Trod

In the mid-1700s, quarryman Moses Rigg used what is now called 'Moses Trod' as a direct route across the fells to Wasdale. He used pack-horses to carry slates masking his cargo of illicitly distilled whisky. The route was the shortest way from Honister to the coast.

The peat water below Dubs quarry was ideal for his purpose, whilst the finished product could be stored in a small hut on an isolated, well-hidden ledge on Gable Crag. Eventually the Customs and Excise caught up with him.

CHAPTER 5
# Lorton Vale and The North West

This is an especially beautiful area of great contrasts. The lush broad Vale of Lorton is walled on the north-east by the exceptionally steep-sided fells of Grasmoor and Whiteside, whilst the low fells on the west provide satisfying viewpoints.

Crummock Water, Loweswater and Buttermere each offer walks of differing character, as do the fells - where Borrowdale Volcanics lie underfoot the way is rough and knobbly; where the softer Skiddaw Slates form the base, paths are often smooth and dry or steep and shaly.

Apart from around Buttermere, walking here is often far less crowded than central Lakeland.

> "There is a Yew tree, pride of Lorton Vale,
> Which to this day stands single, in the midst
> Of its own darkness, as it stood of yore…"
>
> William Wordsworth

*Wordsworth's Yew Tree, Lorton*

# WALK 37:

# Cogra Moss and Blake Fell Circuit

*Cogra Moss and Blake Fell*

**SUMMARY:** Although the fells visited are of modest height this walk has the atmosphere of a good mountain circuit with surprisingly little hard work. The outstanding views make it worthy of a clear day.

| | |
|---|---|
| *Distance:* | 5½ miles (8.8km) |
| *Grade:* | Moderate |
| *Terrain:* | A pleasant mix of forest-tracks and grassy fellpaths with one shorteroded section |
| *Summits:* | Low Pen - 1443ft (440m) |
| | High Pen - 1558ft (475m) |
| | Blake Fell - 1880ft (573m) |
| | Sharp Knott - 1581ft (482m) |
| *Height gain:* | 1355ft (413m) |
| *Map:* | OL 4 |

**HOW TO GET THERE AND PARKING:** 7 miles beyond Cockermouth on the A5086 Egremont road pass the turning to 'Lamplugh Green, Lamplugh Church' and take the next turn L, signed 'Lamplugh Church & Lowes-water'. At the T-junction turn

*to Lamplug & A5086*

**START** P

FELLDYKE

*to Croasda & Ennerda Lake*

R to Ennerdale and in a few yards turn L to 'Croasdale & Ennerdale Lake'. The road makes a series of right angle bends before reaching the Felldyke car park on the left.

**THE WALK:** Leave on the fenced path by the cottage, which leads to an upper lane. There is already a pleasing pastoral scene west. Turn L briefly until two kissing gates on the R lead to a surfaced track leading into the hills. Blake Fell, our objective, is ahead, its impending mountain slopes forming the head of the valley containing Cogra Moss. Enter a plantation, its pathside seat surrounded by spring daffodils, a contrast to the dark, rigid ranks of forest which follow, but soon give way to elderly beeches and the first sight of Cogra Moss. Walk on the track cut into the Skiddaw Slate of Knock Murton on one hand and Cogra Moss on the other. *Cogra Moss is now a redundant reservoir reflecting the fells and their forest skirts. It was planted before more eco-friendly landscaping was established, but nevertheless enhances the vale. Little wonder the lake is a popular fishing venue, stocked with rainbow and brown trout, where the devotees perform for a fee on precarious-looking catwalks.*

At the end of the lake and its old iron fence the path forks. Go R on a small path which climbs a wide forest ride to reach a col between Knock Murton and Low Pen and join a forest road.

Turn R and in a few yards a path branches L. Go on the path then branch L on a narrow path to a 'Robin Hood' gate in the fence. Do not go through, but turn L up the rounded ridge on a good little fence-side path which will conduct us easily through the carpet of moss and heather to the small cairn and wonderful panorama on Low Pen, with the Isle of Man and Galloway set on the horizon.

WHITESIDE          SAND HILL          GRASMOOR          WHITELESS PIKE          NEWLANDS HAUSE          ROBINSON          DALE HEAD

The path continues, still by the fence. Just beyond an old boundary stone a narrow path traverses left, bypassing High Pen and rejoining at the col beyond. (This may be a respite in adverse weather but the height loss from High Pen is but a few feet.) The summit of High Pen is unmarked and noticed only by the enhanced view over the central Lakeland mountains as you roam over the top and down to a shallow col (the traversing path joins here).

Ascend Blake Fell - still following the fence-side path on the broad slope. To the right is Gavel Fell, its fine pinnacle cairn being but an optical illusion formed by converging fence poles. Stones, remnants of the boundary, lie by the fence as it changes direction north. The climb is gradual and the scene continually changes revealing the Lorton Vale containing Crummock Water, Buttermere leading into the deep trench of the Honister Pass, with a hint of Borrowdale beyond. *The vast expanse of peak, crag and lake is bound to give way to friendly rivalry, 'Can you spot Buttermere Gully?' 'Yes, but can you identify Lorton Gully?'* By a stile in the fence an old sheepfold has stones built into a meagre windshelter. Ignore it and breast the rise near a few protruding rocks and the summit is ahead with a more substantial windshelter - and once more the view is fabulous.

Go over the top keeping the same direction (north) and in 25 yards the path forks. Angle L on a small path heading for the cairn on Sharp Knott. (The right fork follows the fence towards Burnbank Fell.) As you descend glance over to the west and scan the return route through the forest to the moss, over the dam and along the Rakegill Beck to Felldyke.

At the col between Blake Fell and Sharp Knott the path bends away right. Note this spot. Go ahead up the short slope to the imposing cairn on Sharp Knott giving a different view over the Solway. (There is a good wind shelter 25 yards beyond the cairn.)

Return to the col and gain the path again which makes a steep descent towards the forest. Another path joins in as the gradient steepens and the forest edge is reached. The path clings to a few collapsing sods as it rounds

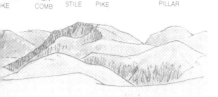

*A vast expanse of peaks from Blake Fell*

the roots of the first trees, but don't grumble. In a few yards find an idyllic wide level green path L and go through the forest along it.

Meet the traversing forest road and turn R. This road is well used by work vehicles and is not as attractive to walk, but provides a quick return as it circles into the valley. Note when the dome of Knock Murton raises its head above the trees. Now watch carefully for a meadow and lake water showing through the tree trunks just before a left bend. Go ahead on a narrow path between fir and larch trees to a fence then on the fence-side path to reach a stile. Go over into the edge of the moss, ahead for a few yards, then turn R and follow the fisherman's path to the dam with the satisfying circle of our walk forming the skyline above.

Climb over a stile, cross the dam and go over the stile leading onto the track. Turn R and retrace the outward route back to the start.

# WALK 38: Loweswater Balcony Path

*At High Nook*

*Loweswater and Carling Knott.*
*The walk traverses the hillside above the woods*

**SUMMARY:** Loweswater is one of the lesser known, quieter lakes of Lakeland set in woodland and surrounded by dumpy little fells. This walk uses a well made path, once a corpse road, which traverses the steep-sided fell and provides a balcony for viewing the higher fells around Crummock Water. The return through the National Trust woods by Loweswater shore is a delight, whatever the season.

**Warning** - The lake may contain blue-green algae and the National Trust notice should be strictly adhered to.

**HOW TO GET THERE AND PARKING:** From the A5086 Cockermouth-Egremont road turn L to 'Mockerkin and Loweswater'. At a T-junction turn L to 'Loweswater'. Pass the Grange Hotel and in ¹/₈ mile park on the right by a telephone box, before reaching the lake.

| | |
|---|---|
| *Distance:* | 5¼ miles (8.5km) |
| *Grade:* | Moderate |
| *Terrain:* | Easy walking on good paths. Lakeshore and fellside. |
| *High point:* | Shoulder of Carling Knott - 1050ft (320m) |
| *Height gain:* | 689ft (210m) |
| *Map:* | OL4 |

THE WALK: Facing the telephone box turn R up the road, and L at a public footpath with kissing gate. The fenced pathway looks out invitingly over Loweswater. Ahead lie the wooded lower slopes of Carling Knott, with the Balcony Path, a thread of shade, above the trees. Go over the stile into the neighbouring field and cross diagonally L to a stile and boarded walkway. Cross an area of rushes, the path swamped by the outlet of the lake. Don't drop off the walkway as the view up the valley is hypnotic. Go over a stile by the field gate into a lane, turn L to climb steeply up towards Hudson Place Farm. Just before the farm, turn R over a stile to 'Fangs Brow' on a bridleway which follows the garden wall to another stile. Go over and turn R along the fence, with newly planted hedge, to find a shaded stile by leaning flagstones. The old path runs beside an aged hawthorn hedge, which stands tiptoe on its eroded roots. At a gap in a cross-wall go diagonally L to a stile, which leads into a hedged path and Jenkinson Place. Looking right across pastoral scene of the lower Loweswater valley stands Darling Fell, with the cairn on Low Fell peering up behind. To the north is Cockermouth, the local market town and birthplace of William and Mary Wordsworth. An old stone water trough still functions in the left-hand wall, if your dog needs a drink, as

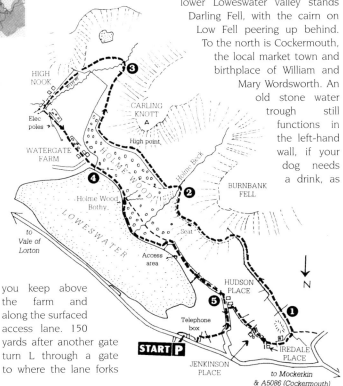

you keep above the farm and along the surfaced access lane. 150 yards after another gate turn L through a gate to where the lane forks

at Iredale Place, branch L up the waymarked bridleway, and through a gate gaining height gradually. The view opens out to the north over the Solway coast. Ignore an old pathway on the left below a water cistern and keep ahead to a ladder stile. Turn L on the bridleway to 'Loweswater & High Nook'. This is the start of our traverse of the western flank of the valley. The three smooth hills lying ahead are (L to R) - Carling Knott, Burnbank Fell and Owsen Fell. The gated and stiled bridleway can be seen well ahead. It roughly keeps above the intake wall, runs over a rise and brings you face to face with a fine aspect along the trough of Loweswater. After a slight dip, the path rises again on the slope of Burnbank Fell. The extra height briefly shows the coast at Flimby, with its array of wind turbines. Turn L over a waymarked ladder stile and onto our Balcony Path.

Fork L on a slightly descending path which dispenses sheer pleasure, a soft green swathe underfoot, the outlook beautiful, and in a short distance a tastefully carved seat to prolong the enjoyment. *The path was once an old coffin road from Loweswater hamlet to St Bees burial ground. Coffins were carried on horseback.*

Our way now bends into the valley of Holme Beck where in summer the slopes above are ablaze with the yellow flowers of dwarf gorse mingling with the purple of heather. Cross the sleeper bridge and continue,

*View from the seat on the Balcony Path*

LOW FELL S.SUMMIT    HOPEGILL HEAD    WHITESIDE    GRASMOOR

LOWESWATER

now along the slopes of Carling Knott beside a stand of windswept larches. (Ignore the path and kissing gate off to the left. This is a steep, short return to the lake shore.) The Balcony Path now runs along the top of a fir plantation, its windward edge protected by a line of hardy pines. The high point of the walk brings open scenery once more with the rugged peak of Mellbreak and the incredible path of Walk 42 rising up it.

The descent now begins as the path turns into the lonely valley of Highnook Beck. A shallow tarn nestles below Black Crag while the beck gathers water from extensive slopes of Blake Fell behind. Just over the bridge the turf spread makes a wonderful picnic spot, the difficulty being to drag paddling children from the water to continue the walk.

The path gradually bends L down the valley and various other paths merge from the right. Looking along the path ahead we appear to be heading straight up the Whinlatter Pass on the horizon until going through a gate in a cross-wall and down to trees lining the beck at High Nook Farm.

Go straight through the farmyard and down the access track for 100 yards then turn L over a ladder stile on a permissive path to Watergate and Loweswater. Cross under the power line to a stile in a fence then head above a strip of trees and through a gate beside a small plantation. The path is raised above field level and shows off the head of Loweswater to advantage.

Pass through the gates at Watergate Farm and cottage, (National Trust warden) and on through a gate to the lake shore and Holme Wood. Our recommended route is to keep on the paths nearest the lake, even on the shore. A gentle stroll now leads under giant beeches along a waterside fringed by tall waving grasses. After crossing a plank bridge leave the wide track and take a R fork past Holme Wood Bothy through shady woodland with glimpses of the lake and beaches of skimming pebbles. At a reedbed the path swings away from the shore to emerge from the trees at the wide track again. Turn R through the access area gate/stone stile and keep ahead going over a stone slab bridge, its stream entering the lake between patches of water lillies. Pass a tree-stump seat by the wall and through a gate into a walled pathway - the roughest bit of the walk. At Hudson Place turn R down the access lane joining the outward route and remember to turn R at the bottom of the hill to the start.

# WALK 39: Low Fell from Thackthwaite (Linear Walk)

*Low Fell*

**SUMMARY:** A there and back walk to the summit of a minor fell with good views over Crummock Water and its surrounding peaks. Much of the way is along a grassy path, a delight to walk, with little effort. This walk can be combined with Darling Fell (Walk 40) to give an entertaining linear walk, useful if others in the party want to loiter on the shores of Loweswater close to the pick-up point.

## HOW TO GET THERE AND PARKING:

**1.** Leave Cockermouth on the B5292. In 3 miles fork R, on the B5289 to Lorton and Buttermere. At Low Lorton turn R over the river, then L to Thackthwaite. Park before (north) of the hamlet on a wide verge. Be alert for cyclists as this lane is on the C2C cycle route.

**2.** From the A66(T) west of Keswick turn L on the B5292 to Braithwaite and Lorton via the Whinlatter Pass. On approaching Lorton turn L to Buttermere and L again on a winding road to a minor road. Go straight across to meet the B5289 at Low Lorton. Turn R for 20 yards then L over the river. Turn L to Thackthwaite.

| | |
|---|---|
| Distance: | 4¼ miles (6.8km) |
| Grade: | Easy |
| Terrain: | Low fell. Good smooth paths. |
| Summits: | Low Fell - 1387ft (423m) |
| | Watching Crag - 1312ft (400m) |
| Height gain: | 1125ft (343m) |
| Map: | OL4 |

**THE WALK:** Note all stiles have a dog flap to Low Fell south summit. Opposite the telephone box in Thackthwaite go up the signed footpath to Low Fell. The path is waymarked as it climbs between pastures and winds round a many-trunked tree which looks out over the Lorton Vale to Whinlatter Pass. Go over a stile and along the ridge of earth beside the old sunken drove road, lined with oaks. Low Fell rises ahead as we mount steadily to a pair of stiles. Carry on up to the stile in the old intake wall and bear R over it to the next stile. Crummock Water glints to the south with the ridges of Whiteside and Grasmoor pushing their grey flanks into the lush green vale. Locate a small plantation to the south along the intake wall then let your eye rise up the craggy hillside to a summit. This is Watching Crag, one of our objectives.

The way is without difficulty on a green carpet which gradually rises and curves from sight around the shoulder of the fell as it follows the valley of the Meregill Beck to its boggy birthplace. At a fork keep L (w/m). Larches and a pine cram into the shelter of the stream bed and a few scattered trees adorn the slope of Fellbarrow ahead. Pass a seat-high boulder and go over the stile in the next fence. Having circled the shoulder of Low Fell the views become increasingly restricted as the path proceeds up the valley, steeper now, and mounts in steady zigzags. It then levels as it approaches the ridge-top fence with Sourfoot Fell, the uninspiring rise terminating the Mere Gill valley.

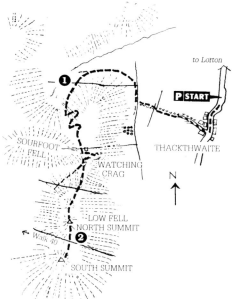

Go over the ridge-top stile and turn L by a ruined sheepfold then bear R to Watching Crag, the insignificant flat-topped hump with a few protruding rocks to its right. The stunning eastward view spreads unrestricted from the central Lakeland mountains to the Solway. Return to the main path.

The wide green path now descends slightly into a depression. Ignore a narrow path branching to the right. Wind round a small stepped crag and steeply up to a stile in a cross-fence and climb to the ridge of Low Fell. Go along the undulating ridge to reach the small cairn with quartz-striped stones at the summit and a splendid view.

Return to the start by retracing the outward route, or visit the nearby south summit for an even better viewpoint.

## LINEAR ROUTE
### To the South Summit

Carry on along the ridge-top path to a stile. Go over and along to the south summit. Do not stop here but go a few yards further to a large viewpoint cairn (see diagram p. 196).

### To Darling Fell

Return to the stile and turn L (west) down the fence-side. (A short-cut path angles left before reaching the fence to save walking two sides of a triangle.) The path hugs the fence descending steeply. Before losing too much height examine the onward route then follow it. We go straight down into the valley of Crabtree Beck, across the beck and straight up the fence-side on Darling Fell. As the gradient eases near the top strike off from the fence diagonally L to a cairn (which disappears temporarily from view). The cairn is not on the summit so, after visiting it for the view over Loweswater to Blake Fell, cover the few yards up the broad grassy ridge to the unadorned high spot, the true summit.

Go over the domed summit and over a stile in a fence then set off down the broad ridge aiming for the wind turbines on the coast (NW). Go straight down, with a few old stumps of fence poles among rushes to the right. At a fence corner continue straight down with the fence on the right. The fence dips downhill and turns left, but the grass is worn where the path cuts left across the corner before joining the fence once more and descending to a small wood. Turn L to a stile in the hedge. Go down steps and turn L down the track. Pass a seat, placed facing a view of pure pleasure. The track descends through pines to the road. Go straight across and down the steep bank to the lakeshore path. Turn R and enjoy the setting until the path turns uphill to rejoin the road. Turn L and after passing a field arrive at the parking area on the left.

# WALK 40 :  **Darling Fell, Low Fell and Loweswater**

*Darling Fell and Low Fell South Summit*

**SUMMARY:** These steep sided, grassy little hills give stunning views to the higher fells on the west and south, a wonderful vista of lake and mountain. This walk is quite tough, for its ascents and descents are steep! In contrast the lakeshore path is positively idyllic.

**HOW TO GET THERE AND PARKING:** Linear car park 100 yards from the north end of Loweswater lake.

**THE WALK:** From the southern end of the car park set off **down** the valley. (Do not be misled because you are facing the mountains of central Lakeland, Dub Park Beck drains Loweswater into Crummock Water and thence via the River Cocker down Lorton Vale to the sea.) At the end of the parking the views are already excellent. Join the road to pass one field then turn R on

| | |
|---|---|
| *Distance:* | 5 miles (8km) |
| *Grade:* | Strenuous |
| *Terrain:* | Grassy fell paths, pleasant lakeshore path, some lanes |
| *Summits:* | Darling Fell - 1282ft (391 m) Low Fell South Summit - 1351ft (412m) |
| *Height gain:* | 1256ft (383m) |
| *Map:* | OL 4 |

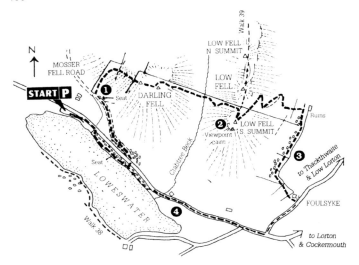

the path running along the shore. Potter along pausing to look over the water to (L to R) Carling Knott and Burnbank Fell, outliers of Blake Fell. Pass a National Trust fishing notice, a report box and a memorial seat, and carry on with yellow poppies and violets peeping between the moss-covered stones. The path winds through a mixture of mature pines and young deciduous saplings swaying their branches in rhythm to the lap of the water. Watch out for a large boulder on the left of the path with a young sycamore leaning on it. Just beyond scramble up a steep path to the road and find a National Trust notice and signpost. Cross the road and take the track to Mosser.

The half-surfaced track climbs gently through the scent of the pines then more steeply as the trees give way to pasture. Scan the skyline for a buzzard as it rides the updraught as the air sweeps in from the Solway Estuary driven by the north-west wind. Take a break at a memorial seat where the outlook excells itself. Ignore the

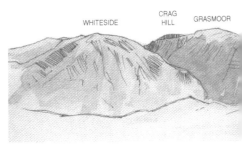

green path branching right which leads to an old quarry. A further 200 yards up the track turn R, up steps and a stile, to Foulsyke.

Make off leftwards towards a small plantation then grind up the fence-side. Be glad the path has abandoned the line of the ROW which makes a beeline straight up the screes. Go straight on where the fence runs away left. The fence turns a corner then we meet it again and turn R along it to its upper corner. There is plenty of fresh air up here to power a line of wind turbines which pick out the coast at Flimby. Go ahead to a post and keep on in the same direction up the wide crest of the ridge to arrive at the fell top and go over its stile. A few yards further is the highest spot and an arresting view of Buttermere, Crummockwater and Loweswater, each surrounded by its high peaks.

To continue, keep ahead but bearing slightly left down a trough, as though making for Grasmoor, to a cairn where you can see the onward route of the ROW path which runs beside the fence about 200 yards away on the left. Make your easiest way across amenably short heather to the fence and steeply down the path to the valley of Crabtree Beck. Cross the beck and stagger up the fence-side on Low Fell. A green path to the right can be used to zigzag up the slope easing the gradient. The lonely bare fellside is broken only by a circular sheepfold in the valley bottom, its perspective shape changing from oval to circle as height is gained.

Where the gradient flattens leave the fence and diverge diagonally R up a green swathe of grass to join the main ridge-top path. Turn R and follow it to the South Summit of Low Fell. Go over the summit and a further 100 yards brings you to a large cairn and wonderful viewpoint.

Return along the ridge path to the fence. Go over the stile and turn R down the fence side. A ROW path goes straight down close to the fence, its wires bent where desperate hands have grabbed to arrest sliding feet. It is far pleasanter to make a long descending traverse on a small trod leading

### *View from Low Fell South Summit*

ROBINSON
ILESS
E
FLEETWITH
PIKE
GREAT
GABLE
HAY STACKS
KIRK
FELL
HIGH
STILE
HIGH
CRAG
RED
PIKE

left to a cairn then back right towards the fence. On reaching an area of rushes where a small stream is collecting turn downhill, then select one of the leftward traversing paths and make another long zigzag arriving back at the stream, where a more pronounced path leads down to trees and a wall. Those doughty walkers who stuck to the fence-path will have to turn L and cross the stream to gain this spot. About 50 yards to the left of the stream is a stile. Go over and straight down the pasture to a cross-path above a ruin, Pottergill, trees and a wall. Turn R over the stream and along an old path overhung with branches. Notice a stile below and go over it into the old path set in a strip of woodland. Pass a 'No Road' sign on a gate, then go over a stile in a cross-fence. Across the vale the northern face of Mellbreak takes on the appearance of a dramatic pyramid. The path now takes a bend to a stile/gate. As it winds along to Foulsyke ignore the first gate in the wall away to the left, and go over a stone slab stile at the second gate. Go along a drive to a surfaced lane at Foulsyke.

Turn R along the lane to the road then R again signed 'to Ennerdale'. Watch out for bikes as we are now on the C2C cycle route. Ignore a left turn, pass Thrushbank, and, at Crabtree Beck Cottage (built 1660), admire the weather-vane. Watch L for the start of the shore path and use it to return to the start.

# WALK 41:  Hen Comb from Loweswater

**SUMMARY:** As one of Lakeland's less visited fells, perhaps due to rather dissmissive comments in other guide books, Hen Comb retains a quiet, remote charm and unworn paths - qualities which the seeker of solitude will recognise. It is a much easier ascent than that of its more majestic neighbour Mellbreak, which will add to its appeal for many.

Choose a dry period, for it is necessary to cross Mosedale Beck to gain Hen Comb's long grassy ridge. In low water this presents no challenge, but the stream can carry a lot of water after prolonged rain. If you follow our route on the descent, the bog of White Oak Moss should pose no problem. Views are very pleasing, particularly down the Vale of Lorton and into the high fells at the head of Buttermere.

**HOW TO GET THERE AND PARKING:** From the B5289 in the Vale of Lorton branch R to Loweswater, cross Scalehill Bridge, and pass two roads signed 'Thackthwaite' on the right. Turn next L on the brow of the hill, at a wooden sign 'Loweswater ½ml'. Go down the narrow lane, National Trust sign 'Maggie's Bridge'. Car park on right. Alternative parking by Church Beck Bridge. (See walk instructions paras 1 and 2.)

**THE WALK:** Set off back over Maggie's Bridge and up the lane, a veritable display of wild flowers in June, to the main road. Turn R and over the right-hand wall the scene is (L to R) Mellbreak, Hen Comb, our return path along the slope of Gavel Fell, and Carling Knott above Loweswater. We appear to be walking away from Hen Comb towards Crummock Water and Grasmoor, but pass the old Loweswater school and turn R to Kirkstile Inn, then the view moves up beyond Crummock Water to the ring of mountains at the head of Buttermere.

Pass St Bartholomew's Church and the inn to a junction. Turn R, signed 'No through road' and cross Church Bridge (alternative parking here) over Park Beck which, having changed its name from Dub Beck, drains Loweswater into Crummockwater and thence via the River Cocker to the Solway Estuary.

Pass Kirkgate farm and go along the walled track beyond.

The green ridge of Little Dodd and Hen Comb beckons happily from the forest in comparison with the dark challenging crags of Mellbreak (Walk 42). Go round two right-angle bends then look over the right-hand

| | |
|---|---|
| *Distance:* | 5½ miles (8.8km) |
| *Grade:* | Moderate |
| *Terrain:* | Lane, low fell, old footpaths. Some bog crossing can be avoided. |
| *Summits:* | Hen Comb - 1670ft (509m) Little Dodd - 1181ft (360m) |
| *Height gain:* | 1410ft (430m) |
| *Map:* | OL4 |

*Hen Comb from Loweswater*

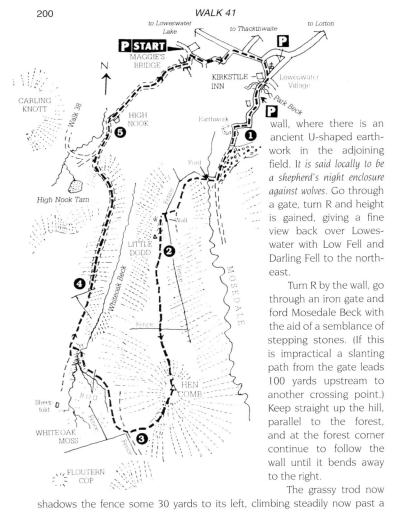

wall, where there is an ancient U-shaped earthwork in the adjoining field. It *is said locally to be a shepherd's night enclosure against wolves.* Go through a gate, turn R and height is gained, giving a fine view back over Loweswater with Low Fell and Darling Fell to the northeast.

Turn R by the wall, go through an iron gate and ford Mosedale Beck with the aid of a semblance of stepping stones. (If this is impractical a slanting path from the gate leads 100 yards upstream to another crossing point.) Keep straight up the hill, parallel to the forest, and at the forest corner continue to follow the wall until it bends away to the right.

The grassy trod now shadows the fence some 30 yards to its left, climbing steadily now past a craggy knoll. Do not neglect the pastoral retro-views down the Vale of Lorton.

Keep an eye on the fence and, leaving the trod at an optimum point, aim off to the R to cross the fence where it meets a short section of wall.

Squeeze between the fence and the wall and continue, with the wall on the left, up Little Dodd.

The obvious path, which is used by the farmer's quad-bike, passes to the left of the summit cone. A short diversion right is needed to mount the summit, but you can still enjoy the same view over the Solway to the Galloway hills from the path.

Take one of the paths on the broad ridge leading towards Hen Comb. The forward view now is over Mosedale to (L to R) High Stile, Red Pike and Starling Dodd. Summer cotton grass (not a grass but a sedge), moss and rushes indicate a boggy strip which can be passed on the left.

The path begins to climb gently through clumps of deer grass and short bilberry. Stride over a cross-fence and make your way up the slope passing a bank of peat. The path is fairly imaginary until you look back and see a clear line, which if continued leads to the summit cairn. In spite of the various uncomplimentary writings about Hen Comb it is a worthy peak with an extensive mountain panorama curtailed by the bulk of Grasmoor and Robinson to the east yet stretching to Snaefell, Isle of Man, to the west.

Go straight over the summit cone on a small path and down the undulations of the descending ridge. Pass a pool, go over a small hump and carry on. Across the valley the dog-leg of Red Gill cuts deeply into the fellside of Great Borne. Down to the right is Whiteoak Moss, the extensive bog which we must avoid to reach the old mine path seen descending the Whiteoak valley.

**Notice** the fence running down the western fellside, across the moss and up the foot of Hen Comb, where it suddenly turns left and runs down towards Red Gill.

Keep down the ridge until reaching the last steeper section. Go down as far as a metal post then a fraction right to the fence corner.

*South-east from the shoulder of Hen Comb*

**Notice** the position of a square sheepfold across the moss. The old path runs from here, more or less level, along the valley. The day-glow green 'ways' across the moss are, as any experienced walker will relate - usually accompanied by a spine-chilling story, sphagnum moss floating on a watery gunge. The path from the sheepfold has also been invaded by strips of mire. We intend to gain the path lower down the valley with dry bootlaces.

From the fence corner turn R on a prominent trod descending to a boulder. Continue the descent, aiming to cross to the path between the moss and the sudden plunge of the valley floor. Keep to the edge of the rushes and rough bog grass on drier ground to reach a fence. Stride the fence, and keep an eye open for twin streams on the opposite hillside. Descend alongside an emerging tributary to its confluence with the Whiteoak Beck. Cross the beck and climb 25 yards up the fell to join the old path left of the twin streams.

Turn R on the old green path, crossing the twin streams. Divert round a very nasty mire at a small spring, and go through a gate entering National Trust land. To the right the valley deepens dramatically, a fitting foreground for a view of our route up Hen Comb. Pass through a slate gateway and it is now easy walking down the gentle gradient.

On leaving the valley behind the path continues on a spur. Below left sparkles High Nook Tarn and ahead is the High Nook valley. The Loweswater balcony Path (Walk 38) merges from the left. Keep ahead through a gate and down the track to High Nook Farm. Go through the yard and along the access track, ignoring a ladder stile on the left. The beckside track leads pleasantly through meadows to a gate. Go over the bridge and turn L to the start and parking.

# WALK 42:

# Mellbreak and Crummock Water Shore

*Mellbreak*

**SUMMARY:** Crummock Water shore is a beautiful place wrapped in mountain scenery as photogenic as any in Cumbria. The first part of the walk is shared with families who enjoy the short woodland stroll to the lake. We continue with a steep and interesting ascent of Mellbreak, the fortress-like peak which dominates the south-western side of the lake. Once on top a plateau is traversed, followed by a much easier descent of its steep far end to visit the entrancing Scale Force, hidden in a verdant gorge but worth seeking out. Surprisingly, it is at its most beautiful when the water is relatively low, its silken thread Lakeland's highest single-plunge waterfall. An easy, but occasionally marshy, shoreline stroll completes our walk.

| | |
|---|---|
| *Distance:* | 7¼ miles (11.5km) |
| *Grade:* | Strenuous |
| *Terrain:* | Rough steep ascent. Boggy lakeside path. Summits: Mellbreak North Summit - 1670ft (509m) |
| | South Summit - 1680ft (512m) |
| *Height gain:* | 1607ft (490m) *Map:* OL4 |

**HOW TO GET THERE AND PARKING:** Pay and Display car park by the River Cocker at Scale Hill Bridge approached from Cockermouth by the Vale of Lorton, then turn towards Loweswater.

**THE WALK:** From the car park a track to the Crummock Water dam runs parallel to the river. Go through the track gate then turn R and walk on the pleasant riverside footpath of your choice to the dam. If the air is calm the scene is truly magical as the receding ridges of the fells reflect symmetrically to watery summits.

Turn R over the first outlet footbridge and, with the clear water gushing in noisy exception to the fish ladder, go over the next footbridge and along the shore path through a lightly wooded meadow abounding in flowers. The retaining wall of the lake makes a good seat to identify the mountain skyline (see drawing) and the shallow water with colourful shingle pebbles of Skiddaw Slate may make you want to take off your boots and go no further. *The forested knoll opposite was one of the viewing stations of 19th-century tourists.* Go over the stile by the pump house. *This is the site of a medieval moated manor house known as Loweswater Pele, a Scheduled Ancient Monument.*

Stay on the lakeside path looking to the right where Mellbreak rises, its steep crags fringing a plateau with the North and South Summits at each end. Across the field on the right a stile is visible, but the mottled mat of moss pierced with tufts of rushes makes the experienced foot loath to take the non-existent path to it. We keep on to a stile by pines. Go through and turn R along the fence to duckboards on the right. Cross the first duckboard and go over a stile (the one ahead was seen previously). Turn L immediately on a path constricted by lush vegetation, jump a soggy ditch and go ahead to meet a wall and stile over a cross-fence. Follow the wall and go over a stile in it. The old path now goes ahead on a raised bank, under a solitary ash tree and, as a green way, rounds a raised knoll past a standing stone to a gate by Park Beck. A shady footpath, pink with campion and balsam, leads to the surfaced lane at Low Park.

Turn R for 20 yards then L on a public bridleway to Ennerdale Water and Crummock Water. Pass Garth Cottage then fork R just before a barn into a walled footpath. Follow this to a gate above High Park. Through the gate the path forks.

Go slightly R on a rising path into the oakwood, at first by the wall then bending away to ease the gradient before running by the wall again. When clear of the trees the challenging face of Mellbreak looms above as we contour below to find a feasible access. To the north Loweswater occupies the vale between Carling Knott and Brunt Fell (west) and Darling Fell and Low Fell (east).

Pass an old gatepost at the corner of a larch plantation and continue to the highest point of the shoulder, where a path emerges on the right from the forest. (For a short return to the start via Loweswater Church turn R.)

Turn L on a broad green path mounting the shoulder towards slopes of yellow and russet scree looming above. On reaching the first stones take a break and look back at our forest-side path, once an old bridleway, which bends south into remote Mosedale on its way to Ennerdale.

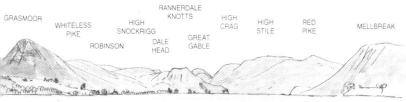

*From the shore at Crummock Water*

*Buttermere from Mellbreak South Summit*

Take the L rising path across the scree and be assured that the zigzag path is reasonably stable and not as gruelling as it looks. Next comes a very short, steep, mobile section so watch carefully as the path reappears, swinging away L then back R under crags towards a fine-stone scree chute spewing from a cleft in the crag. Attack this on the left-hand side where the angle of the rock provides handholds and solid steps. Pass an interesting fold in the rock 3 yards down from the overhanging turf exit. Conquer this as you will, and totter off L to the vantage point declaring it was a doddle and gasping at the wonderful view of the Vale of Lorton.

Keep on the stony ridge path and at a fork

**a)** go ahead up the steep scree or

**b)** turn L on a narrow earth path through the heather. This path is slightly exposed and moves round the mountain-side to a dramatic view of Crummock Water, then up to join the scree way on a grassy platform.

Follow the stony ridge path again and after a bit of perseverance arrive at the summit plateau of Mellbreak. The North Summit has twin cairns - the right-hand one (1670ft/509m) gives an aspect over Mosedale to Hen Comb. The left-hand one offers an excellent view east from the plateau edge a few yards away to the left. Proceed straight on from the left-hand cairn down the grassy path for ½ mile to a broad saddle. At a fork keep L and continue on a rising path which winds its way to the South Summit (1680ft/512m). The numerous array of interlocking mountain profiles separated by the deep trenches of Buttermere, Warnscale Bottom and Honister are an in situ reward for gaining this modest summit. (There is an old iron fence pole 75 yards off to the right [west] and other wooden poles in the direction of Mosedale. Ignore these.)

Continue direction south from the cairn on a path descending between nasty looking boggy pools and parallel to old fence poles away to the left. The path moves briefly along the plateau edge, which makes a startling

RED
PIKE

plunge into Crummock Water, then bends to show the valley of Black Beck with the deep-cut wooded gash hiding Scale Force in the far hillside. The path continues to circle, avoiding crags, then descends more steeply. Go straight down the slope, ignoring traversing sheep trods, and on down the green pathway through bracken. The rising ridge to the left is home to Scale Knott. Go along to a cross-path at the edge of the bracken, then ahead across the ridge of the Knott and heading towards Scale Force.

At a new cross-fence step over the wire (or new stile) and keep straight on the path which then bends right to avoid crags and arrive in the valley. At the main path turn L for 10 yards and sit on the deciding stone.

**Direct path** Follow the left-hand path towards the lake and turn L over a stile near a footbridge.

### Diversion to Scale Force - highly recommended and a very short distance further

Fork R down the slope and on crossing the beck notice that the underlying rock has changed to granophyre - a pink volcanic rock. The path leads up through the bracken to a fence. Step over L to reach the foot of Scale Force. The onward path turns sharp left through old iron gate posts.

*Scale Force, its 100 foot waterfall the highest in Lakeland, is a popular attraction easily reached by tourists from Buttermere. The fall can just about be seen through the foliage when standing on Scale Beck footbridge but a foray into the ravine reveals an exquisite experience, a long silver thread bursting into strands of silk captured between emerald walls. It is seen to best advantage in fairly low water, when you can scramble past the lowest fall into the hypnotic chasm which charms you to linger.*

Return to the old iron gate posts and set off down the valley to cross the footbridge over Black Beck and meet the direct path joining from the left. Continue down the valley for ¼ mile (ignore a stile to the left), pass an almost circular sheepfold and meet the lakeside path near a footbridge. Turn L here.

The path is now straightforward with views over the lake to rocky Rannerdale Knotts (Walk 44). A shingle spit connects the roche moutonnée islet of Low Ling Crag to the shore where the path passes beneath the slabs of High Ling Crag. Take the upper path to avoid the wet area beyond. The next landmark is Iron Stone Rock - a triangular rock protruding from the lake. Above left is the towering rock scenery of Mellbreak and opposite the rough flank of Grasmoor cut by Lorton Gully, a popular scramble. Pass a broken cross-wall. The gate through the next cross-wall is near the shore. If it is too wet underfoot there is dry walking along the shingle beach. Go through the Lilian gate and enter the National Trust area. From here look up the valley where Great Gable can be seen across the distant horizon before the view is masked by trees and the curve of the upper valley. Go through the park-like grassland to the pines gate and retrace the outward path through the flower-filled water meadow to cross the outlet bridges. Go ahead to seats and, with a final look at Crummock Water, turn L along the wide woodland path, ignoring forks leading right, to the start.

# WALK 43: Lanthwaite Woods and Crummock Water Shore

*The boathouse on Crummock Water Shore*

**SUMMARY:** The Victorian tourists appreciated a specially good, easily reached viewpoint and this walk visits Lanthwaite Hill, one of the best in the area with a wonderful panorama over mountain and lake. Linger in the woods by the lakeside and you have a good recipe for a short outing. To make the walk even more worthwhile you can continue along the shore to join Walk 44 over Rannerdale Knotts. Compare the two viewpoints and I think you will agree that Lanthwaite Hill wins.

A tranquil view over Crummock Water to Rannerdale Knotts (Walk 42)

Over Lanthwaite Woods to Crummock Water, a walk for all seasons (Walk 43)

From Lanthwaite Green the path crosses Gasgale Gill (Walk 48)

The raised path over the wet moor to Lord's Seat, above Whinlatter Forest (Walk 49)

RANNERDALE  WALK 43
KNOTTS  HIGH  HIGH STILE  RED  209
GREAT  KIRK  CRAG  PIKE  MELLBREAK
GABLE  FELL

*View from Brackenthwaite Hows*

**HOW TO GET THERE AND PARKING:** In the Vale of Lorton branch L on the B5289 Buttermere road. In 1¼ miles park at Lanthwaite car park (telephone box).

**THE WALK:** Walk along the road past Lanthwaite Farm and turn L over a stile (public footpath sign) into a fenced path leading behind the farm and between the fields. We are facing the woodland ridge of our walk which hides Crummock Water with Mellbreak rising behind. The path bends right to show the flattened dome of Whiteside towering above the oaks of the meadow on the right.

Turn L through a kissing gate and along the wallside where the view of the pyramid of Grasmoor End dwarfs its minute neighbour Rannerdale Knotts. Go through a gate into the wood and along the broad track round a bend (short-cut path up the side of the wall). Fork R towards a wall and along it. Pause to look over the wall into the deep-cut valley of Gasgale Gill. *The spoil heaps merging with the scree at the mouth of the valley were trials to locate the vein of ore from Newlands to Scale Hill where galena (lead ore), containing varying amounts of silver and other minerals, was mined in the early 17th century.* Ignore a forest break on the left, and at fine a old gate with slab supports (a ROW cross-path from Crummock water to the road) go ahead on a narrow ascending path which rises to run above a crag occasionally giving an outlook over the Vale of Lorton. After a brief descent the path leads away from the wall to meet a cross-wall and path. Turn R and go over the stile. Brackenthwaite Hows is ahead. Note this stile for the return.

Go ahead, ignoring paths right and left, by silver birches then winding between gorse bushes onto

| | |
|---|---|
| Distance: | 4¼ miles (7km) |
| Grade: | Easy |
| Terrain: | Woods and lakeshore paths |
| Summits: | Brackenthwaite Hows |
| | (Lanthwaite Hill) - 682ft (208m) |
| Height gain: | 393ft (208m) |
| Map: | OL 4 |

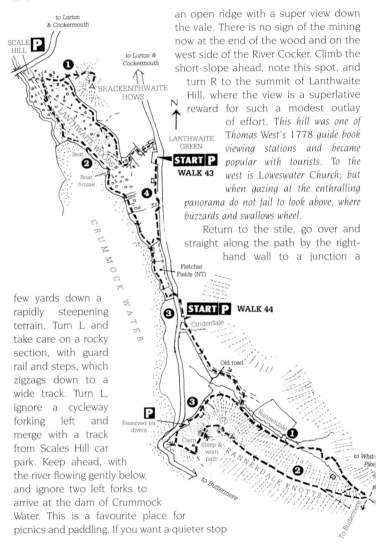

an open ridge with a super view down the vale. There is no sign of the mining now at the end of the wood and on the west side of the River Cocker. Climb the short slope ahead, note this spot, and turn R to the summit of Lanthwaite Hill, where the view is a superlative reward for such a modest outlay of effort. *This hill was one of Thomas West's 1778 guide book viewing stations and became popular with tourists. To the west is Loweswater Church; but when gazing at the enthralling panorama do not fail to look above, where buzzards and swallows wheel.*

Return to the stile, go over and straight along the path by the right-hand wall to a junction a

few yards down a rapidly steepening terrain. Turn L and take care on a rocky section, with guard rail and steps, which zigzags down to a wide track. Turn L, ignore a cycleway forking left and merge with a track from Scales Hill car park. Keep ahead, with the river flowing gently below, and ignore two left forks to arrive at the dam of Crummock Water. This is a favourite place for picnics and paddling. If you want a quieter stop

*Map labels:*

to Lorton & Cockermouth

SCALE HILL **P**

to Lorton & Cockermouth

**❶**

BRACKENTHWAITE HOWS

LANTHWAITE WOODS

N

LANTHWAITE GREEN

**START P**
**WALK 43**

Seat

**❷**

Boat house

**❹**

C R U M M O C K   W A T E R

Fletcher Fields (NT)

**❸**

**START P** WALK 44

Cinderdale

Old road

**P**

Reserved for divers

**❸**

Cairn

Steep & worn path

R A N N E R D A L E   K N O T T S

Rannerdale

**❶**

**❷**

to Whit Pike

to Buttermere

To Buttermere

turn L along the lakeside path, pass a seat with view, and still on the main path reach a little bay with a boathouse and a seat.

The path continues from the shingle beach. Cross a gate and a stile with a brook and go through a plantation edged with heather. A metal gate now leads into bracken country. The view is to Grasmoor End and its Buttermere Gully, whilst Mellbreak across the lake is also impressive. Pass a wall end then at the next wall go over a stile and along the path just above the shore to a memorial seat. Cross a footbridge and proceed a few yards.

**RETURN TO THE START:** Turn L on a narrow path below gorse and up the pasture to a road gate. Instead of walking on the busy road there is a path L which runs parallel. Just before the trees go through a gate onto the road, then follow the broad verge back to the car park.

**TO WALK 44 - RANNERDALE KNOTTS** (via Cinderdale car park) Go ahead on the shore path. After a stile keep to the shingle and on the ensuing path, with footbridges, to a cross-wall. Turn L to the road at the end of the National Trust Fletcher Fields area. Turn R along the road to the **Cinderdale** car park (with summer ice-cream van).

### Cinderdale

Cinderdale is a Scheduled Ancient Monument and the lower car park by the stream is actually on a medieval bloomery site.

# WALK 44: Rannerdale Knotts

*Rannerdale Knotts*

**SUMMARY:** A mountain ridge in miniature with a succession of knobbly peaks and grand views is approached by an easy stroll up Rannerdale. A steep eroded section on the descent comes as a shock for the unprepared but does not last long, although it makes this walk unsuitable for young children unless the outward route is reversed from the summit.

**HOW TO GET THERE AND PARKING:** Half way along the east side of Crummock Water park at Cinderdale car parking. (There are two car parks, north and south, on either side of the Cinderdale Beck.)

**THE WALK:** At the north car park is a small signpost. Set off in its indicated direction, crossing the beck at a ford and gaining a wide green path above the south car park.

Cinderdale is on the left with a waterfall on the beck. *It is named after the cinders left from the bloomery (iron smelter) on this site.* As you gain height on the green path it is possible to look over the lake to the valley of Scale Beck. *Hidden in a deep cleft on its southern flank is Scale Force, the highest single-drop waterfall in Lakeland.* The path gradually

| | |
|---|---|
| *Distance:* | 4 miles (6.5km) |
| *Grade:* | Easy |
| *Terrain:* | Mainly green paths with one nasty steep bit |
| *Summits:* | Rannerdale Knotts - 1164ft (355m) |
| *Height gain:* | 853ft (260m) |
| *Map:* | OL 4 For sketchmap see p.210 |

winds into **Rannerdale** passing though a gate in a cross-wall. Stone edges to the smooth, broad track denote that it was once a well-used road.

Leave the old road and turn R to cross the footbridge over Squat Beck and turn L through a gate in the intake wall. Carry on up the valley on a narrower path. Ignore a bridge and stile on the left, and as we speculate on the whereabouts of the old road we suddenly realise that we are on it again. Cross the stream, pass an old sheepfold and take a short-cut path which leads right onto the ridge of Rannerdale Knotts. Ignoring the short cut is worthwhile as the col is only a short way ahead. On arrival at the cairn on the col is a plunging view into the Buttermere valley leading to Honister Pass (right) and the deep trench of Newlands Hause leading to Keswick (left).

Turn sharp R and amble along the ridge with splendid views across high mountains every step of the way. Make a short climb, a descent then another climb. Scramble onto the crowning rock to a Knott summit cairn and the ongoing path. The view north is restricted by the next Knott so carry on. The path runs to the right of the highest Knott and a brief diversion left to its cairn brings a far better view all round.

To begin the very steep descent keep in the same direction along the cairned zigzaging path. (Note that we do not visit the last and lower Knott.) Turn L, as though tumbling straight into the lake, then bend R under a line of crags and turn L again on a wide grassy path through bracken. Now we come to the bad bit and extreme caution is necessary.

A steep and badly eroded shallow gully must be descended. Keep down grass on its right a few feet, then step left into the trench. Pick your way carefully down the stone chute to reach grass again to the left of two large cairns where you can sit safely and watch others struggling down, enjoying a Buttermere and Crummock Water view at the same time.

Set off again to the L of the cairns and go down the zigzag path moving R when the road is seen below. Descend to it. *This last part is on the old road which went over the knoll before the present lakeside road was blasted out. You may have noticed the grooves in the rock worn by coach wheels.*

Turn R on the road for 50 yards. (It is shorter, but not recommended, to run the gauntlet of the road, which has busy bends and no footpath, back to the start.) Turn R at the divers' Rannerdale parking and along the wallside at the base of the cliffs. Go through a cross-wall gate then fork R away from the wall on a gently rising path into Rannerdale once more. It is a refreshing stroll by the pretty Squat Beck to turn L and cross the bridge used on our outward route. Turn L down the old road, retracing the way to the Cinderdale car parks and start.

**Return to Lanthwaite car park:** Follow the road down the valley using paths on top of the banking which ease the sting of the road walk.

## Rannerdale

The old road once served the village of Rannerdale, where a chapel stood some 200 years ago. The keen eye can pick out grassy humps - sites of the dwellings. Folklore tells of Rannerdale being the site of a fierce battle where the local people ambushed and repelled a Norman force.

# WALK 45:                        Around Buttermere

*The tunnel, Hassness*

**SUMMARY:** A justly popular walk which appears in every guide book! At any time of the year, in any weather, there is a constant stream of walkers. In summer it is almost a throng with numerous families enjoying one of the area's easiest (i.e. virtually flat!) walks. Views are splendid throughout, over lake and mountain. Buttermere has three parking areas, all of which fill rapidly.

| | |
|---|---|
| *Distance:* | 4½ miles (7.25km) |
| *Grade:* | Easy |
| *Terrain:* | Well-maintained paths |
| *Map:* | OL4 |

**HOW TO GET THERE AND PARKING:** Park at Buttermere village:
**1)** above the church on the Keswick road
**2)** in the village to the right of the Fish Hotel (telephone, toilets)
**3)** at Long How, 200 yards north of the village.

**THE WALK:** Parking 1 at a crossroads affords a view over the valley. To the left (south) Buttermere spreads across the glaciated valley floor with the road to Honister Pass and Borrowdale edging along its eastern shore. To the north lies Crummock Water with the River Cocker draining from it to run via the Vale of Lorton through Cockermouth to the Solway. On the east the deep valley of Mill Beck holds the road over Newlands Hause to Keswick. To the west is the village. *Across the flat meadows of Buttermere Dubbs stands Red Pike, High Stile and High Crag, with Fleetwith Pike at the valley head. Under the turf of High Stile's vast fellside the Borrowdale Volcanics meets the Skiddaw Slates whilst Red Pike's Ennerdale granophyre takes over just south of Sourmilk Gill. Look at the church weather vane for the compass points. The whole area is a geologist's dream.*

From Parking 1 go down the hill past the church (built in 1840 - worth seeing the wrought iron shepherd's gate in the porch) and Syke Farm. Turn L just before the Bridge Hotel and through the

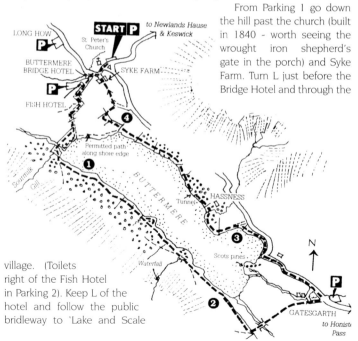

village. (Toilets right of the Fish Hotel in Parking 2). Keep L of the hotel and follow the public bridleway to 'Lake and Scale

Bridge'. The track bends L to a kissing gate facing up the valley to Fleetwith Pike and its prominent ridge path, with the deeply incut Warnscale Bottom on its right. Bend R (ignoring the kissing gate to the right) and follow the track forward towards one of Lakeland's many Sourmilk Gills as the tarn stream cascades from the hanging valley of Bleaberry Combe. Go through the kissing gate into the shore access area and make your way R to go over the outlet stream bridge and the lower Sourmilk Gill bridge, then turn L down to the gate and the shore.

The broad well-maintained path along the western lakeside needs no further description, as you progress through Burtness Wood. Across the water the white house, Dalegarth, is prominent, whilst recessed in their dark chasms are Goat Gills, drawing water from the peak of Robinson and visited at close quarters on Walk 46.

The path splits, the main path running through a plantation but the narrower path forking L along the water's edge. We recommend the L shoreline one, as you can pause on a slight promontory and from a memorial seat enjoy an enthraling watercolour scene down the vale.

Leave the wood at a kissing gate. Up right Combe Beck leaps from Burtness Combe with High Stile the ragged skyline. At the plantation signpost keep ahead but look through a gateway on the left to note how the debris, washed down by the beck, has formed a promontory, though not on such a grand scale as the one which separates Buttermere from Crummock Water.

Stay by the wall and turn L at ruins, joining the path from Ennerdale over the Scarth Gap Pass, to cross the bridge and go along the track to Gatesgarth farm. *The green meadows stretch back into history. In 1267 the Countess of Aumale owned a medieval vaccary (dairy) here with a herd of 40 milk cows.* Go along the signed way to the road.

Turn L and follow the road past Lower Gatesgarth then turn L onto the east shore path. Go through gorse and some trees then glance back up the valley. The renowned stately pines steal the view from Hay Stacks' summits. *Who can resist taking a snap with such a subject before them? A scene which appears in print worldwide.*

The path now leads below Hassness and crosses Goat Gill. Go through a tunnel (hewn in the 19th century to save the landowner, George Benson, a climb over the promontory on his lakeside stroll) to emerge in a pasture with a seat. Just beyond leave the lake and go ahead, through a kissing gate. As you pass some mature oaks watch for a tree-creeper, a small bird which runs up the tree-trunks looking for grubs. Kissing gates lead to a R turn up a rock slab and a fenced field pathway. At the cross-path turn L to the village.

# WALK 46: High Snockrigg via Goat Gill (from Buttermere)

GREAT GABLE
SCAFELL PIKE
KIRK FELL
SCARTH GAP
HONISTER PASS
FLEETWITH PIKE
GREEN GABLE
HAY STACKS

*Looking down from Goat Crag.*
*The walk climbs steeply by the side of Goat Gills on the left*

**SUMMARY:** A short walk which packs a great variety of interest. It includes a leisurely stroll along Buttermere shore, then a very steep climb, where the dramatic rock scenery into the recesses of Goat Gills demands frequent admiring stops. A crossing of the grassy plateau edge of Buttermere Moss culminates in the humble summit of High Snockrigg, to be met with a breathtaking view over Crummock Water. An easy descent of the old peat road to Buttermere completes a highly recommended outing.

| | |
|---|---|
| *Distance:* | 4 miles (6.4km) |
| *Grade:* | Strenuous |
| *Terrain:* | Lakeshore, steep fellside, open moor, old pathway |
| *Summit* | High Snockrigg - 1726ft (526m) |
| *Height gain:* | 1476ft (450m) Map: OL4 |

**HOW TO GET THERE AND PARKING:** Park at Buttermere village:
1) above the church on the Newlands, Keswick road

**2)** in the village to the right of the Fish Hotel. (telephone, toilets)

**3)** at Long How 200 yards north of the village.

**Before starting** For view description and geology summary read Walk 45 Parking 1 p.215*.

**THE WALK:** From Parking 1 go down the hill past the church to Syke Farm gate on the left. From Parking 2 and 3 return to the road bridge, and Syke Farm is well signed just before the church. Turn through the farmyard on the public bridleway to 'Lakeshore Path'. Go between

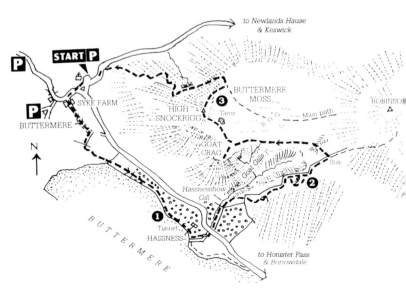

MELLBREAK          DARLING     LOW FELL
                     FELL
       LOWES WATER

*From High Snocking - view over Crummock Water*

two barns, ancient and modern, the old one having door jambs and sills of red St Bees sandstone, probably from the local quarries near Workington (see Walk 29 p. 158).

Go through a gate, pause to read the Herdwick information panel then look up left for a view of High Snockrigg. Turn R into a gated, enclosed footpath and go down the ensuing rock slab, where there is a sudden scene of Buttermere and its enfolding mountains*.

The gated, well-maintained path runs through beautiful lakeside parkland and a tunnel built to avoid a jutting crag. At the other side approach a wall with a kissing gate. Ignore the gate and turn L up the wallside crossing two wooden footbridges to the road. To the left is Hassness, now used by the Ramblers' Association as a holiday centre. Cross the road to a signed gate and, having enjoyed the gentle lake-shore path, the hard work now begins.

The path mounts along the wall through woodland and to the left Hassnesshow Gill runs in its bouldery bed. A more open aspect follows a stile and the Skiddaw Slates rockface of Goat Crag looms large above the deep incisions of Goat Gills. The narrow, yet sound, path indicates that this part of Lakeland is little visited. The next stile leads onto the open fell.

The path steepens, leading through bracken. Ignore side paths left leading to a small dam in the gill and beckoning to the explorer in us. Keep up the fell path which has a good view of the dam and also down to the lake, where the scene has become a panorama. Climb up to and over a ladder stile in a cross-wall (the last shelter spot). The outlook over the void is dramatic.

The path becomes even steeper and runs by a guardian fence which proves useful for handholds. Occasional loops right ease the gradient, and to the left across the chasm the silver thread of the gill cascades from the moor.

The fence and the path bend left round an old iron post, with a redundant elaborate wire-tensioning system. And the climb is almost done. We must carry on well above the gills, so continue to a stile in the fence. The view is now over the Honister valley and the mountains surrounding the head of Buttermere.

Go over the stile and look ahead (north-west) over the top of Goat Crag, to a quick glint of tarns in a col and High Snockrigg. To the right rises the vast shoulder of Robinson which can be climbed from here (a further ½ mile, with 787ft/240m height gain).

A small path leads uphill from the stile at an angle. Go up this path about 150 yards to a ribbon of rock then turn L across the moor to the next rocky rib which bars the onward view. Gain the rock and grass rib and look out towards High Snockrigg. Off to the left is the plunging edge of Goat Gills, and below on the right is Buttermere Moss. We have to drop down from the rib and walk between the edge and the moss on a drier section of moor where sheep trods run. Then, when the gills are well behind, gradually bear left to rise gently up Goat Crag. It is surprisingly easy walking, so go for it.

On approaching Goat Crag the 'summit' itself has disappeared into a blue haze of mountain grass. However its position butting into the valley hosts a wonderful view. Go down a grass slope interspersed with quartz-flecked rocks to a flat-topped promontory for the full experience.

Return to the highest point of Goat Crag and turn towards High Snockrigg. Pass to the left of the little tarns on the col. Ramble up the rigg, looking right down Newlands valley and beyond to Crag Hill and Grasmoor. Prepare yourself for a small cairn with a big surprise for all who approach the summit from this direction. The view is stunning.

Go down the onwards ridge to meet a major path (cairn). This is the path from Robinson via the moss. Turn L and descend the old path, once used for transporting peat from the moor, to the road. Turn L to the village and parking.

# WALK 47:　　　Hay Stacks

*Hay Stacks from Warnscale Bottom*

**SUMMARY:** A very popular low-fell outing with all the rugged qualities of its higher neighbours. The approach up the dramatic combe of Warnscale Bottom is eased by using an old zigzag quarry path which climbs onto the plateau at its head. Thence an invigorating ridge walk winds around rock peaklets and high tarns to Hay Stacks summit. The descent is by a steep but well-made path to join the Scarth Gap pony route for the return.

## HOW TO GET THERE AND PARKING:

**1)** Via Borrowdale and over Honister Pass to Gatesgarth or
**2)** along Buttermere to Gatesgarth at the foot of Honister Pass. Honesty-box parking opposite Gatesgarth farmhouse.

| | |
|---|---|
| Distance: | 4½ miles (7.4km) |
| Grade: | Strenuous |
| Terrain: | Valley and mountain ridgetop. Good paths throughout. |
| Summits: | Green Crag - 1732ft (528m) |
| | Hay Stacks - 1958ft (597m) |
| Height gain: | 1502ft (458m) |
| Map: | OL4 |

**THE WALK:** Set off up the Honister Pass road and just past a white cottage turn R (public bridleway sign). The path leads us towards the crenellated ridge of Hay Stacks, north facing, dark and foreboding. *The volcanic rock is seared by deep gullies*

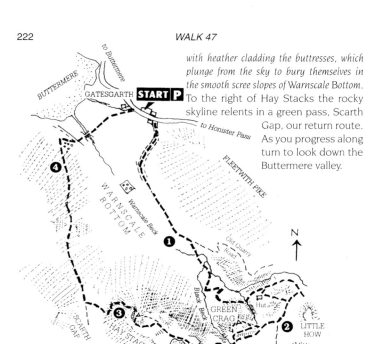

*with heather cladding the buttresses, which plunge from the sky to bury themselves in the smooth scree slopes of Warnscale Bottom.* To the right of Hay Stacks the rocky skyline relents in a green pass, Scarth Gap, our return route. As you progress along turn to look down the Buttermere valley.

*It is a scene of tranquility engineered by glaciers which produced a flat valley floor with steep sides, the spurs of the fells being ground off (truncated) to leave hanging valleys spouting cascading streams. Glacial debris washed down by Mill Beck divided the former valley lake into the Buttermere and Crummock Water we see today.*

Pass a stand of pine and examine the valley head. Warnscale Beck falls in a long series of attractive cascades. To the left of the beck a quarry road slants up the slopes of Fleetwith Pike. To the right of the beck our onward pony path climbs under Hay Stacks. *Both these paths were used to transport slate by laden ponies from the quarries above.*

When level with a sheepfold (left) fork R onto the green pony path (the quarry road forks L). Pass a cairn and cross a footbridge and in a short distance find a place to cross L over a sidestream, one of the resurfacing rivulets of Black Beck, and continue up the path. As height is gained the valley view extends, the crags become gloomier and the waterfalls become prettier. The path bends

R in a long zigzag where we look straight into three deep clefts in the summit rockface. *These were once test-piece challenges for climbers but are now out of fashion.*

At Black Beck the worn path mounts straight for a while to give a view of the shy, slender waterfall, then bends L to become green again and return to the side of Warnscale Beck. After a cairn the path narrows and climbs through old scree. The aspect gradually lightens and, blending with its blue slate rid background, the quarryman's shelter appears above on the right. Go through a broken wall, pass a cairn then make your way R to the hut.

The **Warnscale Head Hut** *is cared for and weathertight. The windows own a view in a million, and according to the hut book many walkers have been grateful to get inside for a short respite: Please leave it clean and tidy.*

From the hut entrance go ahead up the grassy bank (ruins up right) to a cairn and in 10 yards join a major path and turn R (larger cairn by the path on the left). The path is now well cairned and the view to the north splendid. After an initial short climb the gradient eases, and the rock knolls of Little Round How and Great Round How, islands in the marshy moorland plateau, are seen to the south with Grey Knotts behind. Across the moor leftwards we can see the line of the well-known path, Moses Trod, from Honister Pass to Beck Head and Wasdale.

At a cairn keep R and, with a glance at the erratic boulder perched on the far skyline, cross a mix of pebble and water and pass two cairns. The path now divides with a choice.

**a)** The main path tracks round Green Crag.

**b)** For Green Crag summit (recommended) branch R, and at the highest point of the path divert R to scramble easily to the top where there is a brilliant view of (L to R) Great Gable, Beck Head and Kirk Fell. Carry on, pass a small tarn on the left, and at a grassy break bend L to drop down and join the main path.

Turn R along the path where extensive repair work makes the rising balcony path an easy ascent over a brow and along the edge of Innominate Tarn, where Wainwright and other mountain-lovers chose to have their ashes scattered.

Our stony path rises, allowing a view west across Ennerdale to Pillar Mountain, with its famous climbing crag Pillar Rock, and a glance back to the tarn shows it in its splendid setting.

Go over the next rise and, after a brief respite, up again as the path divides and becomes scrambly to mount rock bands then cross a gap. Go to the summit cairn of Hay Stacks, where the view sweeps from the distant Helvellyn range down the ascent route into Warnscale Bottom and round a 360 degree horizon. A place to linger.

Set off north, pass the right end of a summit linear tarn and proceed along the broad ridge. Very soon Scarth Gap will appear close ahead but far below, backed by High Crag dividing Ennerdale and Buttermere. Pass an old fence pole by a folded rock. The very steep descent path has been re-set and leads you easily and safely down the precipitous mountainside. Put the guidebook away as you may need your hands in places.

As the path turns to grass underfoot Scarth Gap is reached (large cairn and a group of old iron gate posts to left). At the cross-path turn R (east) and begin the descent to Buttermere. Go through a wall gap and along to cross a beck. The path improves and at a fork take your pick to the next cairn. The mixture of rock types show a complex geological boundary (see Walk 45 p.215). Go through a gate/stile and at the erosion control area find steep set stones and a footbridge over a beck. Go down the side of the plantation, turn sharp R at the corner and descend to cross an arched bridge to the signpost. Go ahead through a kissing gate, cross the river bridge and carry on along the fenced track to Gatesgarth Farm. Use the narrow walk between the river and the fence to reach the road and the start.

## Warnscale Head Hut

Green Crag Quarry Bothy, as the hut was formerly known, was built in 1860 to provide warmth and shelter for the quarrymen in order to retain the workforce in such bleak conditions. The men sometimes stayed for a week or more working the two small quarries nearby.

*Sledding the slate*

# WALK 48:

# Hopegill Head and The Whiteside Ridge

*The Whiteside Ridge*

**SUMMARY:** This is one of the most rewarding of the higher mountain circuits around Crummock Water. Hopegill, one of Lakeland's quieter little valleys, is approached by a stroll along the edge of Lorton's tranquil vale, on pleasant green tracks. However, the exit from Hopegill is hard won, by a steep though straightforward climb. The sudden emergence onto a dramatic edge is a just reward, followed by a roof ridge amble onto Whiteside, where a steep descent path completes the circuit.

**HOW TO GET THERE AND PARKING:** Park above the north-east end of Crummock Water at Lanthwaite Green parking, B5289 Vale of Lorton.

**THE WALK:** Cross the road to the common and turn L to a National Trust sign just beyond a tiny signpost facing the farm. Branch R on a rough vehicle track. Already you will have noticed the two-humped ridge of Whiteside to the left of

| | |
|---|---|
| *Distance:* | 6 miles (9.6km) |
| *Grade:* | Strenuous |
| *Terrain:* | High fell. Some steep rough walking. |
| *Summits:* | Hopegill Head - 2526ft (770m) |
| | Whiteside east summit - 2358ft (719m) |
| | Whiteside west summit - 2319ft (707m) |
| *Height gain:* | 2404ft (733m) |
| *Map:* | OL4 |

Gasgale Gill and the pyramid of Grasmoor End to its right.

Go along the track until approaching a wall then make a short diversion right onto the common to see the homestead,

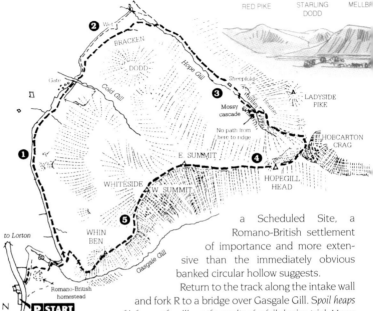

a Scheduled Site, a
Romano-British settlement
of importance and more extensive than the immediately obvious
banked circular hollow suggests.

Return to the track along the intake wall
and fork R to a bridge over Gasgale Gill. *Spoil heaps
higher up the gill are the results of a failed mine trial. Hopes
that the rich vein further east at Force Crag would extend were
unfulfilled.* Cross the bridge and from the onward stone
set path look out west over the valley (diagram). Bend
with the wall, ignoring the rising diagonal path (our return route), and keep on
the level green path which displays the Vale of Lorton. At a fork keep L by the
wall. Wild thyme springs from the pathside turf and, although passing through
bracken, the path is wide and the bracken seldom reaches knee high. Where a
cross-wall rises from the valley notice a reedy
patch over the wall. It is full of orchids in early
summer. Ignore a ladder stile and various
gates in the wall.

Outcropping rocks mark progress down
the valley. Lorton Church and the pele tower
of Whinfell Hall stand out and the dome of
Dodd comes into view ahead right. The path

*View west shortly after crossing Gasgale Gill*

begins to rise, cutting a traverse to rejoin the wandering wall and escapes a converging trap by a gate at Cold Gill. Cross the gill and continue by the intake wall, with the Scottish hills on the northern horizon.

There is now a choice of route as the bracken is higher in mid-summer and may obscure the path.

**a)** Keep on the lower path by the wall and descend to cross Hope Beck. Proceed ahead for a few yards then turn R on a rising path to join the ROW path above on the north side of the gill.

**b)** Fork R on a rising green path which narrows as it bends and traverses bracken into Hope Gill. Follow the path round a dog-leg in the beck to cross at its nearest point to the ROW path.

Turn R up the valley where the saddle-top ridge of Hopegill Head forms a dramatic headwall. The green path rises gently and Hope Beck becomes more lively with cascades and pools. As the bracken of the lonely valley gives way to heather and bilberry don't neglect the retrospective view over Cockermouth to the Solway. On reaching an old sheep bield you may be wondering how we are going to get out of this deep valley, so sit and survey the problem. In the col between Hopegill Head and Ladyside Pike (left) is a small triangular rocky peaklet. We aim to join the ridge path at its right-hand side. It is a 1250ft climb to get there.

Set off up the beck towards a patch of erosion where you step across the beck and carry on up the defile. A backward glance at the overlapping

*Looking back to central Lakeland from the Whiteside Ridge*

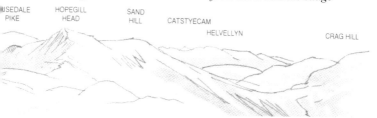

slopes of the fells confirms that the height is wearing away. When the way is barred by a rocky cascade, cross back left and zigzag up the earth and scree bank until out of the ravine, and it is possible to make your way parallel to the beck up the untracked bilberry slope. (Note: Tiny white flowers of milkweed indicate the grass has been cropped by the sheep and make for easier walking than on the bilberry). Do not be misled by sheep trods. A few rests, a few grumbles and the ridge path is reached. Go no further as a few yards ahead are the plunging cliffs of Hobcarton Crag, a special protected site of rare alpine flowers, especially the alpine catchfly, unique in the British Isles. Turn R along the ridge path and climb the slabs ahead (not as formidable as they appear). Take care at a viewing 'platform' overlooking the sheer crags and gullies. Walk, or scramble, where the rock strata forms natural steps up a dyke to the summit of Hopegill Head. The panorama is superb, however; look down to the minute sheep bield and feel the satisfaction of achievement.

Turn R (west) along the ridge. To the left across the void of Gasgale Gill is Grasmoor with a typical glaciated combe, Dove Crags, on its north face. Here the gullies long hold snow and ice, and are much favoured by ice climbers. Take care on a steeper descent section followed by a view down Hope Gill which will bring speculation on whether our ascent route could have been improved.

Gradually ascend to the summits of Whiteside. This is a chance to look east, where the path up Helvellyn is visible, and from the west side of the cairn Loweswater comes into view.

Continue along the ridge bearing slightly L and in a few yards a steep descent begins and our starting point appears but a bird-swoop below. The path winds about overlooking the gully-ridden Gasgale Crags yet for such a steep gradient the path is remarkably stable and easy to follow. Please respect the conservation efforts by keeping to the main path. Make a brief rise to the top of Whin Ben then another steep descent. The way now becomes a green path bending right and leading down to the Gasgale Gill Bridge. Retrace the outward path to the start.

# WALK 49: Lord's Seat and Broom Fell

*The walk goes up the valley of Aiken Beck*

**SUMMARY:** The back of Whinlatter is tranquil and the walk up the valley of Aiken Beck is surprisingly pleasant for much of it lies along forest road. Lord's Seat is easily attained and is the only place you are likely to meet many other walkers. The stroll along the broad grassy ridge over Broom Fell leads to the only difficulty on the whole route - a short, steep forest path descent through plantation to regain easier terrain, with a finish along the Spout Force Trail. The stream is heard in its ravine but is elusive to view. Do not miss the diversion to the only good viewpoint of the falls.

Much of the walk is in a working forest and paths may be temporarily closed due to tree felling.

**HOW TO GET THERE AND PARKING:** From the summit of Whinlatter Pass descend west towards Lorton for 1¼ miles. Spout Force Walk parking is on the right.

| | |
|---|---|
| Distance: | 5½ miles (8.8km) |
| Grade: | Moderate |
| Terrain: | Forest tracks and grassy fell-top |
| Summits: | Lord's Seat - 1811 ft (552m) |
| | Broom Fell - 1673ft (510m) |
| Height gain: | 1319ft (402m) |
| Map: | OL4 |

**THE WALK:** Set off along the forest road with yellow waymarkers and take in an immediate view west of the Vale of Lorton and the deep-cut wooded valley of Aiken Beck to the left. Ignore the

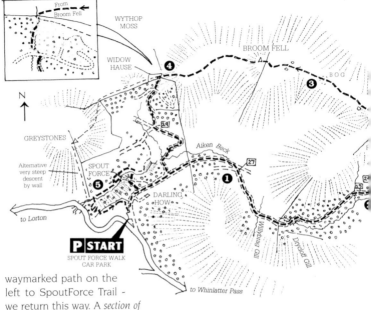

waymarked path on the
left to SpoutForce Trail -
we return this way. A *section of
forest has been harvested* (1999) *and more sympathetically planted, with future glades of
hardwoods already in place.* Pass Darling How Farm and stride on up the valley
with the spreading ridge of Broom Fell, with a squat cairn on its summit,
filling the scene.

At a T-junction go straight on, leaving the waymarkers. The road rises
gently up the peaceful valley and when the plantation appears on the right
Lord's Seat, our first summit, comes into view ahead. Arrive at a four-way
junction where logs are assembled. Go straight across along the forest
edge and into the secluded upper valley. The silence is disturbed only by
the crunch of your boots and intermittent bird cries. It is hard to imagine
that Keswick is buzzing only 5 miles away.

Stay on the road as it bends L (ignore a path following the forest edge).
Cross Willybrag Gill and go through a gate into the forest. The trees are not
oppressive as the road climbs, more steeply now, to cross Drycloff Gill. Top
the rise where the open aspect (right) shows the bleak undulating skyline of
Whinlatter Fell with no familiar hills to recognise.

Pass post 25 then turn L just before post 24 on a rising green path, leaving the road to wind its way over to the Forest Visitor Centre. As the path climbs, Grisedale Pike and Hopegill Head (L to R) appear to the south-west. Exit onto the peaty moor confronted by Skiddaw and meet a cosseted path at post 6.

Turn L on the path which leads, surprisingly quickly, to a stile and the remains of an old iron gatepost on the summit of Lord's Seat. From here you can see Keswick in its wonderful mountain setting.

Three paths meet on the summit. A popular path arrives from Barf to the east. We leave to the north-west, left from our approach, in the direction of Broom Fell's pepperpot cairn. The path descends steeply; pass a fenced area and continue along the broad moor with Bassenthwaite Lake down in the Derwent valley to the right. Cross the col and stride up the broad grassy slope with spectacular horizons plucking at the eye until attention is needed to cross the stile at the summit fence on Broom Fell.

A neat circular cairn crowns the summit and the stones of an old wall have been shaped into a somewhat airy windshelter. On a clear day Criffel, across the Solway, appears closer than its 27 miles. At the northern foot of Broom Fell lies the Wythop valley, its flat floor, Wythop Moss, being the largest bog in Lakeland. Sale Fell is the low fell beyond.

Set off again in the same direction (at right angles to the fence) on a path which descends gently at first then more steeply to a col with pools.

*Iron gatepost on Lord's Seat*

The path narrows and bends slightly L to climb over a rise. There is now a view over the Aiken valley recalling our outward route. Keep on the broad ridge, sighting Blake Fell over Lorton Vale to the west. Come over a rise to find a col and forest ahead. Descend to a wall junction.

Step over a fence and the wall. Then, ignoring the more prominent path which branches left, keep on the descending trod along the forest edge towards a small stream. Follow the trod into the forest and wind down between the trees getting closer to the stream, until it is possible to cross it and gain a forest road near a T junction. Go R a few yards then turn L onto a green little used old forest track. This drops gently at first until making a steeper descent onto a major forest road at pole 29.

Turn L and follow the road round the bend, cross the bridge over Aiken Beck and carry on to meet the outward route. Turn R and walk along until opposite a white building of Darling House Farm.

### Return via Spout Force Trail
(recommended)

Turn R on a path leading through trees and down a spur to a short steep descent R down the bank of the beck. Cross the stream (if it is not in flood) on a raised 'causeway' of stones to gain a path climbing up towards and entering more mature forest. The path now rises then descends, to the gradually increasing noise of tumbling water until stopped by a fence shielding the gorge. The viewing platform is on the left. Turn L down the streamside path and cross L over the footbridge. A steep stepped path zigzags up to a stile. Continue up through the field keeping by the left hand fence which leads to the parking area at the start.

If you do not visit Spout Force, continue on the forest road, through the gate to the start. Hungry-walker-type refreshments can be found 1 mile up the road at the Whinlatter Forest Centre.

# WALK 50: Dunthwaite and Watch Hill

*Isel Bridge over the River Derwent*

Commission's stewardship scheme opened this walk in 1994, using paths previously accessible only to anglers. It wanders along a very beautiful park-like stretch of the River Derwent, before climbing to the top of a modest fell which affords excellent views of the western Lakeland fells around the Vale of Lorton to Skiddaw.

The walking is mainly on close-cropped smooth grass in peaceful surroundings, different in character from other walks in this book. An excellent choice for families - let the youngsters find the way. The first half of the walk is very well waymarked, the extension over the fell is unmarked but easy to find.

| Distance: | 5½ miles (8.8km) |
| | Short return 3¼ miles (5.3km) |
| Grade: | Easy/moderate |
| Terrain: | Grass paths, open grassed fell, forest tracks and road |
| Summits: | Setmurthy Common - 823ft (251m), |
| | Watch Hill - 754ft (230m) |
| Height gain: | 620ft (189m) |
| Map: | OL4 |

**HOW TO GET THERE AND PARKING:** From the A66 at the north end of Bassenthwaite Lake turn onto the

B5291, signed Castle Inn, Dubwath. Almost immediately turn R to Castle Inn. Go along the end of the lake to a junction and ahead towards Higham Hall (do not cross the river). At the next junction turn R to Isel. Ignore a junction to the left and continue for 2 miles. Turn R to Isel, Blindcrake and Sunderland. Park in the layby just before the River Derwent bridge.

The walk has good stiles with dog flaps on the short version and is well waymarked. It is a suitable exercise for youngsters to find the route from the guidebook whilst the parents keep a check from the waymarks.

**THE WALK:** Go through the kissing gate by the fishing returns box and gravitate to the path on the river bank. Walk upstream along a park-like meadow. At an oak tree the bank becomes fenced. Keep by the fence side (waymark), where the slight rise reveals the fells towards Caldbeck, with Skiddaw rising majestically above and the rounded hump of Binsey, the last outlier of Lakeland's northern fells. Go over the stile into a well-made fenced pathway which takes an intriguing route above a bend in the river to a memorial seat with a refreshing view over the valley. Ascend to the road near Kirkhouse. Ignore the road stile and turn L still on the path which descends to a stile by the riverside again.

The path stays at the waterside until reaching a section fenced off to prevent erosion. Turn R following the fence With Dunthwaite House standing well-sited on the higher ground to the right. Go through a stile at

the end of the erosion area and follow the bank to a fisherman's shelter. Pass two yellow waymarks, then at the third pole turn R through a stand of mature oaks and press on up the hill, passing through a gateway with an old red sandstone gatepost, into an upper field. Go straight ahead, passing the pylon, and under the power lines. The white house on the left is Shepherd's Field, with Elva Hill ahead. Go over the stile, turn L and shadow the edge of the field to reach a kissing gate. Turn R on the drive to the road.

Turn R along the road for 650 yards and find a waymarked stile by a holly

*Grey heron*

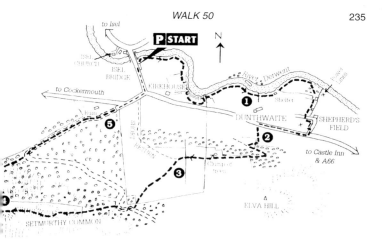

giving a L turn into a rising pasture. Go straight up the hill to the wood. Discover a stile to the R below the corner of the woodland. Turn L to the stile/gate into the wood.

   The woodland path gains height in easy sweeps to a fell gate where the path continues along the top of a plantation, still gaining height, and passes the remains of an old wall topped by struggling hawthorns. Pass a clump of old pines, plus five of the next generation, to a gate in the fence on the horizon ahead. Look out over the Derwent valley to the skyline mast on Moota Hill. This acts as a pointer down to the fine building of Isel Hall. Go through the gate into the National Trust open access area.

**Short Return** (waymarked route)
Follow the broad green path which bends slightly R then makes a gentle descent across the fell to a pole in the distance. Follow waymarks to the road rejoining the route at *.

**To Setmurthy Common and Watch Hill**
From the gate a small, definite path (there are several sheep trods casting about) rises diagonally L over the fell, crossing an old groove heading towards the forest in the distance and passing some emaciated hawthorns on the line of an old wall. When the forest road is in sight look for a stile (no dog flap) in the forest fence 25 yards left of a red and white pole. Enter the trees briefly to reach the road.

Now in the Setmurthy Plantation turn R along the road for 50 yards then take the unsigned path L climbing straight as an arrow up the hill. (Ignore a forest ride branching left a few yards after leaving the road.) The climb is short but steep between contrasting evergreen and deciduous trees. On reaching the planting of young pines turn to admire the forest, the sitka spruce, old pines and young pines, dressed in their individual shades of green, making a worthy foreground to the distant slopes of Skiddaw.

Carry on until a stile leads onto the hilltop of Setmurthy Common. If you step a few yards to the left the view unfolds along the Vale of Lorton to the Buttermere Fells with the M-shaped peak of Mellbreak above Crummock Water and a westward scan over Cockermouth to the Solway.

The path now runs on the crest of the wide ridge, with the breeze riding unhindered from the Irish Sea, and the plantation over to the right. Pass a few old diggings then contour to the L of the next hummock on the green path, and although the view is now somewhat one-sided there is plenty to hold the interest until reaching the flat summit of Watch Hill overlooking Cockermouth. Pass above a shallow quarry hole and turn R to the forest fence corner. Follow down its side to a major cross path.

We now join the Allerdale Ramble, a 50 mile waymarked route from Seathwaite in Borrowdale to Grune Point on the Solway, on its Keswick to Cockermouth stage. Turn R through the forest gate/stile to be confronted with a curving track and branch L along it, making a pleasant, easy descent towards the valley (ignore various paths and tracks to the sides) to merge with the forest road. Keep ahead, and if you catch the sweet smell of coconut it is the gorse which lines the wayside. Pass a ruined barn in the left-hand field, a sign that the road gate is near.

Turn R on the road for 100 yards. Short return rejoins here. In another 100 yards at the junction turn L to Isel and the start.

## Isel Church

Go over the bridge, turn L past Bridge House and L again to the church. It dates from the early 12th century and has some interesting Norman features.

# LISTING OF CICERONE GUIDES

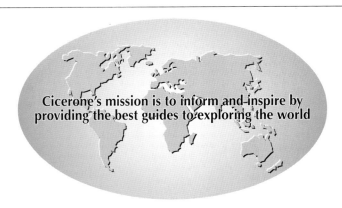

Cicerone's mission is to inform and inspire by
providing the best guides to exploring the world

Since its foundation 40 years ago, Cicerone has specialised in publishing guidebooks and has built a reputation for quality and reliability. It now publishes nearly 300 guides to the major destinations for outdoor enthusiasts, including Europe, UK and the rest of the world.

Written by leading and committed specialists, Cicerone guides are recognised as the most authoritative. They are full of information, maps and illustrations so that the user can plan and complete a successful and safe trip or expedition – be it a long face climb, a walk over Lakeland fells, an alpine cycling tour, a Himalayan trek or a ramble in the countryside.

With a thorough introduction to assist planning, clear diagrams, maps and colour photographs to illustrate the terrain and route, and accurate and detailed text, Cicerone guides are designed for ease of use and access to the information.

If the facts on the ground change, or there is any aspect of a guide that you think we can improve, we are always delighted to hear from you.

**Cicerone Press**
2 Police Square  Milnthorpe  Cumbria  LA7 7PY
Tel: 015395 62069  Fax: 015395 63417
info@cicerone.co.uk  www.cicerone.co.uk

CICERONE